Exploring

THE EPISTLE
OF JAMES

THE JOHN PHILLIPS COMMENTARY SERIES

THE JOHN PHILLIPS COMMENTARY SERIES

Exploring

THE EPISTLE OF JAMES

An Expository Commentary

JOHN PHILLIPS

KREGEL
MINISTRY

Exploring the Epistle of James: An Expository Commentary

© 2004 by John Phillips

Published by Kregel Publications, 2450 Oak Industrial Dr. NE, Grand Rapids, MI 49505.

ISBN 978-0-8254-3395-5

Printed in Colombia

10 11 12 13 14 / 29 28 27 26 25 24 23

Summary Outline

Introduction

James was a Jew. He might, perhaps, have considered himself a completed Jew; but he was a Jew for all that and as such was bound by his Jewishness to both the Mosaic Law and the traditions of the rabbis. His Christianity never did rise much above Judaism, even though it was Judaism at its best. The Judaism of James was long-standing. Moreover, it was probably a major factor in his rejection of the claims of Christ for so many years.

James was the Lord's brother and therefore had the awesome privilege of being reared in the same home that God chose to house His incarnate Son. That someone could live in the same house as the Lord Jesus for so many years and remain an unbeliever seems incredible, but so it was.

Peter said that the Lord Jesus "went about doing good" (Acts 10:38). We can be sure that He did the same at home. He was transparently honest, unfailingly compassionate, and ever ready to help others. He was sinless. He displayed the highest kind of wisdom. He was as brave as a lion and as bold as an Old Testament prophet. He was impeccably good, perfectly poised in every situation, and flawlessly balanced in His decisions and reactions at all times. He was perfect when He was a babe, a child, a youth, and a man. His sinless perfection was exhibited in the home, in the classroom, in the synagogue, and in the marketplace. He was never prudish, never pushy, and never proud. He was never rude, never critical, and never selfish. He excelled at school, in sports, at His trade, and in His knowledge of the Word of God. He discriminated unerringly between right and wrong and between truth and error. He saw through the legalism of the synagogues, the man-made traditions of the rabbis and the scribes, the extremism of the Zealots, the hypocrisy of the Pharisees, the opportunism of the Herodians, and the rationalism of the Sadducees. Day by day, moment by moment, He set

7

before His brothers and sisters, His mother and foster father, His neighbors, and His customers and friends the wonder of a perfect life. He was Man inhabited by God, God manifest in the flesh. And James failed to see that fact. For that matter, neither did the other brothers in that Nazareth home see it. That says something about the blindness of the unregenerate human heart.

We do not know at what age James decided that Jesus could not be the Messiah. Surely he must have known the remarkable circumstances that surrounded the birth of Jesus and that now comprise the Christmas story. What was it that convinced James that Jesus was not the Messiah? Was it jealousy, perhaps—the same kind of envy that stirred the hearts of Joseph's brethren (Gen. 37:11)? Was it James's growing zeal for the Law as expounded by the rabbis and as expressed in thousands of rabbinical rules, regulations, and traditions? Many discussions about these things must have ensued around the supper table and in the carpenter's shop.

Perhaps it was at an early date that James made up his mind. If Jesus once publicly expressed His views on the synagogue and the Sanhedrin, not to mention the Scriptures, there would be an explosion—indeed, the first expression of it came in the Nazareth synagogue itself and led to the first attempt upon the life of the Lord (Luke 4:14–30). Long before that, however, James had settled for the Law and all of its trappings and traditions.

Not until the risen Lord sought him out did James realize how wrong he had been about Jesus. How like Jesus to seek him out! What a pity that we do not have a chapter or two on that historic meeting instead of just a passing comment by Paul (1 Cor. 15:7). Even so, the legalism that James had practiced and promoted all of his life died hard, and he carried it over with him into his church life.

James was a man whom the Jerusalem church, a thoroughgoing Jewish church, much loved and honored. In the early days, he also commanded the respect of the Jewish secular and religious authorities.

Eusebius recorded the following statement from Hegesippus, who lived in the second century, not far removed from apostolic times:

> James, the brother of the Lord, who, as there were many of this name, was surnamed the Just by all, from the days of our Lord until now, received the government of the church with the apostles. This man was holy from his mother's womb. He drank neither wine nor strong drink, and abstained from animal food. A razor never came upon his head, he never anointed himself with oil, and never used a bath. He alone was

allowed to enter the sanctuary. He never wore woolen, but linen garments. He was in the habit of entering the temple alone, and was often
found on his bended knees, and asking for the forgiveness of the people;
so that his knees became as hard as camels' in consequence of his ha-
bitual supplication and kneeling before God. And, indeed, on account
of his exceeding righteousness, he was called "the Just."[1]

We cannot say how much of this account was true and how much was the
embroidery of tradition. If by "sanctuary" Hegesippus meant the holy place of
the temple, then the statement is obviously dubious because James was of the
tribe of Judah, not the tribe of Levi. It is certainly not true that he was holy from
birth, and it is doubtful that he was a lifelong Nazarite. Just the same, the statement doubtless has some foundation. The designation "the Just" would endorse
his reputation for observing rigidly all of the religious Mosaic ritual. The book of
Acts confirms this fact (15:19–21; 21:18–25).

The impact of the powerful personality, genius, scholarship, education, and
Holy Ghost anointing of Paul upon James must have been considerable. James
was forced to consider the fact that Gentiles were not Jews and that it was unreasonable to expect Gentiles to become Jews to become good Christians. Such
practices as circumcision, Sabbath keeping, and eating only ritually clean food
were irrelevant to Gentiles. James modified his views on these issues as a concession to Paul's impassioned convictions, but he was not prepared to dilute them
for Jews who became Christians. Nor was James willing to give the Gentiles
absolute freedom. Although he was solidly behind the Magna Charta of the church
for Gentile believers, he was probably also behind the appended restrictions at
the end of the letter signed by the leaders of the Jerusalem church (Acts 15:28–
29). For the sake of peace, the Holy Spirit endorsed them. Paul accepted them as
inevitable.

One suspects that James was always uncomfortable around Paul. Peter was a
more pliable man. John was a dreamer. But Paul was equally as strong a man as
James. Moreover, he was far better educated, an intellectual genius, an extraordinary soul winner, a church planter, a motivator, and a teacher, and was widely
traveled. James must have felt his own parochialism very keenly when Paul came
to town, usually accompanied by a phalanx of Gentile converts from all over the
Roman world. James did not intend to give up his Jewishness.

An all-out fight between these two men could have wrecked the church. That

---

1. Eusebius bk. 2.23.

they avoided it is remarkable. We can imagine how Paul must have felt, for instance, over the situation that developed at Antioch. Peter had been having some great times of fellowship with the Gentile believers in that city. They had wined and dined him all over town. Then some Judaizers arrived from Jerusalem. They are said to have come "from James" (Gal. 2:20). They thoroughly intimidated Peter, who at once broke off all social intercourse with the Gentile Christians, causing confusion and offense everywhere. Paul exploded! And Peter experienced a very uncomfortable half hour or so with a righteously indignant Paul. Of course, the Jerusalem emissaries might have exceeded their commission, but it seems certain enough that they did come armed with some instructions from James.

The ingrained legalism of James came out again on the occasion of Paul's last visit to Jerusalem. James could not resist reminding Paul of the "many thousands of Jews . . . which believe; and they are all zealous of the law" (Acts 21:20). Nor could he resist prodding Paul to affirm his own Jewishness. Rather than fight with James, Paul gave in, with disastrous results. The broad-mindedness of Paul contrasts with the narrow-mindedness of James.

James wrote his letter long before these events took place. When he wrote, the church was still largely Jewish, and still hardly any difference existed between Christianity and Judaism in its best and most biblical form. His letter contains hardly any distinctively Christian expressions and no "Christian" doctrine. All of the great truths of the faith, so common in Paul's letters, are missing from the epistle of James. The Lord's name occurs only twice (1:1; 2:1). James had not as yet grasped the fact that Christianity had ushered in a new dispensation and that the rending of the temple veil had rendered Judaism obsolete. He had no conception of the universal church. To James, a Christian was not a Spirit-baptized member of the mystical body of Christ but rather a genuine Israelite, a "completed Jew."

James wrote from Jerusalem and before the Jerusalem conference that took place in A.D. 50–51. James likely wrote between 44–50. He wrote his letter as from one Christian Jew to other Christian Jews. Its purpose was to insist on a belief that behaves. Because most of what James had to say was of a highly practical nature, its teachings apply to all Christians in all places and at all periods. His letter, indeed, seems to be an exposition of the Sermon on the Mount.

Perhaps Paul read the letter before setting out for the Jerusalem conference. It contained nothing with which he would disagree. Rather, it would give him an appreciation for the zeal and integrity of the man whom he must win to his side at the coming conference if it was to be at all successful.

The letter of James, then, was the first New Testament document. James deserves full marks for that task—for being the first person in the New Testament era to begin writing down the teaching of the church. Because he was not an apostle, that feat says a lot for James. His letter was inspired, "God-breathed" by the Holy Spirit Himself. Evidently, the Holy Spirit thought very highly of James to give him a place of such high honor and to enable him to write a book that will last forever.

Complete Outline

b. The crown ensured (1:12b)
B. The temptations of the Christian life (1:13–16)
 1. The source of temptation (1:13–15)
  a. What we must realize (1:13)
   (1) Recording a common error (1:13a)
   (2) Refuting a common error (1:13b)
  b. What we must recognize (1:14–15)
   (1) The mother of sin (1:14–15a)
   (2) The method of sin (1:15b)
   (3) The maturity of sin (1:15c)
 2. The subtlety of temptation (1:16)

PART 3: THE CHRISTIAN AND HIS BIBLE (1:17–27)
A. God's Word is likened to a gift (1:17–18)
 1. A gift that brings divine light (1:17)
  a. The nature of the gifts (1:17a–c)
   (1) Their monopoly (1:17a)
   (2) Their majesty (1:17b–c)
    (a) Godlike in their purity (1:17b)
    (b) Godlike in their perfection (1:17c)
  b. The nature of the giver (1:17d–e)
   (1) He is unchallengeable (1:17d)
   (2) He is unchangeable (1:17e)
 2. A gift that brings divine life (1:18)
  a. According to the will of God (1:18a)
  b. According to the Word of God (1:18b)
  c. According to the wisdom of God (1:18c)
B. God's Word is likened to a graft (1:19–22)
 1. To effect a change in our talk (1:19–20)
  a. Be swift to respond to speaking (1:19a)
  b. Be slow to resort to speaking (1:19b–20)
   (1) A first principle (1:19b)
   (2) A further principle (1:19c–20)
    (a) The rule (1:19c)
    (b) The reason (1:20)
 2. To effect a change in our walk (1:21–22)
  a. What to reject (1:21a)
  b. What to receive (1:21b)

a. A very great principle (2:9–11)
  (1) An example (2:9)
  (2) An explanation (2:10–11)
    (a) The fact declared (2:10)
    (b) The fact demonstrated (2:11)
b. A very good policy (2:12–13)
  (1) God's magnanimity (2:12)
  (2) God's mercy (2:13)
    (a) A general rule (2:13a)
    (b) A gracious reminder (2:13b)

PART 5: THE CHRISTIAN AND HIS BELIEFS (2:14–26)
  A. The approach (2:14)
    1. The false claim is quoted (2:14a)
    2. The false claim is questioned (2:14b)
  B. The appraisal (2:15–18)
    1. A case to consider (2:15–16)
      a. The need discerned (2:15)
      b. The need dismissed (2:16)
        (1) A foolish assertion (2:16a)
        (2) A foolish assumption (2:16b)
    2. A conclusion to consider (2:17–18)
      a. A pontifical conclusion (2:17)
      b. A pragmatical conclusion (2:18)
  C. The application (2:19–20)
    1. Faith displayed (2:19)
    2. Faith disputed (2:20)
  D. The appeal (2:21–26)
    1. The proof of the contention (2:21–25)
      a. The case of Abraham the Hebrew (2:21–24)
        (1) A great triumph (2:21)
        (2) A great truth (2:22)
        (3) A great trust (2:23a)
        (4) A great testimony (2:23b)
        (5) A great test (2:24)
      b. The case of Rahab the harlot (2:25)
        (1) What is declared of her (2:25a)

(2) What was done by her (2:25b)

2. The point of the contention (2:26)

a. A dead body (2:26a)

b. A dead belief (2:26b)

PART 6: THE CHRISTIAN AND HIS BEHAVIOR (3:1–4:12)

A. Sin in the life revealed (3:1–4:5)

1. Sin in the mouth (3:1–12)

a. A word about the teachers (3:1)

(1) Don't multiply teachers (3:1a)

(2) Don't misunderstand teaching (3:1b)

b. A word about the tongue (3:2–12)

(1) A divine standard (3:2)

(2) A devastating statement (3:3–12)

(a) The unbridled tongue (3:3–5a)

i. The illustration (3:3–4)

a. How a beast is controlled (3:3)

b. How a boat is controlled (3:4)

ii. The application (3:5a)

(b) The untrammeled tongue (3:5b–6)

i. The illustration (3:5b)

ii. The application (3:6)

a. How decadent it is (3:6a)

b. How defiling it is (3:6b)

c. How destructive it is (3:6c)

d. How devilish it is (3:6d)

(c) The untamed tongue (3:7–10)

i. The illustration (3:7)

ii. The application (3:8–10)

a. The tongue and its disloyalty (3:8)

1. How pugnacious it is (3:8a)

2. How poisonous it is (3:8b)

b. The tongue and its dichotomy (3:9)

1. Its ability to bless God (3:9a)

2. Its ability to berate man (3:9b)

c. The tongue and its duplicity (3:10)

1. Repetition (3:10a)

2. Repudiation (3:10b)

    (d) The unredeemed tongue (3:11–12)

        i. The illustration (3:11)

        ii. The application (3:12)

2. Sin in the mind (3:13–18)

  a. Wisdom and its course (3:13–14)

    (1) The main stream of wise behavior (3:13)

    (2) The muddy stream of wicked behavior (3:14)

      (a) A bitter spirit (3:14a)

      (b) A belligerent spirit (3:14b)

      (c) A boastful spirit (3:14c)

      (d) A blind spirit (3:14d)

  b. Wisdom and its source (3:15–17)

    (1) The source of human wisdom (3:15–16)

      (a) Its outflow (3:15)

        i. Its secular source (3:15a)

        ii. Its sensual source (3:15b)

        iii. Its satanic source (3:15c)

      (b) Its outcome (3:16)

        i. Unrest (3:16a)

        ii. Ungodliness (3:16b)

    (2) The source of heavenly wisdom (3:17)

      (a) Its basic characteristic (3:17a)

      (b) Its benevolent characteristics (3:17b–d)

        i. Its motivation (3:17b)

        ii. Its moderation (3:17c)

        iii. Its mediation (3:17d)

      (c) Its bountiful characteristics (3:17e–f)

        i. In the thoughts it entertains (3:17e)

        ii. In the things it espouses (3:17f)

      (d) Its balanced characteristics (3:17g–h)

        i. Absolutely unbiased (3:17g)

        ii. Absolutely unblemished (3:17h)

  c. Wisdom and its force (3:18)

3. Sin in the members (4:1–5)

  a. The first question (4:1–4)

    (1) The question asked (4:1)

B. Boasting about our prosperity (5:1–6)
1. The rich men's woes described (5:1–4)
   a. The prophetic declaration (5:1)
   b. The prophetic details (5:2–4)
      (1) The depreciated value of their wealth (5:2)
      (2) The damning voice of their wealth (5:3a)
      (3) The detailed vision of their wealth (5:3b–4)
         (a) As to the day of reckoning (5:3b)
         (b) As to the details of reckoning (5:4)
            i. Their fraud described (5:4a)
            ii. Their fraud discerned (5:4b)
2. The rich men's wickedness disclosed (5:5–6)
   a. Their pleasure (5:5a)
   b. Their plunder (5:5b)
   c. Their power (5:6)
      (1) Its abuse seemingly unprevented (5:6a)
      (2) Its abuse seemingly unpunished (5:6b)

PART 8: THE CHRISTIAN AND HIS BURDENS (5:7–20)
A. The burden of poverty (5:7–11)
1. A call for simple patience (5:7–8)
   a. The prospect (5:7)
      (1) A biblical reason for patience (5:7a)
      (2) A biological reason for patience (5:7b)
   b. The promise (5:8)
      (1) Be still (5:8a)
      (2) Be strong (5:8b)
2. A call for sufficient patience (5:9)
   a. Beware of complaining (5:9a)
   b. Beware of condemnation (5:9b–c)
      (1) Because of the prophesy of the judgment (5:9b)
      (2) Because of the proximity of the judge (5:9c)
3. A call for sublime patience (5:10–11)
   a. The prophets (5:10)
      (1) Their exhortations (5:10a)
      (2) Their example (5:10b)
   b. The patriarch (5:11)

(1) A point to ponder (5:11a)

(2) A person to ponder (5:11b–c)

    (a) What Job endured in his body (5:11b)

    (b) What Job endorses in his book (5:11c)

B. The burden of proof (5:12)

  1. What to avoid (5:12a)

  2. What to avow (5:12b–c)

    a. The requirement (5:12b)

    b. The reason (5:12c)

C. The burden for prayer (5:13–18)

  1. The hypotheses (5:13–14a)

    a. The man who is overwhelmed: let him speak (5:13a)

    b. The man who is overjoyed: let him sing (5:13b)

    c. The man who is overcome: let him send (5:14a)

  2. The healing (5:14b–16)

    a. The prayer (5:14b)

    b. The procedure (5:14c–d)

      (1) The sanctifying oil (5:14c)

      (2) The sovereign name (5:14d)

    c. The promise (5:15)

      (1) What is asserted (5:15a–b)

        (a) The authority of the prayer involved (5:15a)

        (b) The authority of the person invoked (5:15b)

      (2) What is assumed (5:15c)

    d. The postscript (5:16)

      (1) A requirement (5:16a)

      (2) A response (5:16b)

      (3) A reason (5:16c)

  3. The hero (5:17–18)

    a. Elijah and his passions (5:17a)

    b. Elijah and his prayers (5:17b–18)

      (1) His first prayer answered (5:17b)

      (2) His further prayer answered (5:18)

D. The burden for people (5:19–20)

  1. The careless backslider (5:19a)

  2. The concerned believer (5:19b)

  3. The consequent benediction (5:20)

PART 1

James and His Biography

James 1:1

J ames, a servant of God and of the Lord Jesus Christ, to the twelve tribes
which are scattered abroad, greeting."

James! He at once owns Jesus both as Lord and Christ and as God, and he owns himself as His *doulos,* His slave. That is a different James than the man who for so long refused even to consider the claims of Jesus.

Much controversy has revolved around the question of whether James was really the son of Mary and, therefore, the Lord's half brother (Gal. 1:19). The three views on this issue are usually named after their respective authors. First is the *Hieronymian view,* the view espoused by Jerome and the Roman Catholic Church. According to this view, the "brethren" of the Lord Jesus (John 7:5) were really His cousins. Supposedly, they were the sons of Alphaeus and Mary, the sister of Mary, the Lord's mother. This view suits the Church of Rome, which upholds the dogma of the perpetual virginity of Mary. It also clears the way for Rome's efforts to exalt the Virgin Mary to divine status and for Rome's vested interest in promoting celibacy.

Second is the *Epiphanian view,* proposed by Epiphanius, that these "brethren" were sons of Joseph by a previous marriage. This view also plays into the hands of Rome. Little commends it because no historical proof exists that Joseph was a widower with a family.

Finally, the *Helvidian view* posits that the "brethren" of Jesus were just that— the children of Joseph and Mary. Strong support for this view comes from the Gospels themselves. We read of Joseph that he "did as the angel of the Lord had bidden him, and took unto him his wife [Mary]: and knew her not till she had brought forth her firstborn son . . ." (Matt. 1:24–25). The expression *knew her* is a well-known Hebrew idiom for "cohabitation." The word *till* shows clearly that she had children afterward. The word used means "not till then," or "afterward." Luke gives similar evidence: "And she brought forth her firstborn son . . ." (Luke 2:7). The word *prōtotokos,* "firstborn," is never used of an only son.

The family circle at Nazareth was made up of five brothers—Jesus, James, Joses, Judas, and Simon (Mark 6:3; Matt. 13:55)—and some sisters. So it was a fairly large family. Jewish boys started school at the age of six. We can be sure that the spiritual education of James began before that in the home in which he was reared. At school, religion was the primary subject. Attention was paid to languages—

Hebrew, Aramaic, and Greek with some Latin for good measure. James wrote in Greek with a smattering of Hebraisms.

James apparently rejected the Lord's messianic claims. No doubt, he felt keenly the hostility of his Nazarene neighbors toward Jesus after the incident when the Lord declared boldly who He was (Luke 4:16–30). James seems to have become alarmed at the growing hostility of the Pharisees toward the Lord's claims. Rumors were being circulated that Jesus was insane. The authorities accused Him of being in league with Beelzebub (Matt. 12:23). So the Lord's brothers, accompanied by Mary, sought to interfere in His work and bring Him back home out of harm's way (Mark 3:31; Matt. 12:46; Luke 8:19). The Lord's only response was to declare that those who responded to His message were more truly His mother and His brethren than those who were His by natural ties (Mark 3:34; Matt. 12:49).

As time passed, the hostility of James and the other brothers of the Lord seemed to grow. Six months before His death they sneered at Him and offered Him some advice, which He rejected (John 7:2–5). John says that "neither did his brethren believe in him" (v. 5). Possibly James was the ringleader in this domestic tragedy. Is it surprising, then, that at His death the Lord Jesus committed the care of His mother, not to His brother James but to the apostle John?

All of this rejection was changed, however, after the Resurrection. The Lord appeared to James (1 Cor. 15:7). James was instantly transformed from an unbeliever to a committed believer. James then seems to have rounded up the family and led his brothers to faith in Christ. In any case, the whole family was in the Upper Room soon afterward (Acts 1:14). The apostles passed over James as a possible successor to Judas, and they chose Matthias by lot (Acts 1:15–26). Just the same, James was in the Upper Room on the Day of Pentecost.

James soon moved up in the ranks of the Jerusalem church. He was included in the councils of the Twelve. Paul met him when he visited Jerusalem after his conversion (Gal. 1:19). James could have been one of the people who mistrusted Paul at that time. Indeed, Barnabas was the only one who had faith in him and the courage to stand by him. Peter responded at once (Gal. 1:18), but we do not know how James responded.

The next reference to James was at the time of the murder of the apostle James and the imprisonment and miraculous escape of Peter. Peter made his way to the home of Mary, the mother of John Mark (Acts 12:12) before removing himself from Herod's power. "Tell these things to James and to the brethren," he said. Evidently, by this time, James was in a position of leadership in the Jerusalem church.

He remained in charge of that church throughout the remaining period covered by the book of Acts. He presided at the critical Jerusalem conference (Acts 15:14–21).

And he was still in charge when Paul made his last fateful visit to Jerusalem (Acts 21:18). James was the one who urged Paul to prove his Jewish integrity by paying the costs involved in terminating the Nazarite vows of certain Jews. Those costs were considerable. James, perhaps judging by the size of the offering that Paul had brought in support of the Lord's work in Jerusalem, money collected from Gentile churches, seems to have decided that Paul was affluent.[1]

Paul, anxious not to split the church over an issue that he deemed to be unimportant, went along with James's suggestion (Acts 15:28–29). In the temple the next day, he was assaulted and beaten up. The Romans took him into protective custody and eventually imprisoned him in Caesarea—but not until he barely escaped with his life from a plot to kill him.

It would have been pleasant if Luke had been able to record a concerted effort by James and the Jerusalem church to rally to Paul's side at the time of his arrest. A mention that James visited him in prison to minister to his needs would likewise have been heartwarming. But all that we have is silence. Possibly the Jerusalem church felt itself well rid of Paul. As Saul of Tarsus, he had threatened their stand for Jesus. Now, as Paul the Apostle, he threatened their Jewishness. In light of the intensely practical nature of James's epistle, we can hope that he did try to do something for Paul.

The death of James is not recorded in the Bible. Various traditional accounts have been preserved. According to Josephus, Ananus, the Jewish high priest, took advantage of the period between the death of the Roman governor, Festus, and the arrival of Albinus, his successor, to get rid of James. Ananus is said to have convened a meeting of the Sanhedrin, arraigned James before it, accused him and some others of breaking the law, condemned him to death, and had him stoned. According to the account of Clement of Rome, James was thrown from the gable of the temple and then beaten to death with a club by a fuller. He is said to have been buried on the spot beside the temple. The year is thought to have been A.D. 62. Eusebius says that Josephus believed that the martyrdom of James precipitated the events that resulted in the destruction of Jerusalem, although many people think that this comment is spurious.

Regardless of how James died, we must agree that he was not the kind of man who could be ignored. On the contrary, he was a very forceful person,

---

1. It would have been pleasant if Luke had been able to record an expression of thanks for that offering. There was none; at least none is recorded. Probably James and the other leaders considered such contribution their due.

activated by the highest motives and genuinely concerned about the spiritual welfare of his flock.

His readers were not primarily his own local parishoners. He was concerned about "the twelve tribes of the diaspora," Christian Jews scattered far and wide around the world. Those whom he addressed had not ceased to be Jews upon becoming Christians. Some of them had been present in Jerusalem on the Day of Pentecost and had responded to Peter's preaching. They had carried home with them only the most rudimentary knowledge of Christianity: Jesus was the Messiah; He had been crucified, buried, and raised from the dead; He had ascended on high; He was the promised Kinsman-Redeemer; and salvation was in Him and Him alone. Those who had been scattered abroad at the time of Stephen's martyrdom understood more. However, even at that time, the gospel was being preached "to none but Jews only." Christian communities were being formed within the Jewish communities in all major cities. At this stage, however, these Jewish Christians were still members of local synagogues. These were the people whom James had in mind when he wrote his letter.

James addressed himself to "the twelve tribes which are scattered abroad," ignoring the Old Testament separation of the Hebrew people into the nations of Judah and Israel. As for the modern idea that the scattered ten tribes of the northern kingdom were "lost," James gives no support to that theory. By New Testament times, the word *Jews* was in common use to describe *all* Hebrew people, and the word *Israelites* was synonymous. To all Jewish Christians in the far-flung dispersion of the Hebrew people, James sends his greetings. From both their annual pilgrimages to Jerusalem and their participation in the meetings of the Jerusalem church, many of the Christian Jews would be familiar with James.

PART 2

The Christian and His Battles

James 1:2–16

A. The testings of the Christian life (1:2–12)
   1. Testings are for a purpose (1:2–11)
      a. For our enlargement (1:2–4)

James addresses himself to half a dozen basic issues of the Christian life. He discusses the Christian and his *battles* (1:2–16), the Christian and his *Bible* (1:17–27), the Christian and his *brethren* (2:1–13), the Christian and his *beliefs* (2:14–26), the Christian and his *behavior* (3:1–4:12), the Christian and his *boasting* (4:13–5:6), and the Christian and his *burdens* (5:7–20). He begins with the *testings* and *temptations* that assail the godly. As to our temptations, they are for a *purpose* (1:2–11) and for our *profit* (1:12). James could see three reasons why God allowed His people to be tested: for our *enlargement* (1:2–4), for our *enlightenment* (1:5–8), and for our *ennoblement* (1:9–11).

They are for our enlargement. They are intended, for instance, *to move us:* "My brethren, count it all joy when ye fall into divers temptations" (1:2). Testings jolt us out of the comfortable ruts into which we tend to settle. They provoke a reaction. The way we respond to testings tells us a great deal about our spiritual condition. The word translated "temptations" refers primarily here to trials. The word pictures an assayer who puts gold in the fire to test its purity. James has in mind the external trials that overtake us on our journey home. He sees "divers" or "manifold" trials. The word for "manifold" denotes "many-colored" or variegated trials—trials of all sorts. The classic Old Testament example of a saint being tested by all kinds of adversities is Job. In a series of inexplicable disasters, he lost his wealth and his health, his family, the sympathy and fellowship of his wife, and the goodwill of his friends. Job came out of his trials a wiser and better man.

James does not urge his readers to react positively *if* they fall into trials but *when* they fall into trials. Trials are not electives in God's school; they are required courses. Sooner or later, testings *will* come. They are not intended to give God an opportunity to see how we are doing but to let us see how far we have come—or failed to come.

Moreover, testings are designed *to mellow us:* "Knowing this, that the trying of your faith worketh patience" (1:3). That is why James tells us to "count it all joy" when these testings come. They are not mindless, senseless woes unleashed upon us by a cold and impersonal fate. They are permitted by a wise and loving heavenly Father, who is too caring to be unkind and too wise to make any mistakes. Satan was not allowed to touch Job at any time or in any way apart from God's express permission. Moreover, each time he obtained permission to attack God's beloved servant, God drew the line in the sand beyond which Satan could not go.

One great objective that God has in mind in allowing us to face the trials of life is to teach us patience. The word for "trying" can be translated "proof." The idea behind the word is that of something being put in the crucible. It also carries the thought of a yoke of oxen being put to the test (Luke 14:19). This "trying of our faith" works "patience." The word used here for "patience" means literally "to abide under" something. We find it very hard to remain quiet under adverse circumstances, but God expects us to endure them cheerfully. No one knew how to do this better than Paul. When he and Silas were flogged at Philippi, then jailed, and then subjected to the torture of the stocks, they *sang!* Indeed, they sang to such effect that their influence and testimony not only held their fellow prisoners enthralled but also led to the conversion of their jailer (Acts 16:19–31).

James knew that Hebrew Christians were frequently being persecuted for their faith. The author of the epistle to the Hebrews (presumably the apostle Paul) encouraged Hebrew Christians not to give up their boldness. He reminded them that they "took joyfully the spoiling of your goods" (Heb. 10:34). To this day, Jewish Christians often pay a high price for their confession of faith. It is not uncommon for other Jews to ostracize them. Sometimes they are counted as already dead and are treated accordingly: a dead person cannot be married, cannot own property, and cannot hold a job. He is dead. The key to survival under such testing is patience.

The third purpose of testing is *to mature us:* "But let patience have her perfect work, that ye may be perfect and entire, wanting nothing" (1:4). Testing is a process. It has to go on and on until full maturity is reached and we become people of demonstrable Christian character.

The word for "perfect" is *teleiōs.* It indicates something that has reached its end, something that is finished. It carries the idea of being fully developed, of being complete, or of being initiated. The word was applied to people who were fully instructed in something in contrast to those who were mere novices. Paul used the word when writing to carnal and immature Corinthians to describe a believer who had advanced beyond the need of elementary teaching (1 Cor. 2:6–7). James has in mind patience leading to perfection in performance—a "perfect work." The word for "entire" is *holoklēros.* Paul used the word when he wrote to the Thessalonians. He told them that, in view of the coming rapture, they should be whole in spirit, soul, and body. The idea is that every grace present in Christ should be manifested in the believer. Or, as James puts it, "wanting [lacking] nothing."

Patience is a farmer's word. The farmer plows and plants his field, but then he has to wait patiently for the harvest.

Patience is a photographer's word. We see him as he goes into the wilds to get videos of a cuckoo putting its eggs in another bird's nest or of a crocodile tenderly picking up its newly hatched young in her mouth. He has to find the right spot, build his blind, set up his cameras—and then settle down to wait.

Patience is an astronomer's word. His calculations tell him of the impending visit of a comet or the coming of an eclipse. In no way can he hurry the process. If he wants to see the comet or the eclipse, he must wait.

Patience is nature's word. A time exists in the ripening process of a peach or an orange when it has all of its various parts. It is as much a peach or an orange as it is ever going to be, but it is not yet ripe. If the fruit is picked at that stage, it will be hard and bitter. Much fruit that is sold today is like that. The tomatoes are red and round and ripe—or so they seem. The peaches are beautiful in color, shape, and texture, but they have been forced in the growing process, and they have been picked too soon. The result is disappointing. The tomatoes are hard and dry, the oranges are sour, and the peaches are tasteless. They have been picked before they are ripe. Impatience has spoiled the process.

Patience is God's word. God is never in a hurry. God's word to us is "Wait!" It takes time for the earth to complete its journey around the sun. It takes time for the tide to come in. It takes time for a child to grow into a man or a woman. And it takes time to bring a person to full maturity in Christ.

We live in the day of fast-food restaurants, instant news, and instant entertainment. We try to carry all of this hurry over into spiritual life. A celebrity professes to be saved. He is lionized, promoted, hurried from place to place to give his testimony, and applauded on every hand. A young man shows promise as a preacher. He is invited here, there, and everywhere to preach his half a dozen borrowed sermons. He gets on the conference circuit and ascends the pulpits of the megachurches. Then, crash! Down he goes. God's word on all of this hurry is "Wait!" He says, "Not a novice, lest being lifted up with pride he fall into the condemnation of the devil" (1 Tim. 3:6). Patience!

> b. For our enlightenment (1:5–8)
>   (1) Wisdom required (1:5a)

Life's testing times can be perplexing. The great question that looms in our lives at such times is "Why?" It was the first thing that Job said after cursing the day of his birth (Job 1:11–12, 23). It was a question that his friends tried to answer for him, although their conclusions only aggravated Job, who knew them to be false. When God finally answered Job, it was with a series of unanswerable questions of His own centering on the word *who*. It is the mark of growth when we stop asking "Why?" and start asking "Who?" Job's attention was thus weaned from his sorrows to God's sovereignty. No wonder that his book found its way into the Word of God as containing the highest wisdom!

We learn from James that we need wisdom when the strong tides lift and the cables strain. "If any of you lack wisdom . . ." he begins (1:5). Not all of God's people are wise, and even the sagest of them can collapse when the fiery trial comes. The word for "wisdom" is *sophia*. It is more than knowledge. A person might memorize the *Encyclopedia Britannica*—and yet act like a fool. Wisdom is more than the intelligent apprehension of knowledge acquired. A person might earn half a dozen doctorates and be totally blind toward spiritual things. Einstein, one of the great geniuses of all time, is said to have been much put out by the "Big Bang" theory of the beginning of the universe because that line of reasoning would force him to face the fact of a creator.

With James, wisdom has to do with applying the circumstances of life to Christian living. We are to live like Jesus lived—in step with the will of God. The Lord went to the cross with all of its agony, suffering, and pain because He trusted the wisdom and eternal purpose of God. The cross was God's will, part of the plan. The Lord Jesus accepted that fact (1 Cor. 1:17–2:16).

James knew that many Christians lack this kind of wisdom. The word for "lack" is *leipō*, the same word as in the preceding verse. It means to be destitute, wanting, or defective. If we are defective in wisdom, we will not know how to handle problems when they arise. And who has not felt totally inadequate at times to deal with situations that have arisen? James has a solution for this state of affairs.

(2) Wisdom requested (1:5b)

"[L]et him ask of God, that giveth to all men liberally, and upbraideth not." God is a generous giver. Moreover He does not embarrass us when we come to Him. The word for "ask" is *aiteō*, which means to ask for something to be *given* (as distinct from *erōtaō*, which means to ask for someone to *do* something). The word *aiteō* is commonly used of an inferior who is addressing a superior. The word for "liberally" is *haplōs*. The word can mean either that God gives unconditionally, without bargaining, or it can mean that God gives generously. The word for "upbraideth" is *oneidizō*. God does not reproach those who appeal to Him.

God gives liberally to all men, as the Lord Jesus makes clear in the Sermon on the Mount. He points to God's matchless goodness, generosity, and impartiality. God "maketh his sun to rise on the evil and on the good, and sendeth rain on the just and on the unjust" (Matt. 5:45). Likewise, His salvation is generously made available to all (John 3:16; 2 Peter 3:9). In the same generous way, He gives wisdom to those who appeal to Him. How much more, then, will He grant the request for wisdom when it is one of His own dear children who is appealing to Him?

The classic biblical example of a man's turning to God for wisdom is Solomon. The Lord appeared to Solomon when he was crowned king of Israel and asked him what He should give to him. Solomon said, "Thou hast made thy servant king instead of David my father: and I am but a little child: I know not how to go out or come in. And thy servant is in the midst of thy people which thou hast chosen, a great people, that cannot be numbered nor counted for multitude. Give therefore thy servant an understanding heart to judge thy people, that I may discern between good and bad: for who is able to judge this thy so great a people?" (1 Kings 3:7–9).

God gave him wisdom beyond anything that Solomon could have imagined. Proof of this fact came shortly afterward when two women came before him and presented him with a very difficult case. (See 1 Kings 3:16–28.) Each shared the same home. Each had given birth to a son. One of the sons had died. Now each woman claimed that the surviving son was hers.

Solomon said, "Bring me a sword. Cut the living child in two and give each woman half."

One woman applauded Solomon's judgment; the other was horrified. Rather than allow such a thing to happen, she said that she would renounce her claim to the child.

"That's the mother!" Solomon said. The Holy Spirit adds, "And all Israel heard of the judgment which the king had judged; and they feared the king: for they saw that the wisdom of God was in him" (v. 28).

No such godlike wisdom was seen again in Israel until the Lord Jesus came. His verdict on giving, or not giving, tribute to Caesar is another classic example of wisdom (Matt. 22:16–22). So was His verdict in the case of the woman taken in adultery (John 8:1–11).

(3) Wisdom received (1:5c)

"And it shall be given him," James says. God does not scold us for either our lack of wisdom or our folly. On the contrary, He offers us a full measure of wisdom. Much of the wisdom that we need, and for which we pray, is to be found in His Word. It is already ours, available to us in hundreds of precepts, proverbs, parables, and principles. The Law of Moses contains 613 commandments, many of them still relevant to human life and society. Solomon wrote a whole book of proverbs, pithy sayings full of the distilled wisdom of heaven for life on earth. The parables of the Lord Jesus are gems of wisdom. The great principles unfolded in both the Sermon on the Mount and the Epistles are sublime. The Bible is full of wise counsel. It speaks authoritatively to all aspects of human life. It deals with our social life, our secular life, our sex life, and our spiritual life. It speaks clearly. It makes no mistakes. It is infallible and unerring in its judgments. All we have to do is read it, study it, meditate upon it, memorize it, and obey it.

We need to come to God, as little Samuel did, saying, "Speak, LORD; for thy servant heareth" (1 Sam. 3:9). Or, as the old chorus puts it,

> Speak Lord, for Thy servant heareth,
> Speak just now,
> Some message to meet my need
> Which Thou only dost know.
> Speak, now, through Thy Holy Word,
> And make me see,
> Some wonderful truth Thou hast
> To show to me.[1]

God has other ways to make us wise, but, for the most part, He simply refers us to His Word. To ask God to make us wise and yet to ignore the great Book of wisdom that He has placed in our hands is unreasonable. The great Hebrew poet declared, "Thou through thy commandments hast made me wiser than mine enemies: for they are ever with me. I have more understanding than all my teachers" (Ps. 119:98–99).

(4) Wisdom refused (1:6–8)

Receiving wisdom requires following certain rules. For various reasons, our prayers can be denied and our request for wisdom refused. One such reason is *indecision:* "But let him ask in faith, nothing wavering" (1:6a). James flings wide

---

1. E. H. G. Sargent, "Speak, Lord," *Scripture Union Choruses (Books 1, 2, and 3 Combined)* (London: Scripture Union, 1964).

open the door of prayer. Then he slams it shut again because praying has rules just as everything else has rules. One rule is that our prayer must be in line with God's "good and acceptable and perfect" will (Rom. 12:2). A prayer for wisdom certainly comes within that condition, but it must be tendered to the throne of God in faith. We must be trusting totally in God. Faith is defined for us as "the substance of things hoped for, the evidence of things not seen" (Heb. 11:1). The Holy Spirit adds that "without faith it is impossible to please him: for he that cometh to God must believe that he is, and that he is a rewarder of them that diligently seek him" (Heb. 11:6).

Few people needed wisdom more than Moses when he became Israel's kinsman-redeemer. God forewarned him that he would have a titanic struggle with Pharaoh. At first, his faith faltered because Pharaoh responded to his initial demand by making life ten times more difficult for his captives than it was before. The elders of Israel reproached Moses bitterly (Exod. 5:7–23), and he flew back to God in dismay. But his faith grew with exercise. As plague after plague fell upon Egypt, Moses' assurance blossomed.

Notice, for instance, the contrast between Moses and the people of Israel at the Red Sea. *Their* hearts failed, but Moses, with the sea before him and the Egyptian army behind him, said, "Fear ye not, stand still, and see the salvation of the LORD" (Exod. 14:13). In answer to Moses' heart cry, God said, "Wherefore criest thou unto me?" (v. 15) Evidently, Moses was perplexed. He knew that God was going to deal with the Egyptians because God had already told him so (Exod. 14:4). His wavering brought a rebuke, but it also brought a gracious word of command, which must have tested Moses' faith to the utmost: "[S]peak unto the children of Israel, that they go *forward*" (Exod. 14:15, emphasis added). Into the sea! When Moses dared to put God to the test, the sea parted before him. God gave Moses wisdom at the Red Sea to know what to do. He did not give him that wisdom, however, until he needed it.

At each crisis, Moses asked direction from God and wisdom to know what to do: at Marah, where the water was undrinkable (Exod. 15:22–25); in the wilderness, when they had nothing to eat (Exod. 16:1–4); at Rephidim, where they had no water at all (Exod. 17:1–6); and, worse, when Amalek fell upon the unprepared host in war (Exod. 17:8–16).

So, then, we are to "ask in faith." The situation might be desperate and the need for wisdom great. We turn to God, ask for wisdom, and take for granted that the Lord will show us the next step. Sometimes the light comes as a sudden flash of insight—as when God saw through the treachery of Herod and instructed the wise men not to return to Jerusalem but to go home a different way (Matt. 2:12); and as when God instructed Joseph to take Jesus and Mary to Egypt to escape Herod's murderous intent (Matt. 2:13–15). Sometimes the needed wisdom comes as events unfold. Sometimes it is not until much later that we can look back and see how wonderfully God overruled and led in a given situation.

When David went into the valley to fight Goliath, God gave him wisdom. We can be sure from what he said to the giant that David had been asking God about this whole situation (1 Sam. 17:45–47). God put it into David's heart not to fight the giant neither with a sword (v. 50) nor arrayed in Saul's armor (vv. 38–39). He would have been an easy prey for Goliath, indeed, if he had sallied forth to battle dressed in Saul's oversized gear. No, God had a better way. He gave David the wisdom to fight Goliath with a sling and a stone (v. 45) and then to cut off the giant's head with the blasphemer's own sword (v. 50). Years later, David declared that it was the Lord who taught his hands to war (Ps. 18:34; 2 Sam. 22:35).

"Nothing wavering," says James. The word used has to do with doubt. It suggests not so much weakness of faith but lack of it altogether. Paul used it in connection with Abraham's faith when, at the age of one hundred, both he and Sarah were far beyond the years of childbearing, but God told them that they were to have a son: "And being not weak in faith," Paul says, "he considered not his own body now dead, when he was about an hundred years old, neither yet the deadness of Sarah's womb: he staggered *(diakrinō)* not at the promise of God through unbelief; but was strong in faith, giving glory to God" (Rom. 4:19–20). We want wisdom? Then we must have no doubt whatsoever that, when we ask God to give it to us, He will do so.

Another reason our request for wisdom might be refused is for *illustration:* "For he that wavereth is like a wave of the sea driven with the wind and tossed" (1:6b). It is an apt illustration. Nothing is more uncertain, unpredictable, and unstable than a storm-tossed wave. It heaves this way and that, at the mercy of each howling gust of wind, and blowing now from this point of the compass and now from that. The man who looks to God for wisdom, then rushes for counsel to this person and that person, tries this angle and then that angle, rushes down this path and then that path, and tries this door and then that door is making a mockery of his prayer for wisdom.

A third reason is for *information:* "For let not that man think that he shall receive anything of the Lord. A double minded man is unstable in all his ways" (1:7–8). God does not play our little games. Much that passes for counseling falls into this very category because often people will not act on the counsel that they receive. Instead, they run from one counselor to another, hoping to get the kind of advice that they can accept comfortably.

The word for "double minded" means literally "double souled," indicating a man of divided loyalty. The word for "unstable" can be translated "restless."

Perhaps James had in mind the warm word of commendation given to the tribe of Zebulun at the time of David's accession to the throne. The warriors of Zebulun were "expert in war, with all instruments of war, fifty thousand, which could keep rank: they were not of double heart" (1 Chron. 12:33). The Hebrew idiom is literally "a heart and a heart."

The double-minded person cannot make up his mind. He comes to a fork in the road, and he cannot decide which way to go, so he perishes at the crossroads. Life does not stand still. If we refuse to make a decision when the time comes, circumstances take over and make the decision for us. A man stands undecided at the bus stop. The bus arrives, the passengers alight, people around him push on board, and still the man hesitates. The doors close, and the bus moves off. His indecision was a decision, after all—a decision to do nothing. Many a double-minded person has forfeited salvation that very way. Indecision is culpable when a person is unable to make up his mind about God and the things that God has to say. God's Word says, "Choose!" (Josh. 24:15; Hos. 10:12).

c. For our ennoblement (1:9–11)
   (1) Rejoice in advancement (1:9)

Testings are for our enlargement and for our enlightenment. They are also for our ennoblement. James now looks at the way circumstances affect our lives and how we should react to them, especially if we have sought wisdom from the Lord and the results have—or have not—been what we expected. First is the case of unexpected advancement: "Let the brother of low degree rejoice in that he is exalted."

The word for "low" can be rendered "low estate." The classic example is Mary, the mother of our Lord. In her great Magnificat, she exclaimed, "My spirit hath rejoiced in God my Saviour. For he hath regarded the *low estate* of his handmaiden" (Luke 1:47–48, emphasis added). The same word is used there as is used in James 1:9. Although Mary was a direct descendant of David, she was a poor peasant woman. She rejoiced in her unexpected exaltation: "[F]rom henceforth all generations shall call me blessed" (Luke 1:48).

"Blessed!" Thus had the herald angel addressed her (Luke 1:28), as did her cousin Elizabeth (Luke 1:41–42) and one of the Lord's followers (Luke 11:27).

The thought behind James's statement is that the brother who is poor, or lowly, can be glad because God has given him true riches and true rank in the kingdom of God.

(2) Rejoice in adversity (1:10–11)

To rejoice in adversity is a whole lot harder! James gives us a *vivid example:* "But the rich, in that he is made low: because as the flower of the grass he shall pass away. For the sun is no sooner risen with a burning heat, but it withereth the grass, and the flower thereof falleth, and the grace of the fashion of it perisheth." He also gives us a *valid expectation:* "so also shall the rich man fade away in his ways."

There is nothing particularly spiritual about being poor, and there is nothing particularly sinful about being rich. Temptations exist at both extremes. In His parable of the sower (Matt. 13), the Lord Jesus pointed to the thorns that choked out part of the harvest. He said that the thorns represented "the care of this world," the great problem of the poor, and "the deceitfulness of riches," the great problem of the rich (v. 13). Worry on the one hand and wealth on the other, both of which "choke the word" (v. 22). The wise man prayed, "Give me neither poverty nor riches; feed me with food convenient for me: lest I be full, and deny thee, and say, Who is the LORD? or lest I be poor, and steal, and take the name of my God in vain" (Prov. 30:8–9). Of the two economic extremes, James seems to prefer poverty. The Lord Jesus Himself was poor (Matt. 8:20; 2 Cor. 8:9).

The word for "that is made low" is used in the Septuagint version of Isaiah 53:7, the passage that the Ethiopian eunuch was reading when Philip led him to Christ: "In his humiliation ['low estate,' referring to the whole period of the Lord's sojourn on earth] his judgment was taken away . . ." (Acts 8:33). Paul used a kindred word in describing our Lord's earthly pilgrimage: "And being found in fashion as a man, he *humbled* himself, and became obedient unto death, even the death of the cross" (Phil. 2:8). Paul also used the same word in describing his whole attitude toward the proud Corinthians: "Have I committed an offence," he asked, "in *abasing* myself that ye might be exalted?" (2 Cor. 11:7, emphasis added).

In any case, James foresaw the possibility of the rich man's being leveled suddenly by adverse circumstances. His graphic illustration is that of grass withering before the fierce heat of summer.

The gospel always seems to appeal to the poor rather than to the rich. For instance, the wealth of the rich young ruler turned out to be a snare to him. It kept him from following Christ (Mark 10:17–22). Jesus commented on the man's reaction, "How hardly shall they that have riches enter into the kingdom of God! . . . It is easier for a camel to go through the eye of a needle, than for a rich man to enter into the kingdom of God" (Mark 10:23–25).

The disciples were astonished at this revolutionary teaching. "Who then can be saved?" they asked (Mark 10:26).

Some people have deliberately renounced rank and riches to join the ranks of the poor. Take Francis of Assisi, for example. He was born to prosperous parents. They looked askance at their son when he adopted a lifestyle foreign to the one in which he had been reared. They were outraged at the squalor in which he lived and at his prodigal way of giving to the poor. His father locked him up in the cellar of their home and then hauled him before the local bishop and demanded that he renounce his new infatuations. Francis seized the opportunity to confirm his revolutionary new views. He took off all of his clothes and returned them to his father! He had on a hair shirt under his robes, over which he put an old smock that had belonged to a farmer. It was fitting enough clothing, he thought, for a beggar and a follower of Christ.

He founded the Franciscan order, which is now the largest religious order in the Roman Catholic Church. He preached and practiced austerity and good works and disciplined his body severely. Although he forbade moroseness, he loathed laughing. He ministered especially to lepers, people for whom he had once entertained a great horror. He conquered his aversion, gave them large sums of money, and kissed their hands. He made a custom of fasting the forty days of Lent, as well as at other times. At times, he would lie all night in a ditch full of icy water to punish his flesh and often slept sitting up outside on the ground. At a lonely vigil at Mount La Verna, he is said to have received the *stigmata*—wounds in his hands, feet, and side. He suffered from a chronic eye infection. He preached to everyone who would listen, even to the birds! He wrote a canticle about "Brother" Sun. Throughout his career, he was fascinated by the poverty of Christ and His disciples. Those who wished to join his order had to give away all of their possessions and join the ranks of the very poor. He would often meditate, holding a human skull in his hand to remind him of his mortality and that Jesus had been crucified at the place of a skull. Just before his death, he added a stanza to his "Canticle of Brother Sun." It was a stanza in praise of "Sister Bodily Death." When death came, it found him blind, diseased, and emaciated. He is thought to have died from tuberculoid leprosy.

The Roman Catholic Church has a long roll call of such men. There was Simon Stylites, for instance, who achieved incredible feats of asceticism. He crowned all of his other acts by moving to a hillside, where he sat chained to a pillar six feet high and with a heavy iron collar around his neck. From time to time, he would increase the height of his pillar until, at length, his disciples had to climb a tall ladder to bring him such scraps of food as he would condescend to eat. There he perched throughout the bitter frosts of thirty Syrian winters and the scorching heat of thirty burning summers, disdaining any shelter from the weather.

There was also Francis Xavier, a Spanish cavalier who was born in a palace on the slopes of the Pyrenes, a man who enjoyed pleasure and was the applauded darling of society. He moved to Paris and became a teacher, only to find himself haunted by an ungainly, deformed pupil. That pupil was determined to make a conquest of his witty and popular teacher. That pupil was Ignatius Loyola.

Xavier did not have a chance against the pitiless logic of his pupil. He renounced the world, became a monk, and flung himself into the cause of world evangelism. He went to India, then on and on to other distant lands, learning language after language. He was ridiculed, stoned, and persecuted, but on he went. He tumbled across oceans, preaching to sailors and soldiers on the high seas. He preached to robbers and to slaves, to lepers and to those who were dying of loathsome pestilence. Kings and cannibals alike heard him preach, raising a cross in one hand and ringing a bell with the other to summon the crowds. He was fearless and tireless, allowing himself only three hours of sleep a night. He took burning deserts and precipitous mountain paths in his stride, and neither earthquake nor volcano could stop him. At last—worn out and an old, old man of forty-five— he died on a beach in Siam.

Not that Rome has any monopoly on those who have surrendered fortunes for the cause of Christ. Charles T. Studd was born to wealth and was educated in England's most prestigious schools—Eton and Cambridge. He achieved fame as a sportsman. Then along came D. L. Moody, and C. T. Studd was converted. He gave away his fortune and went to China. He and his companions donned Chinese garb and lived with the Chinese people. When his health was broken he returned to England, but not for long. Off he went to India and then to Africa, where he set out to penetrate the heart of the continent. In "the hungry thirties," at the height of a great global economic depression, he issued the following statement of his financial principles.

> I would solemnly lay before you the absolute necessity of nobody, man or woman, coming out here who does not recognize the absolute necessity of super-sacrifice of self, and demand it. If people want pretty houses and elegant furnishings, for God's sake and ours, let them stay at home in the nursery. If they are afraid to cycle or walk and need to be carried about in sedan chairs, let them remain in a lady's boudoir at the seaside. . . .

If a man joins our mission, he comes out on God. God is his Father; to God he looks for supplies whether in money or in kind. If God sends much, he is rather cast down, thinking God is afraid to trust him to suffer in patience. If God sends little, he thanks God and takes courage that after all he may be in the apostolic succession. If he has nothing, then he shouts hallelujah, for he knows he has come to the very entrance of the heavenly kingdom where there is neither eating nor drinking, but righteousness, peace and joy and loving service forever and ever.

What is done, God does. What is given, God gives. What is withheld, God withholds. . . .

Some people inquire as to the houses we live in and the food we eat. Our houses are mostly the counterpart of those the government provides for their officials in this district. They are all thatched with grass or leaves. My personal residence has walls of elephant grass. Others are made of stucco, clay, or bamboo. Our European furniture comprises beds, chairs, tables, bookshelves and the like. We live as much as possible on native food: fowls, eggs, rice, maize, bananas, pineapple, guava, potatoes, cocoa, cornflower, macaroni. European tinned food we reserve as much as possible for time of sickness.

But if the reputation of Protestant missions depends on such things as the houses they live in, the furniture they use, the filthy lucre—as the apostle calls it—that they receive and the food they eat, the sooner they die the better. Are houses, furniture, food, the foundation of an excellent missionary reputation? I observe that Christ said to his disciples, "Take no thought for your life, what ye shall eat . . . drink . . . put on!" And Paul wrote to Timothy, "Having food and raiment let us be therewith content." "Endure hardness, as a good soldier of Jesus Christ."

We are only ashamed that the little sacrifices we have made are so terribly small as to be invisible. When we think of the life of our Lord and Savior and God, who came to earth to redeem us, who was born in a manger, who had nowhere to lay his head, who died a felon's death on the Cross, who said "Follow me," then great shame oppresses us, because we are such terrible caricatures of Christ and his apostles.[2]

---

2. See *Decision* magazine, July 1961.

Rich or poor, the important thing is to keep close to the Lord. Paul could say, "I have learned, in whatsoever state I am, therewith to be content. I know both how to be abased, and I know how to abound: every where and in all things I am instructed both to be full and to be hungry, both to abound and to suffer need. I can do all things through Christ which strengtheneth me" (Phil. 4:11–13).

2. Testings are for our profit (1:12)

James has shown us that testings are for a purpose (1:2–11). He now shows us that they are also for our profit. First, he shows us the *crisis endured:* "Blessed is the man that endureth temptation (trials)" (1:12a). The word for "blessed" is the same word that the Lord used in the Sermon on the Mount (Matt. 5:3–12). To the Lord's eight beatitudes James adds another: "Blessed is the man that endureth temptation."[3] Like its Old Testament counterpart, the word for "blessed" that is used here means "to make large," or "to be happy."

The word for "endure" suggests someone bravely bearing up under suffering— "to bear up courageously," or to take things patiently. It also carries the idea of waiting.

The great demands of the Sermon on the Mount are far beyond our own poor ability to achieve. In that same sermon, the Lord gave to His disciples the principles of holy living, but not until Pentecost did they receive the power to live the Christian life. In the Upper Room, the Lord taught the mystery of being "in the vine" (John 15:1–8), but Paul translated that mystery into everyday experience (Rom. 6–8) and related everything to the indwelling Holy Spirit.

"Blessed is the man that endureth temptation," says James.

Paul asks, "Who shall separate us from the love of Christ? shall tribulation, or distress, or persecution, or famine, or nakedness, or peril, or sword? As it is written, For thy sake we are killed all the day long; we are accounted as sheep for the slaughter. Nay, in all these things we are more than conquerors through him that loved us. For I am persuaded, that neither death, nor life, nor angels, nor principalities, nor powers, nor things present, nor things to come, nor height, nor depth, nor any other creature, shall be able to separate us from the love of God, which is in Christ Jesus our Lord" (Rom. 8:35–39).

Paul wrote out of a vast experience of trial and suffering (2 Cor. 11:23–33).

---

3. Much of James's letter is based on the Sermon on the Mount, if it is not simply an exposition and application of that great statement.

Next James shows the *crown ensured:* "for when he is tried, he shall receive the crown of life, which the Lord hath promised to them that love him" (1:12b). The word for "crown" here is *stephanos,* the crown of triumph that was given to victors in the Olympic games and other such events. The Greek games were common in Palestine in the days of Herod the Great. They were even held in Jerusalem itself. The "crown of life" stands here in contrast with the Lord's crown *(stephanos)* of thorns (Matt. 27:29). The only other place where the crown of life is mentioned is in the ascended Lord's promise to the persecuted saints at Smyrna: "be thou faithful unto death, and I will give thee a crown *[stephanos]* of life" (Rev. 2:10). We can win other crowns—the crown of righteousness (2 Tim. 4:8), for example, and the crown of glory (1 Peter 5:4).

James offsets the ups and downs of life, along with its troubles and trials, by promising a reward, a crown, to those who love the Lord unreservedly. It is a powerful incentive.

Some years ago, at the Moody Bible Institute's annual Founder's Week Conference, Dr. Howard Hendricks of Dallas Theological Seminary recounted an experience that he once had with the town's champion checkers player. He was a young fellow at the time and so confident of his prowess that he decided to take on the old veteran. He was given the first move and decided to set the pace. After a few moves, his adversary put a piece in the line of fire. "Jump me!" he demanded.

Hendricks did so, scooping the piece triumphantly off the board. He thought that he had the game in the bag when his opponent put another piece in jeopardy. "Jump me!" he said.

Hendricks gleefully took the piece. Then it happened. The older man picked up one of his pieces. Jump! Jump! Jump! Jump! His piece raced down the board, scooping up Hendricks's pieces with relentless precision. His piece arrived at king territory. "Crown me!"

After that, young Hendricks didn't have a chance. Piece after piece was pounced on until he had lost them all.

Dr. Hendricks made the point. "No good checker player minds losing an occasional piece," he said, "so long as he is heading for king territory." James seems to have thought much the same. The occasional trial or loss can be taken in stride ao long as we keep in mind "the crowning day that's coming by and by."

The crown of life is promised "to them that love him." That's all it takes. Ah! but then, love "bears all things, believes all things, hopes all things, endures all things. Love never fails" (1 Cor. 13:7–8 NKJV).

B. The temptations of the Christian life (1:13–16)
  1. The source of the temptation (1:13–15)
    a. What we must realize (1:13)

Sin is a serious business. It is universal and deadly. James now puts the whole question of sin and temptation into focus. He begins by *recording a common error:* "Let no man say when he is tempted, I am tempted of God" (1:13a). We are not to blame God for our bad behavior. In the Garden of Eden, Eve blamed the serpent, and Adam blamed both Eve and God.

"The serpent beguiled me," Eve said, trying to shift the blame (Gen. 3:13).

Adam was even more brazen: "The woman whom thou gavest to be with me, *she* [the word is emphatic] gave me of the tree, and I did eat" (Gen. 3:12). Adam tried to shift the blame for his disobedience to God.

Modern psychology has invented all kinds of ways for guilty people, suffering mentally from the consequences of their own bad behavior, to shift the blame to their parents, their partners, or other people in general. But God refuses to allow us to get away with such evasions. The desire to shift the blame, however, is as old as Adam.

God will not let people blame Him for their sin. It is a libel on the character of God. God is holy. He hates sin in all of its forms. Temptation arises from various sources, within and without, but never from God, who is "of purer eyes than to behold evil, and canst not look on iniquity" (Hab. 1:13). The whole of God's nature militates against sin. It would never occur to Him to tempt anyone. Testings often come from Him, but *temptations* do not. God tests us to bring out the good; Satan tempts us to bring out the bad. For instance, all of Satan's attacks on Job were designed in Satan's nefarious, twisted mind to tempt him to curse God. At the same time, God was testing His beloved servant and refining him.

James now goes on to *refute a common error.* He says, "God cannot be tempted with evil, neither tempteth he any man" (1:13b). The words *cannot be tempted* come from *apeirastos,* meaning that God is "incapable of being tempted." Paul says that the Old Testament Israelites "tempted" *(peirazō)* God (1 Cor. 10:9), that is, their wicked behavior militated against His holy nature. All they did was bring down upon them the righteous judgment of a God whose holiness compels Him to take action against sin wherever it raises its head.

A magnet cannot attract a piece of silver, a golden coin, or a lump of lead. It can attract only iron—because iron has the same nature as the magnet. Just so, nothing in God's character can respond to temptation. On the contrary, the most terrifying holiness emanates from Him. He is described as "a consuming fire"

(Deut. 4:24), and His ministers are likewise "a flame of fire" (Heb. 1:7). So awesome is the outshining of His holiness that the sinless seraphim themselves, sons of light that they are, hide in their wings before Him and cry, "Holy, holy, holy, is the LORD" (Isa. 6:1–3).

God finds sin utterly repulsive in all of its forms, and His whole being burns against it. We find sin attractive, however, because we have fallen natures. God's nature is one of absolute and active goodness. A snowflake approaching the sun would have a better chance of survival than Satan would if he were to approach God with a temptation. We laugh and jest and make jokes about sin. God is not amused.

Temptation arises from quite another source, as James now tells us.

b. What we must recognize (1:14–15)

James points out three phases of the temptation-sin-death process. He begins with *the mother of sin:* "But every man is tempted, when he is drawn away of his own lust, and enticed. Then when lust hath conceived, it bringeth forth sin" (1:14–15a). The father of sin is the devil; the mother of sin is lust. Before a baby can be born, impregnation must take place. It is the same with sin. Once let lust be impregnated, and there will be a birth. Moreover, once that sin is brought to birth, it will have a vigorous life of its own.

It is popular today to attribute human wrong behavior to genetics. A massive hunt is under way, for instance, to find the gene, the blueprint, and the code that predetermines whether a person will become a homosexual. That is a very convenient way to justify sodomy. The Bible does not treat sodomy as a sickness, a psychosis, or a genetic problem; it treats it as sin, and a very flagrant sin at that (Gen. 19). In the Old Testament, God's law pronounced the death penalty on people who practiced sodomy, adultery, bestiality, and incest (Lev. 18:1–30; Deut. 22:22; 27:20–24; Lev. 20:10–16). God did not condemn people to death for being sick or for behaving according to the dictates of their genes. He condemned them to death for practicing soul-destroying, society-polluting sins.

The Lord Jesus knew which genes can control us, what aspects of life are predetermined, and what aspects of life we can control. He said, "Which of you by taking thought can add one cubit unto his stature?" (Matt. 6:27). That is a genetic function. To the woman taken in adultery, He said, "Go, and sin no more" (John 8:11). Hers was responsible, volitional, chosen, and culpable behavior.

The teaching of James has to do with behavior for which we are responsible. Satan sows a thought, either personally or through one of his human or demonic emissaries, and lust responds. We have the embryos of all kinds of lust in our fallen natures. Satan comes along and plants the living factor of temptation along-side the latent factor of lust, and germination takes place. Alongside the porno-graphic lust he plants a dirty book, a filthy movie, or a suggestive picture. Instantly, the latent lust and the lewd temptation are positioned so that conception can take place in the soul. It does not happen at once. Something else must happen first, but now the situation is ripe for conception to take place and for a sin to be born.

Similarly, alongside the anger lust, he lays an insult or a disappointment. Instantly, the latent lust and the luring temptation are in a position for conception to take place and for a temper to explode.

However, the two things must first fuse together. The temptation is there, and the lust is there, and the two ingredients are there. The situation is ripe for conception to take place. When does that happen? When the will gets involved. Once the will responds, impregnation takes place. Lust conceives. Sin is born.

The first temptation, in the Garden of Eden, illustrates what happens. The first thing we learn, both from the temptation of Adam and Eve and from the temptation of Christ, is that Satan can *persuade,* but he cannot *push.* He can dangle the bait, but he cannot ram it down our throats.

In the case of Eve, the *suggestion* came first. The serpent drew Eve's attention to the tree and persuaded her to listen to what he had to say. That was her first mistake. When she listened, she made room for the devil's words to be debated in her mind. It was the first step to becoming involved. Before long, not only was Eve's mind engaged in the wrong thoughts but also her desires were quickened. She saw that the tree was "good for food, and that it was pleasant to the eyes, and a tree to be desired to make one wise" (Gen. 3:6). Suddenly, the forbidden fruit seemed to be unexpectedly delightful, delectable, and desirable. Satan had successfully impregnated lust. Millions of people now involved with drugs, drink, and immorality took the first step when they listened to an evil suggestion.

Then came the evil *insinuation.* Satan insinuated to Eve that God had not told her the real truth about that tree—that its fruit would open her eyes and make her wise. He insinuated further that God was not really interested in her welfare because He was withholding from her something that was desirable. She could become as one of the gods. She could have a more abundant life and enjoy a dimension of living beyond anything that she had ever known or imagined.

The third step was *rationalization.* Eve came to believe that right was wrong and that wrong was right. Moreover she accepted Satan's lie that no penalties were attached to "doing her own thing." No harm would come to her. She could indulge her desire and get away with it. Such are Satan's lies. He set her up. He took her mind, the will gave way, and lust was impregnated. "Then, when lust hath conceived, it bringeth forth sin," James says (1:15). Once we allow lust and temptation to fuse, we can expect the inevitable: a birth. A sin will be born. Apart from God's intervening grace, that diabolical offspring will be ours forever.

James now moves us on to the next step. We are told about *the method of sin:* "and sin, when it is finished . . ." (1:15b). The sin, now conceived, grows and develops. The word that James uses for "finished" *(apaoteleō)* means "to bring to maturity," or "to become full grown." Every sin grows in sinfulness. As Paul puts it, sin becomes "exceeding sinful" (Rom. 7:13). It grows in strength, and its malign influence spreads progressively. Sin is joined to sin. They bind us with iron chains. The man who drinks becomes a hopeless drunkard. The man who smokes marijuana goes on to cocaine and heroin. The man who indulges in sex becomes a companion of pimps, prostitutes, and perverts.

Samson, for example, thought that he could play games with Delilah. She won! She saw him blinded and bound, grinding corn for the Philistines, the sport of his enemies and the mockery of the world. The sin grows in size, it spreads, and it cannot rest until it has others in its coils. No sooner was Eve a sinner than she became a seducer.

But James has not finished. He tells us about *the maturity of sin:* "for sin, when it is finished, bringeth forth death" (1:15c). It puts its hand upon morality and kills it. It puts its hand upon character and kills it. It puts its hand upon health and kills it. It is the great destroyer of the human race. Every hospital, every prison, every battlefield, and every graveyard cries out that sin is deadly. It kills.

"Thou shalt surely die," God said to Adam.

"Thou shalt not surely die," the serpent said to Eve.

Sin has a thousand agents. Those who become involved in sexual immorality expose themselves to venereal diseases and AIDS, diseases that have reached epidemic proportions in the world. Venereal diseases such as syphilis, gonorrhea, and the other more than twenty companion diseases, such as herpes, strike some fifteen million Americans every year, with a new infection occurring every forty-five seconds. They bring with them pain, blindness, arthritis, infertility, brain damage, insanity, and death.

2. The subtlety of temptation (1:16)

Because the whole issue of sin is surrounded by deception, James concludes this statement regarding temptation thus: "Do not err, my beloved brethren" (1:16). We might wonder how James came to have such a thoroughgoing acquaintance with the dynamics of sin. He derived it from a study of his own heart. He was held in the bondage of unbelief, a particularly malevolent form of sin (Rev. 21:8) all through the years that he spent in the same home, synagogue, and workshop as Jesus. Throughout those years, he was held in error concerning the nature, person, personality, and ministry of the Lord. He was completely deceived.

When the serpent is first introduced into the Bible story, the Holy Spirit gives us fair warning. "The serpent," He says, "was more subtle than any beast of the field . . ." (Gen. 3:1). The Hebrew word can be rendered "wise" or "crafty" (Job 5:12; 15:5). The serpent allowed itself to become the agent of fallen Lucifer, the most brilliant of all created intelligences. Lucifer was a high-ranking member of the order of the cherubim. However, his wisdom has turned into craftiness, subtlety, and guile. He has a thousand devices for making sin attractive to us and for deceiving us. We must be on our guard.

James goes on to tell us how to avoid being deceived by the Evil One (1:17–27). We must heed the Word of God. We cannot have too serious a view of sin, or of our own personal susceptibility to and accountability for it. James tells us bluntly that we cannot blame someone else for our sins. The graffiti scrawled across a wall gives us the modern attitude: "Humpty Dumpty was pushed." That was not so. He fell. The old nursery rhyme calls it "a great fall." He had no business being on the wall in the first place.

PART 3

The Christian and His Bible

James 1:17–27

A. God's Word is likened to a gift (1:17–18)
1. A gift that brings divine light (1:17)
a. The nature of the gifts (1:17a–c)

Every good gift and every perfect gift is from above." Anything that is good in us comes from God. He gives only good gifts. The Lord introduced this subject in the Sermon on the Mount: "What man is there of you, whom if his son ask bread, will he give me a stone? Or if he ask a fish, will he give him a serpent? If ye then, being evil, know how to give good gifts unto your children, how much more shall your Father which is in heaven give good things to them that ask him?" (Matt. 7:9–11).

Perhaps the Lord had in mind His own temptation experience in the wilderness. After a forty-day fast, when He was famished and weak with hunger, Satan came and offered Him a stone (Matt. 4:1–4)—along with the suggestion that He exercise His deity to take care of the needs of His humanity. Jesus knew that, at that moment, it was the good and acceptable and perfect will for Him that He be hungry, and He quoted the Word of God to the devil to prove it.

God gives only good gifts. All that is good in our lives comes from God. God is good, and He alone is absolutely good. Far from being the source of temptation to do evil, God is the Source of all that is good.

b. The nature of the giver (1:17d–e)

God is *unchallengeable.* He is "the Father of lights," and He is *unchangeable:* "with whom is no variableness, neither shadow of turning." God's first work in creation was to command the light to shine out of darkness. "Light, be!" He said, and light was. Later, He commanded the sun, the moon, and the stars to shed their light upon the earth. Fallen man, in his abysmal folly, soon forgot the One from whom all light comes, "the Father of lights," and substituted the sun, the moon, and the stars themselves as objects of worship. In Egypt, for instance, the reigning pharaoh was believed to be the son of the sun, the incarnation of Ra, the sun god. The Babylonians invented astrology and the worship of the stars. Abraham himself came from Ur, a Chaldean center of moon worship.

The great stars that burn and blaze by the countless billions in the sky are merely the handmaidens of the living God. David knew! He sang, "The heavens declare the glory of God; and the firmament showeth his handiwork . . . There is no speech nor language, where their voice is not heard" (Ps. 19:1, 3). The starry heavens have well been called "God's oldest testament." Psalm 19 is a great Hebrew hymn designed by the Holy Spirit to compare God's testimony to Himself in the stars with His testimony to Himself in the Scriptures.

God bears witness to Himself. With Him is no "variableness," James says. The Greek word tells us that with God there is not the slightest variation—in contrast with the sun that seems, to the eye, to move across the heavens, rising in the east and setting in the west.

With God, furthermore, there is "neither shadow of turning." The reference here might be to the sundial, one of the oldest instruments devised by man for keeping track of time. It marks the shadow cast by the sun on the dial as the sun proceeds upon its way. The reference might also be to the sun as it sets swiftly in a ball of flame behind the western horizon and casts lengthening shadows upon the earth as it sets.

God does not change; He casts no shadows. The wise man of old declared, "The path of the just is as the shining light, that shineth more and more unto the perfect day" (Prov. 4:18). Jesus said, "I am the light of the world: he that followeth me shall not walk in darkness, but shall have the light of life" (John 8:12).

2. A gift that brings divine life (1:18)

James now gives us his version of the new birth. He sees it as being related to *the will of God:* "Of his own will begat he us"; to *the Word of God:* "with the word of truth"; and to *the wisdom of God:* "that we should be a kind of firstfruits of his creatures." The will of God takes us back to a dateless, timeless past when the members of the Godhead decided to act in creation. The Word of God is our current point of reference, the instrument of the Holy Spirit in revelation and regeneration (Heb. 1:1; 1 Peter 1:23). The wisdom of God embraces His future purpose in exhibiting us as "the firstfruits of his creatures."

People have raised all kinds of difficulties regarding the sovereignty of God as related to the will of man. The Bible clearly teaches that God acts sovereignly and of His own volition in arranging for the regeneration of certain members of the human race. However, Peter balances that truth by reminding the redeemed that they are "elect according to the foreknowledge of God" (1 Peter 1:2). Paul says much the same thing (Rom. 8:29–30). We might never resolve the issues involved in the two great issues of divine sovereignty on the one side and human volition and accountability on the other. The fact is certain that the initiative in our salvation is God's. The Lord Jesus is presented to us as "the Lamb slain from the foundation of the world" (Rev. 13:8). Calvary was no afterthought with God. When the members of the Godhead decided to act in creation, they knew that the time would come when they would have to act in redemption. It was all foreknown, including God's omniscient knowledge of who of Adam's race would respond to the gospel.

The actual process of bringing the redemptive work of the cross home to our hearts is bound closely with "the word of truth." The Word of God is the Holy Spirit's instrument to bring us under conviction of sin, to open our eyes to the person and work of Christ, and to bring about the miracle of regeneration in a believing heart.

Doubtless, many reasons exist why God has brought various members of the human race into the sphere of redemption, reconciliation, and regeneration. James presents just one of them: the redeemed are to be "a kind of firstfruits of his creatures." We are the first specimens, so to speak, of His new creation.

James was thoroughly familiar with the Old Testament annual Feast of Firstfruits (Lev. 23:10–14). It took place on "the morrow after the sabbath." On the Sunday after the Passover, the Hebrews had to present a sheaf from the harvest field and wave it before the Lord. Plenty more grain was in the field, but the wave-sheaf was set apart especially for God. Even James, as devoted as he was to the Sabbath, must surely have seen the significance of the fact that the wave-sheaf was connected with the first day of the week, with the day on which Christ rose from the dead, and thus with the church itself. At some time between Passover and Pentecost, the risen Lord appeared to James. It might well have been on the resurrection day itself, the same day on which He appeared to backslidden Peter.

The church is the antitype of the Old Testament type of the Feast of Firstfruits. It occupies a unique place among the various companies of the redeemed. The Old Testament believers were redeemed; the 144,000 witnesses, who will witness for Christ during the Tribulation, will be redeemed; the countless multitude of those who will be won to Christ by the ministry of the 144,000 will be redeemed; and the people who will respond to the preaching of the apocalyptical angel (Rev. 14:6–7) will be numbered among the redeemed. But the church is unique, set apart from all other companies of the redeemed.

Perhaps James had caught a glimpse of this fact from David's great Calvary psalm (Ps. 22). In the second half of the psalm, the Divine Sufferer looked forward to a day beyond the cross. "My praise shall be of thee," He tells His father, "in the great congregation" (Ps. 22:25). God has many congregations. Indeed the psalmist has already mentioned one of them (Ps. 22:22). But He has a *great* congregation. David did not know anything about that congregation, but the Holy Spirit did. The great congregation is the church. It stands apart from all other congregations of God's people in ages past and ages yet to be.[1] James described it as "a kind of firstfruits of his creatures."

It was left to the apostle Paul, however, to set before the church the significance of its unique place in the annals of eternity and its high and holy calling in the purposes of God. Note his word to the Ephesians: "That in the dispensation of the fulness of times he might gather together in one all things in Christ, both which are in heaven, and which are on earth; even in him: in whom also we have obtained an inheritance, being predestinated according to the purpose of him who worketh all things after the counsel of his own will: that we should be to the praise of his glory, who first trusted in Christ" (Eph. 1:10–12). He continues later in the epistle, "To the intent that now unto the principalities and powers in heavenly places might be known by the church the manifold wisdom of God, according to the eternal purpose which he purposed in Christ Jesus our Lord" (Eph. 3:10–11).

B. God's Word is likened to a graft (1:19–22)
   1. To effect a change in our talk (1:19–20)

James resorts now to another illustration. God's Word is not only a gift but also a graft. James speaks of "the engrafted word." When we accept God's Word at its face value, it will change our conduct, and our conversation by changing our character. James says that we should *be swift to respond to speaking:* "Wherefore, my beloved brethren, let every man be swift to hear" (1:19a). This is a lesson that Peter had to learn on the Mount of Transfiguration. The heavenly vision burst upon his sight, and he caught a glimpse of the Lord in conversation with Moses and Elijah. Then he opened his mouth and blurted out some sheer nonsense! It was too bad that he did not simply *listen* because Luke tells us that the two visitors from glory were talking with the Lord about the death that He was soon to accomplish at Calvary. If Peter had listened to that conversation, he might have given us another epistle! He should have been "swift to hear," to respond to what was being said in respectful silence and with eager attention. Instead, God Himself had to tell Peter to hold his tongue and listen to the Lord (Matt. 17:1–5).

---

1. See John Phillips, *Exploring Psalms* (reprint, Grand Rapids: Kregel, 2002).

The art of listening is one that we all need to acquire. The Lord Jesus often used this expression: "He that hath ears to hear, let him hear." The words are His alone in the Bible. In Scripture, no mortal man ever used them, but He alone who spoke with the authority of God (Matt. 7:29). He used the expression seven times while on earth (Luke 8:8; Matt. 11:15; 13:9, 43; Mark 4:23; 7:16; Luke 14:35—in chronological order) and eight times from heaven (Rev. 2:7, 11, 17, 29; 3:6, 13, 22; 13:9). Most of us are poor listeners. God speaks, however, to those who have ears to hear.

A famous naturalist, walking through a city park with a friend, said suddenly, "Did you hear that cricket?"

"No," his friend replied, "I heard nothing. How could you possibly have heard a cricket with all of this roar of traffic enveloping us?"

Said the naturalist, "You hear what you train yourself to hear. Watch!" He pulled some coins from his pocket and threw them on the sidewalk. Instantly, several passersby slapped their pockets and looked to see if they had dropped some money.

When he was still a small boy, the young Samuel learned a great lesson from his elderly guardian, the aged priest Eli. One night, God called to little Samuel. The boy thought that Eli had called him, and he ran to see what the old man wanted. After this same thing happened three times in a row, it dawned on the aged priest that God was calling the boy. He said to him, "Go, lie down: and it shall be, if he call thee, that thou shalt say, Speak, LORD; for thy servant heareth" (1 Sam. 3:1–10). It was good advice.

If we are to be swift to respond to speaking by cultivating the habit of being "a good listener," we are also to *be slow to resort to speaking* (1:19b–20). James sets forth two principles. The *first principle* is "Be slow to speak" (1:19b). One of the things that aggravated Job was the eagerness with which his friends tore into him with their various views about what had happened to him. Indeed, Job was so provoked by Zophar's first speech that he turned on him and said, "O that ye would altogether hold your peace! and it should be your wisdom" (Job 13:5). Zophar was an arrogant, bigoted man and the most cutting and scathing of Job's critics. In effect, Job said to him, "If you would keep your mouth shut, some-body might make a mistake and think you were wise!" Job could have said much the same to all of his wordy friends. They all spoke out of ignorance.

James advocates "an eloquent silence." The Lord Himself might have spoken to Pilate in his own native dialect and opened his eyes. He might have told him that, in His kingdom, He was served by ministers who were a flaming fire. He might have told him of legion upon legion of mighty angels, standing with swords already drawn, in the unseen world. He might have told him of a throne, high and lifted up beyond a billion teeming galaxies in space. He might have answered Pilate's cynical question, "What is truth?" by an exposition of all of the follies of all of the philosophers of Athens and Rome.

But He did nothing of the kind. For the most part, He said nothing, and that terrible silence spoke more loudly to Pilate than any words. The reason the Lord was so silent was simple. He had nothing to say. Pilate knew perfectly well the innocence of his prisoner. He knew fully the motives and the malice of the Sanhedrin, and he knew where his duty lay. That was all there was to it. Pilate had never before met a prisoner who defended himself so brilliantly by saying little or nothing at all.

When James says, "Be slow to speak," he means, perhaps, that we would do well to think twice before we speak. When Nathan the prophet came to David with the story of the rich man who had stolen a poor man's one little lamb, to provide a feast for a visitor, David exploded, when he should have been slow to speak. His anger "was greatly kindled," the Holy Spirit says. "As the Lord liveth, the man that hath done this thing shall surely die: and he shall restore the lamb fourfold," he blurted—and, in so doing, he condemned himself.

"Thou art the man!" Nathan said. David had angrily and unexpectedly pronounced judgment of himself (2 Sam. 12:1–13).

James now moves on to the *further principle* (1:19c–20). He states *the rule:* be "slow to wrath" (1:19c); he gives *the reason:* "for the wrath of man worketh not the righteousness of God" (1:20). All too often, unguarded speech gives expression to an inner turmoil in our hearts. Jesus said, "Out of the abundance of the heart the mouth speaketh" (Matt. 12:34).

The word for "wrath" here referred originally to any natural impulse. In time, it came to represent anger, the strongest of all of the passions. The word can be rendered "temper." James adds an explanation. Losing one's temper can never achieve anything, least of all the righteousness of God in one's life.

There is such a thing, of course, as righteous anger. When the Lord was in the synagogue one Sabbath, His enemies eyed Him, waiting to see if He would heal a man there who had a withered hand. He knew their thoughts and challenged them. They held their tongues and waited. We read, "When he had looked round about on them with anger, being grieved for the hardness of their hearts," He healed the man (Mark 3:5). The miracle, and the imagined breaking of the Sabbath, so provoked His enemies that they began to plot His death. James, however, was not talking about that kind of anger, wrath against sin, the reaction of a truly good person. The Lord Jesus did not lose His temper, although He let people see His great displeasure at the hardness of their hearts. James was warning us against bad temper.

The classic biblical example of a man's wrath working not the righteousness of God is found in the story of Moses, whose meekness and self-control was displayed on scores of occasions, even under the severest provocation. But on one notable occasion, he lost his temper completely. The Israelites had come back to Kadesh. It was the first month of the fortieth year after the Exodus. Nearly all of the people who had come out of Egypt were dead. A new generation now stood before Moses, and the history of the Hebrew people was about to begin again. No history had been recorded since the last fateful arrival at Kadesh, except for a sad list of wanderings (Num. 33).

Back at Kadesh, they found no water to drink. The people turned on Moses at once. Moses turned to God. God told Moses to *speak* to the rock and water would flow. On the previous occasion, God had told him to *smite* the rock, but all that was needed now was that he speak to it. The typology is perfect. It reminds us that the great Rock of Ages, the Lord Jesus, was smitten at Calvary so that the life-giving water of the Holy Spirit might flow. He will never be smitten again. All that is needed now is a simple appeal.

But Moses lost his temper. He stood before the rock, and he "spake unadvisedly with his lips" (Ps. 106:33). He cried, "Hear now, ye rebels; must we fetch your water out of this rock?" Then he "lifted up his hand, and with his rod he smote the rock twice" (Num. 20:10–11). God graciously gave the water, but He passed the sentence of death on Moses and locked him out of the Promised Land (Num. 20:12). He had ruined the type. He had lost his temper and had failed to "sanctify" the Lord before the people. His behavior is actually called "rebellion" (Num. 20:24; 27:14). Moses, who had tried to excuse himself from becoming Israel's kinsman-redeemer at the beginning of his ministry by saying, "I cannot speak" (Exod. 4:10), was kept out of Canaan for speaking far too much. The man whose meekness was proverbial (Num. 12:3) was solemnly punished for displaying what James calls "the wrath of man."

2. To effect a change in our walk (1:21–22)

The Word of God, as a graft, is God's instrument for changing our behavior. James tells us *what we must reject:* "Wherefore lay apart all filthiness and superfluity of naughtiness" (1:21a). The word for "filthiness" suggests dirt, filth, and impurity. The word for "superfluity" suggests "an exceeding measure," or something above and beyond the ordinary. The picture is of something overflowing, referring here to wickedness. The word for "naughtiness" (a much diluted word in our modern English vocabulary) refers to wickedness, depravity, and one's vicious disposition and desires. We are to be done with these things.

But that is easier said than done, given our fallen, Adamic nature. Evil wells up from within. James did not have the theological mind of Paul, nor did any of the Lord's disciples. It would remain for Paul to write his epistle to the Romans, especially chapters 6–8, before the great truths of positional and practical sanctification would be developed. But James had the right idea. The things that belong to the old nature cannot be allowed to hold sway in a believer's life. James tells us to "lay apart" these things. Paul tells us to "put off" the old man and his deeds and to "put on" the new man (Col. 3:9–10). The act is volitional. James links the action to the Word of God; Paul links it to the Spirit of God (Rom. 8:1–4).

James tells us *what we must receive:* "receive with meekness the engrafted word" (1:21b). W. E. Vine points out that in the New Testament meekness is treated as an inwrought grace. Its exercise is first and foremost godward. Meekness accepts all of God's dealings with us as good. It was a quality of life characteristic of the Lord Jesus, who described Himself as being "meek and lowly in heart" (Matt. 11:29). It is this spirit that embraces "the engrafted word." The word for "engrafted" indicates something sown, rooted, or implanted. James saw the Word of God as a living plant, taking hold of the believer's life and changing his behavior.

He tells us, also, *what we must resolve:* "But be ye doers of the word, and not hearers only, deceiving your own selves" (1:22). There has to be willing cooperation on our part, obedience to the Word, if the Word is actively to transform us. As practical as ever, James pours scorn on merely listening to the Word of God. We must *do* what it says.

The Lord Jesus gives us the most graphic illustration of what James has in mind, as He drew His famous Sermon on the Mount to a close. He said, "Therefore whosoever heareth these sayings of mine, and doeth them, I will liken him unto a wise man, which built his house upon a rock: And the rain descended, and the floods came, and the winds blew, and beat upon that house; and it fell not: for it was founded upon a rock. And every one that heareth these sayings of mine, and doeth them not, shall be likened unto a foolish man, which built his house upon the sand: And the rain descended, and the floods came, and the winds blew, and beat upon that house; and it fell: and great was the fall of it" (Matt. 7:24–27).

Some people read the Bible to admire it as magnificent literature. Where in the world, indeed, can we find such wonderful stories, such vivid poetry and imagery as in the Bible? Some people read the Bible to verify its history. A whole science of archaeology has grown up around the inerrant way in which the Bible touches on the histories of men and nations. Other people study the Bible to seek out its teachings on nature, science, philosophy, and psychology. No other book deals so accurately with matters that fall within the province of science.

Some people make a lifelong study of the great legal codes of Scripture. The Mosaic Law is an acknowledged masterpiece of legislation and the foundation of many of our modern legal systems. Some people study the Bible to uphold or to disprove the soul-destroying theories of the so-called higher critics. Some people spend their time disproving the teachings of the various cults of Christendom, most of which claim to be based on the Bible. Some people study the Bible to become expert in its Hebrew, Greek, and Aramaic vocabularies and grammar and, in so doing, compile vast concordances and lexicons with which to weigh each jot and tittle of the text. Some people study the Bible devotionally, others study it doctrinally, some study it analytically, some study it synthetically, and still others study it homiletically.

Nearly all of these ways or reasons for studying the Bible have their place. But over all of them James writes the words, "Be ye *doers* of the word, and not hearers only, deceiving your own selves." Bible study is not an end in itself; it is a means to an end. The Bible calls for a response. We must do what it says. Obviously! It is the Word of God. If we don't do that, it is like pouring water into a sieve.

C. God's Word is likened to a glass (1:23–27)
    1. A challenging experience (1:23–24)

James introduces a third illustration—the Word of God, he says, is like a mirror. He introduces a *foolish condition:* "For if any be a hearer of the word, and not a doer . . ." (1:23a). James has just told us that we are not to adopt that attitude toward the Word of God. He had doubtless seen plenty of believers, however, who did just that. They would sit under the soundest preaching, listen to the most penetrating and practical teaching, and nod their heads in agreement. They would even come forward occasionally to make public declaration of their resolve to put the truth into practice. But then they would do nothing about it.

The classical biblical example is Jonathan. Like all of his fellow soldiers, he had trembled as, day by day, the great Philistine giant of Gath hurled his challenge across the Valley of Elah and blasphemed the living God of Israel. Then David, the Lord's anointed, had come with a message of hope and salvation to all who had ears to hear. He preached that message to his brothers and to King Saul, all of whom were skeptical. Then he went into the valley of death and destroyed Goliath—

he who had the power of death. He returned victorious from that fight, and the people responded with their songs of praise: "Saul hath slain his thousands, and David his ten thousands" (1 Sam. 18:7).

Jonathan, however, saw that there was more to it than that. He gave his heart and life to David. In a singular act of dedication, he put his robe, garments, sword, spear, and girdle at David's feet. He said to him, "Whatsoever thy soul desireth, I will even do it for thee" (1 Sam. 18:1–4; 20:4). It was a blank check of promised loyalty, service, and devotion. But that was it! Jonathan never went with David, never shared in his rejection, never joined him in the cave, and never became a partner in the long and perilous wanderings over the next dozen years. Whatever his motives were in hanging around the palace, they were wrong. His failure to go with David led, eventually, to an untimely death in the service of his father, the David-rejecting Saul (1 Sam. 31:1–2).

So James's *if* is a weighty one. Even a public commitment to do the will of God, as expressed in the Word of God, is of little value if it is not followed by deliberate daily steps of obedience.

The Lord Jesus, in one of His parables, illustrated the folly of being a mere hearer of the Word. "A certain man had two sons," He said, "and he came to the first, and said, Son, go work today in my vineyard. He answered and said, I will not: but afterward he repented, and went. And he came to the second, and said likewise. And he answered and said, I go, sir: and went not. Whether of them twain did the will of his father? They say unto him, the first" (Matt. 21:28–31). Then came the Lord's scathing denunciation of the religious leaders of His day, who were, indeed, hearers but not doers of the Word.

James now sets before us a *forceful comparison:* "he is like unto a man beholding his natural face in a glass: for he beholdeth himself, and goeth his way, and straightway forgetteth what manner of man he was" (1:23b–24). We can picture a man waking up one morning, taking a look in the mirror, and looking at his face. He sees a day's growth of beard and a head of tousled hair. He yawns and says to himself, *I'd better have a shave and comb my hair.* Instead of taking care of his ablutions, however, he goes into the kitchen to see what he can dig up for breakfast. Then he notices the clock and realizes that he has overslept and needs to leave right away or be late for work. He forgets all about his appearance.

He sits down at his desk and gets on with his work. The boss comes in and glances around the office. He stops in front of the man's desk. "Don't you have a mirror in your house?" he asks.

The man replies, "Yes, sir. As a matter of fact, I looked in it when I got up this morning."

The boss asks, "Don't you have a comb and a razor?"

The man says that he has a very good razor and produces his comb from his back pocket.

The boss gives him a cold look. "The next time you look in the mirror," he says, "do something about it. That's my advice to you."

"Now then," says James, drawing the comparison, "the next time you look into the Word of God, and God shows you something about yourself, you'd better do something about it." That is James's advice to us. We should not just glance in the mirror of God's Word; we should take a good, hard look at ourselves while we are about it.

Paul has a word about that: "But we all, with open face beholding as in a glass the glory of the Lord, are changed into the same image from glory to glory, even as by the Spirit of the Lord" (2 Cor. 3:18). That is one of the remarkable properties of the Word of God as a mirror. It not only shows us our Savior but also puts in our heart the desire to be like Him. The *glance* saves—as the children of Israel learned when they were bitten by the fiery serpents. Their eyes were directed to the uplifted serpent on the pole. "Look and thou shalt live," Moses said (Num. 21:6–9), as the Lord reminded the religious Pharisee Nicodemus (John 3:14). But if a glance can save, it is only the *gaze* that sanctifies.

So we are to gaze into the mirror of God's Word, to see both ourselves and our Savior, and to catch a vision of what we are and what we ought to be. This was the principle behind the use of a laver in the tabernacle worship. It stood between the brazen altar and the tabernacle itself. At the far end of the tabernacle, in the Holy of Holies, God sat enthroned in glory upon the mercy seat. The priest, in approaching the tabernacle, came first to the brazen altar. There he offered the appropriate sacrifice. Blood was shed as he realized that he needed a *radical* cleansing for sin. He took a few steps more and came to the brazen lever. Just those few steps, and he was already defiled! He needed a recurrent cleansing from sin. The laver was made from the donated mirrors of the women, and it also held the water of cleansing. So it both revealed and removed his defilement. Failure to appropriate the cleansing available at the laver was a serious matter.

We need not only that radical cleansing in the blood of the Lord Jesus (1 John 1:7) but also that *recurrent* "washing of water by the word" (Eph. 5:26). The one is made available to us by the Son of God (1 Peter 1:18), the other by the Spirit of God (2 Cor. 3:18).

2. A changing experience (1:25–27)
   a. A call to behold (1:25)

James continues with his illustration of the mirror. He draws our attention again to the twin truths of discerning and doing: "But whoso looketh into the perfect law of liberty, and continueth therein, he being not a forgetful hearer, but a doer of the work, this man shall be blessed in his deed."

The word for "looketh" here means literally "stooping down" to look. The idea is that of looking at something more closely. The word is used of John when, on the resurrection morning, he arrived at the empty tomb a few steps ahead of Peter. Peter blundered right on in. John, however, paused. "And he stooping down, and looking in [the same word as that in James], saw the linen clothes lying . . . and the napkin, that was about his head, not lying with the linen clothes, but wrapped together in a place by itself. . . . saw, and believed" (John 20:4–8). Peter saw what John saw, but it was the one who "stooped down" thoughtfully to look who grasped what it signified, and he believed.

That is the way we should read the Word of God. We should stoop, as it were, over the sacred page to comprehend, believe, and obey.

The "perfect law of liberty" is God's law, the law that sets us free. The Mosaic Law was a temporary provision. It made provision for sin to be covered until such time as it could be canceled altogether. It contained 613 separate edicts designed to organize society, under God, so that people could be delivered from harmful things and evil people. It included both moral laws and ritual laws. The Sabbath laws, for instance, along with the various laws governing feast days, were designed to give the people time for rest and refreshment. The ceremonial laws taught, in the form of illustrations, truth regarding cleansing from sin and holy living. The rabbis had added thousands of rules and regulations to the Mosaic Law and had turned it into an impossible burden for anyone to bear. At the Jerusalem conference, Peter reminded James and the other elders of the Jerusalem church of how onerous a thing rabbinical Judaism and traditional law keeping had become (Acts 15:6–12). The endless pettifogging details and minutia, which the rabbis had added to the law of the Sabbath, for instance, turned the day from being a blessing to being a burden. In the hands of the rabbis, the simple law about not seething a kid in its mother's milk evolved into a rigid system of rules and regulations that made cooking a nightmare for the conscientious Jew.

James saw the law as perfect, something designed by a benevolent God to bring liberty. However, in James's view, it was necessary to "continue" in a law-abiding lifestyle if the benefits and blessings of the law were to be realized. The word for "continueth" means "to abide by," to persevere in doing something. We are to "make a habit" of abiding by God's law, of putting into practice the things that we read in God's Word.

Life without law can become a burden. In a sequel to *Mutiny on the Bounty*, authors Charles Nordhoff and James Norman Hall recount the settlement of Pitcairn Island by a handful of mutineers, a few native men, and some women. For lack of law and a firm hand to enforce it, the existence of the small population on the island, though blessed with an abundance of life's necessities, descended into chaos. Drunken brawls broke out. Immorality became a frequent occurrence. Suspicion between the whites and the native men gave rise to mass murder and a war of extermination. One of the seamen went mad. Another became a hopeless drunkard and committed suicide in a fit of the horrors. The women became desperate and built a fort, barricading themselves, determined to shoot on sight any man who came within range. Such was life without law.

Then someone found a copy of the Bible, and those who survived the years of unbridled lust, drunkenness, wickedness, and debauchery settled down to live new lives, set free by "the perfect law of liberty." A new generation arose, ruled by God's Word; and a new society emerged where law and order and decency and respect became the rule of life.

How much more ought attention to God's Word bring peace and blessing to a regenerate heart!

James admonishes us yet again not to be "a forgetful hearer, but a doer of the word." The word for "forgetful" points to a hearer who is chronically forgetful, a hearer characterized by absentmindedness. We can all have an occasional slip of memory, but it is a serious matter to be one who forgets habitually.

Such a man was John Newton in his unregenerate days. As a boy, he was thrown from a horse and nearly lost his life. He soon forgot his close call. He and some friends made a date to visit a naval vessel at anchor in the bay. They were to row out to the ship together. Something happened, and Newton did not arrive on time, so his friends left without him. Their boat capsized, and they were drowned. He went to their funeral, and it pulled him up short. But he soon forgot. He had a vivid dream that disturbed him greatly and haunted him for a while. Once more he forgot. His mother died when he was seven. Every day of his childhood, she had prayed for and with him. After her death, however, he soon forgot her prayers. He fell in love with Mary Catlett. Her love and prayers pursued him on his wild career; that was the one anchor that saved him from total shipwreck as he went from bad to worse on the high seas, sinking lower and lower into sin.

Then came his conversion in a terrible storm at sea when it was only through God's mercy that the ship did not sink. That night, John Newton sought mercy for himself and found it. He went on to become a clergyman of the Church of England. He lived for God and wrote hymns that we sing to this day, some 250 years later. After his conversion, he put the following text on the wall of his study: "Thou shalt *remember* that thou wast a bondman in the land of Egypt, and the Lord thy God redeemed thee."

In his hymn "Pardoning Love," Newton recounts his conversion. When he cried for mercy from the hold of that storm-tossed ship, the Lord Himself seemed to search his very soul. He wrote,

> Sure, never till my latest breath,
> Can I forget that look;
> It seemed to charge me with His death,
> Though not a word He spoke.

James would have approved of the converted John Newton. "Be not a forgetful hearer," he says, "one who habitually forgets." If we do cultivate a quickened memory for the Word of God, it will bring its own rewards: "This man shall be blessed," says James, "in his deed." When we put into practice the precepts and principles of the Word of God, we find that this is indeed the way to true happiness.

b. A call to behave (1:26–27)
(1) A pretended religion described (1:26)

Merely listening to God's Word leads to dead religious activity and deception. James confronts us with *the test:* "If any man among you seem to be religious, and bridleth not his tongue . . ." (1:26a). He confronts us also with *the truth:* "but deceiveth his own heart, this man's religion is vain" (1:26b). The word for "seem" can be rendered "to be of the opinion." If a person "thinks or supposes that he is religious" is the idea. This is the view he has of himself.

The word for "religious" occurs only here in the New Testament and rarely, if ever, in classical Greek. The "religious" person is the one who follows carefully the observances connected with his belief. That is, he is concerned with all of the outward aspects of worship, especially the ceremonial demands of religion. A kindred word is used of the religion of the Jews (Acts 26:5).

The Lord Jesus did not come to found a religion. Old Testament Judaism was a religion, one that was ordained of God. For fifteen hundred years, the Hebrew people were called upon, not only to adhere to the moral law but also to observe punctiliously the rituals laid down in the ceremonial law. They had feast days and fast days and Sabbaths. They had sacrifices and offerings. They had a tabernacle and then a temple. They had priests and Levites and robes, rules, and rituals—all of the paraphernalia of religion. All of it was symbolic and pictorial, all pointing down the ages to Christ. This was the law as a system, as distinct from the law as a standard. Getting caught up in the system was all too easy. All of the "religious" part of the Mosaic Law was abolished at Calvary by the rending of the temple veil (Matt. 27:52; Heb. 10:19–23).

Christianity is not a *religion;* it is a *relationship.* It is Christ! The law, Paul says, was our schoolmaster to bring us to Christ. Christ alone lived the life that the law demanded (as expounded in the Sermon on the Mount). He fulfilled all of the types inherent in the rituals. The genius of Christianity lies in the fact that the Lord Jesus, by His Holy Spirit, indwells every believer and lives His life in that person. Only gradually did the church add its own man-made rites and rituals, obscuring the simplicity of New Testament Christianity and evolving a form of baptized Judaism. This trend reached its height in the Roman Catholic Church. The Reformers jettisoned much of Rome's doctrine but retained much of its preoccupation with magnificent buildings, elaborate rituals, an organized calendar, and a religious hierarchy.

James had strong leanings toward the law and its religious observances. He could see, however, their danger. A person could be religious and miss the whole point of Christianity altogether.

To James, it all boiled down to bridling one's tongue—and he will have much more to say about that later (3:1–12). The word for "bridleth" means "to lead by a bridle," hence, "to hold in check," "to restrain." In ancient times, a bridle was merely a loop on the halter rope that passed around a horse's lower jaw. The test of true religion, according to James, lay, in part, in a person's ability to curb his tongue. According to him, a person who seems to be "religious" but who cannot control his tongue is self-deceived. His religion is useless.

The classic biblical example of people whose religion was vain, and who demonstrated that fact by their wicked words, is found in the scribes and Pharisees. They accused the Lord of performing His miracles by allying Himself with Beelzebub, the prince of demons (Matt. 12:24). The Lord accused them of committing the unpardonable sin of blaspheming the Holy Spirit (Matt. 12:31–32). At once, He adopted a new form of parabolic teaching designed to conceal truth from such people while revealing it to His own. Later, He exposed their religion for what it was (Matt. 23:1–39).

(2) A practical religion described (1:27)

Finally, James summarizes his concept of true religion. It is revealed in *unstinted giving:* "Pure religion and undefiled before God and the Father is this, To visit the fatherless and widows in their affliction" (1:27a). It is also revealed in *unstained living:* "and to keep himself unspotted from the world" (1:27b). The word for "visit" here means literally "to look out" for someone, to "select" someone. It carries the idea of "inspection," to exercise oneself as an overseer or shepherd. It means "to visit with help." It is used of visiting the sick and the afflicted (Matt. 25:36, 43). The Lord will use the criteria Himself in a coming day at the judgment of the nations in the Valley of Jehoshaphat, to separate "the sheep" from "the goats." In other words, the only kind of religion that James would accept as genuine was that which expressed itself in pure conversation and practical conduct; naturally, one would not go empty-handed to visit orphans and widows.

The apostle Paul demonstrated this "religion" to James, its chief proponent in Jerusalem. At the end of his third missionary journey, Paul made his last visit to Jerusalem, bringing with him a handsome financial gift from the Gentile churches that he had founded. In his heart, he carried a burden for the widows and orphans of the Jerusalem church. Many of them had been made widows and orphans as a result of his persecution of the church in his unregenerate days. More recently, and for well over a year, he had organized a vast giving project among the Gentile churches, especially in Achaia and Macedonia, for the relief and welfare of the widows and orphans of Palestine and Jerusalem. A representative contingent of Gentile believers accompanied him to Jerusalem to make the presentation (Acts 20:3–5). That was "true religion."

James and the elders seem to have taken the gift as their due. We have no record that they ever thanked Paul or the churches that gave to them. Rather, they were concerned with the outward trappings of religion. They told Paul of the "many thousands of Jews" who had become believers and who were "all zealous of the law." They urged Paul to demonstrate, as a Jew, his own zeal for the law. How should he do it? By paying the cost for four zealous Judaistic believers who wanted to terminate a Nazarite vow. This cost was not small by any means. According to the Mosaic Law, the Nazarite had to shave his head and bring to the priest a male lamb of the first year for a burnt offering, one ewe lamb of the first year for a sin offering, one ram without blemish for a peace offering, a basket of unleavened bread, cakes of fine flour mingled with oil and wafers of unleavened bread anointed with oil, along with their respective meal and drink offerings (Num. 6:13–15). Multiply all of that by four, and that was the demand that

James and the others made on Paul's pocketbook! A lesser man than Paul would have exploded. Paul revealed both his "pure religion" by curbing his tongue and his extraordinary grace and willingness to go the extra mile by doing what was demanded of him; he viewed that as the price for peace.

Along with the ability to hold one's tongue and a heart of compassion for others, James lists a clean life as a further evidence of true religion. The person who practices it keeps himself "unspotted from the world." The word for "unspotted" can be translated "unstained." The word is used of the Lord Jesus as a Lamb.

We are living in a very dirty world, just as polluted, in fact, as the pagan world that reveled in uncleanness during James's day. The gods of Greece and Rome were vile and lustful gods. Pagan society and religion sanctioned every imaginable form of immorality. When Paul wrote to the Romans, he did so from Corinth, one of the most debauched cities of antiquity. The sins that he denounces in the first chapter of that epistle were sins that he saw being practiced all around him every day as part of the pre-Christian, pagan lifestyle. Our modern world is vile, just as was the world of imperial Rome. Mass media and the marvels of modern technology have helped inundate our world with every form of filth. It is easily accessible, too, by mail or at the corner store, by book, by movie, by video, and by television. It can be conveyed by mail or by computer. It ranges from the indecent to the unbelievably decadent. It is such big business that modern governments make little effort to curb it.

How can we keep ourselves clean? We can stay away from much of the filth of the world. But when we do become defiled accidentally, we have recourse to the cleansing blood of Christ and the purifying Word of God. Then, too, the Father, the Son, and Holy Spirit are on our side. If we want to do so, we can keep ourselves unspotted from the world.

PART 4

The Christian and His Brethren
James 2:1–13

A. Partiality: a sin against the Lord (2:1–7)
   1. The problem stated (2:1–3)
      a. An indication of the problem (2:1)

M y brethren, have not the faith of our Lord Jesus Christ, the Lord of glory, with respect of persons."

That is an awkward sentence. It can be rendered, "Stop holding the faith of our Lord Jesus Christ with respect to persons." In other words, faith in the Lord Jesus is incompatible with partiality and discrimination. We cannot combine snobbery with faith in Christ. The two do not mix.

Paul used the word for "respect of persons" to remind the Roman church that "there is no respect of persons with God" (Rom. 2:11). God is neither partial nor prejudiced in His dealings with the human race. The color of a person's skin, the size of his bank balance, the number of degrees he has after his name, or the place he holds in the social hierarchy leaves God completely unimpressed. The Lord Jesus was as polite to the woman at the well (John 4) as He was to Nicodemus (John 5). He was as gracious to the woman who touched the hem of His garment as He was to Jairus, the ruler of the synagogue. He was as open to poor, blind Bartimaeus as He was to the rich young ruler. He had no "respect of persons." He was as honest and forthright with the Syro-Phoenician woman as He was with Pilate. He treated everyone with the same love, the same interest, and the same care and concern. He was not condescending when He was dealing with the publicans and sinners, and He was not cowed or compromising when He was dealing with those who occupied the seat of power. He gave the outcasts and the untouchables the same gentle, loving compassion that He extended to the scribes and the Pharisees. Sometimes the Lord did not approve of peoples' behavior, but He looked beyond that to the individuals and their deepest needs and treated them with dignity no matter what.

    b. An illustration of the problem (2:2–3)

James parades three people before us. First, he shows us *the prosperous man:* "For if there come unto your assembly a man with a gold ring, in goodly apparel . . ." (2:2a). The word for "gold ring" is *chrusodaktulios.* It occurs only here. It means literally "a gold-ringed" person. The implication is that he let everyone see that he has a gold ring. It was on display. He was also wearing "goodly" apparel. The word is *lampros,* meaning "bright," or "shining." The word is used of the "gorgeous robe" that Herod and his soldiers flung in mockery over the shoulders of Christ (Luke 23:11). The word means "resplendent." Cornelius used the same word in describing the "bright clothing" in which his heavenly visitor was arrayed (Acts 10:30). We get the idea that the man whom James describes was outstandingly well dressed.

Then James show us *the poor man:* "And there come in also a poor man in vile raiment" (2:2b). The word here means to be destitute or in want. It is used of Lazarus, the beggar, who sat at the gate of the rich man, hoping eagerly that some crumbs from the rich man's table might fall his way (Luke 16:20). The poor man's clothes are described as "vile raiment." The word suggests old, shabby clothing. This man, evidently, was "down at the heels."

Both of these men arrive at the local church at the same time. (The word used is *sunagōgē,* the usual word for a synagogue. At the time James wrote, Jewish Christians possibly were still attending worship at the synagogue to hear the Law of Moses read [Acts 15:21], just as Jewish Christians in Jerusalem still attended the temple.) However, James refers to "your" synagogue, which suggests that, whether in the synagogue or somewhere else, a distinctively Christian gathering is indicated. When Gentiles began to enter the church in large numbers, the active hostility of unbelieving Jews took fire against the entire Christian body. This invasion of the church by Gentiles troubled the Christian Jews too.

In any case, both men arrive at the meeting place simultaneously. The prosperous man appears and, behind him, *the pitiful man.* The usher apparently had a well-developed "respect of persons": "And ye have respect to him that weareth the gay [*lampros*] clothing," James declares, "and say unto him, Sit thou here in a good place; and say to the poor, Stand thou there, or sit here under my footstool" (2:3). Both men, it would seem, are strangers. The preferential treatment in the one case and the punitive treatment in the other case were based solely on the outward appearances of the two men. Regard and attention was lavished on the well-to-do man. He was ushered to his seat as though he were a prince. The poor man, however, was given short shrift and dumped in the most undesirable seat in the meeting place.

And it still happens. Some years ago, I met a woman who liked to put this kind of behavior to the test. She would select a fashionable church and put on old, ill-fitting clothes, shabby shoes, and a dowdy hat. She would arrange her hair in an unsightly bun and present herself at the church. Her main interest was in finding out what kind of treatment she would receive at the door, either upon arrival or at the end of the service. Usually, little or no attention was paid to her at all. No one cared if she came or went. Usually, she received a perfunctory handshake at the door; the preacher's eyes being busy elsewhere.

The next Sunday, she would present herself at the same church in a different guise, with styled hair, and wearing an expensive suit with a mink fur stole and expensive jewelry. On the way out, the pastor would be effusive.

"We're so glad to have you with us. This must be your first visit. We do hope you'll come back. What is your name?"

She would look at him. "Oh, no, this is not my first visit. I was here last Sunday. As a matter of fact, you shook hands with me at the door then too."

"Surely not!"

"Oh yes. But, you see, last Sunday I dressed in old clothes, and you really didn't see me at all. You said a perfunctory, 'Good morning.' Then you hurried on to the lady behind me, who was much more stylishly dressed than I was. And, no, I shall not be back."

2. The problem studied (2:4–7)
   a. The Christian perspective conveyed (2:4–6a)

First, *the indictment is recorded:* "Are ye not then partial in yourselves, and are become judges of evil thoughts?" (2:4). Aren't you making class distinctions in your mind? Aren't you setting yourselves up as able to judge the true quality of other people? Aren't you having evil thoughts?

These are serious indictments. Just because a person is better dressed than another person or has a better vocabulary and more refined manners does not prove him to be a better person.

After C. S. Lewis became a Christian, he decided that it would be appropriate for him to join a local church. There he found himself in the company of that very collection of his neighbors he had formerly sought diligently to avoid. The local grocer came sidling up to him to unctuously present him with a hymnbook. He looked around him and noticed that the man over there had boots that squeaked, the woman in front of him was wearing a ridiculous hat, and the man behind him sang off-key. He found himself drawing the unwarranted conclusion that these peoples' faith must somehow be ridiculous. Only later did he learn that some of these people were, in fact, devout, well-taught, and valiant Christians—believers whom Satan himself had reason to fear. It is a great mistake to judge people by their appearance.

Next, *the indictment is reviewed:* "Hearken, my beloved brethren, Hath not God chosen the poor of this world rich in faith, and heirs of the kingdom which he hath promised to them that love him?" (2:5). Of course, He has. All of the apostles were poor men; so were many of the prophets. James himself was a poor man. The book of Judges teems with "nobodies" whom God chose to use.

A person might be poor financially or socially but "rich in faith." That condition represents *present* wealth. A person who is rich in faith holds in his hand the key to the vaults of heaven. The unlimited resources of the Godhead are at his disposal to accomplish the plans and purposes of God. A person might be poor in this world and yet be no less an heir to the kingdom of God! That's *prospective* wealth, to be "a joint-heir with Jesus Christ," as Paul would put it (Rom. 8:17).

Moses was a poor man. Admittedly, he had been raised in a palace on the Nile, but he was the son of a slave, and, when God found him, he was a fugitive with a price on his head, a mere shepherd who was wandering on the back side of the desert. But he was rich in faith. His faith had cost him the throne of Egypt (Heb. 11:24–26), but he was heir to a kingdom just the same—as Pharaoh discovered when Moses reappeared armed with might and miracle.

David was a poor man, the youngest son of an insignificant farmer, with nothing but a song in his heart and a sling in his hand. But he was rich in faith and able to proclaim that faith in the dark valley itself. And he was heir to the kingdom of Israel—something that drove King Saul to frenzy.

Jacob was a poor man. His father was rich, true enough; but he himself was a penniless nobody when he showed up at Padan-Aram. He was so poor that he had to sell himself as an indentured servant to his Uncle Laban to get the wife he wanted. But he was rich in faith and had an eye on the Abrahamic covenant. That was something that Esau so discounted that he sold whatever rights he had to it for a bowl of stew. Jacob, however, became heir to the kingdom, and his sons became the patriarchs of the tribes and of the purposes of God.

We could go through all of the annals of Israel and the church to show how God has "chosen the poor of this world" to accomplish His purposes down here. Martin Luther was a poor man. John Bunyan was a poor man, and so were D. L. Moody and George Müller. Yet, they were all rich in faith and heirs of the kingdom! That is not to say that God cannot and does not use some great and gifted men who are rich in this world's goods. But they are the exception rather than the rule. It is the height of folly to despise poor people, especially in the church. We ought, rather, to sing with Hattie E. Buell the song of the Christian poor, "A Child of the King":

I once was an outcast stranger on earth,
A sinner by choice, and an alien by birth!
But I've been adopted, my name's written down,
An heir to a mansion, a robe and a crown.

Finally, *the indictment is repeated:* "But ye have despised the poor" (2:6a). James cannot seem to let the matter rest. The word for "despised" here suggests that the people in the church were insulting the poor and shaming them. The same word is used to describe the Jerusalem apostles after the authorities had imprisoned them, beaten them, and threatened them. They "departed from the presence of the council, rejoicing that they were counted worthy to suffer *shame* [to be dishonored] for his name" (Acts 5:41).

The Lord used the same word in the parable of the faithless husbandmen, a parable that depicts the attitude of the nation toward God's prophets in the past and toward God's Son in the present. The Lord says that one of God's messengers they treated *"shamefully"* and sent him away empty (Luke 20:11). The Lord also used the word when the Jews accused Him of being a Samaritan and having a demon. He said, "I have not a devil; but I honour my Father, and ye do *dishonour* me" (John 8:49).

Snobbery seems to have reached epidemic proportions in the Jerusalem church. Evidently, James thought it necessary to hammer home the fact that such behavior was reprehensible in a believer. No room existed in the church for racial discrimination, class distinction, or economic differences.

b. The Christian perspective confirmed (2:6b–7)

James adds a practical note. Some rich people, he says, *bully Christians:* "Do not rich men oppress you, and draw you before the judgment seats?" (2:6b). Something about great wealth is corrosive to character. Money can buy most things in this world. People who can command large sums of money often become arrogant. People whom they cannot buy, they bully. Those whom they cannot bully, they belittle. Those whom they cannot belittle, they try to bury. The word that James uses here for "oppress" means literally "to exercise power" over someone. The word is used to describe the Lord's healing of "all that were *oppressed* of the devil" (Acts 10:38). The Bible gives many and varied examples of this oppression of the enemy (Luke 13:16; 2 Cor. 12:7; Rev. 2:10). In James's experience, rich men often enough were willing to do Satan's work for him. It was not only silly but also sinful, then, to give preferential treatment to a person just because he was rich.

Some people not only bully Christians by "exercising power" over them and oppressing them but also *blaspheme Christ:* "Do not they blaspheme that worthy name by the which ye are called?" James says (2:7). Because rich people often become intoxicated with their power to manipulate their fellowman, some of them go on to blaspheme the Lord Himself. In the days of the early church, when James lived, the rich and powerful Sadducees were the ones who persecuted the church, dragging Christians into court and saying the most terrible things about the Lord Jesus.

So, then, partiality is a sin against the Lord.

    B. Partiality: a sin against the law (2:8–13)
        1. The royal law defined (2:8)

"If ye fulfil the royal law according to the scripture, Thou shalt love thy neighbour as thyself, ye do well." This is a direct quotation from the Law of Moses: "Thou shalt not hate thy brother in thine heart: thou shalt in any wise rebuke thy neighbour, and not suffer sin upon him. Thou shalt not avenge, nor bear any grudge against the children of thy people, but thou shalt love thy neighbour as thyself: I am the LORD" (Lev. 19:17–18).

Doubtless, James had often heard the various commandments of the law discussed at home and had heard much of the Lord's teaching on the question of the law. It is not necessary for us simply to imagine that the Lord's teachings and parables were spontaneously thought up and delivered on the spur of the moment. He had spent His whole life pondering the Word of God and formulating His doctrine and beliefs. In His public teaching, He drew on a vast storehouse of knowledge. That He had not discussed His thoughts and conclusions at home and at work, around the supper table and at the carpenter's bench would be most unlikely. Although James might have heard from the apostles the Lord's precepts, parables, and principles, doubtless he would have been familiar with many of them from many years of his personal and intimate relationship with Jesus as a member of the same family.

There is, of course, the Lord's famous parable of the Good Samaritan. He delivered it in response to the challenge of "a certain lawyer." It was a parable against racial and religious prejudice. The lawyer had put Christ to the test, asking Him what he should *do* to inherit eternal life. The LORD threw the ball back to him: "What is written in the law?" He asked.

The lawyer knew his Bible: "Thou shalt love the Lord thy God with all thine heart, and with all thy soul, and with all thy strength, and with all thy mind," he said, giving the commandment (Deut. 6:4–5) that summarizes man's duty to God. He added, "and thy neighbour as thyself," giving the commandment that summarizes our duty to each other.

The Lord bluntly replied, "Thou hast answered right: this do, and thou shalt live" (Luke 10:25–28).

If we are going to get to heaven by *doing* something, that is heaven's minimum requirement. The astute lawyer knew that he could keep neither of these commandments, so he looked for a loophole. "Who is my neighbour?" he demanded.

The Lord replied with a parable that showed the utter hypocrisy of both priest and Levite (the lawyer who was challenging Jesus was a Levite) when confronted with a man in desperate need. Then along came a Samaritan who might have been motivated understandably, by both racial and religious prejudices, to pass by the unfortunate man. Instead, he helped him fully and freely.

The Lord then challenged the lawyer. "Which now of these three, thinkest thou, was neighbour unto him?"

Grudgingly, and refusing to acknowledge the fact that the benefactor was a detested Samaritan, the lawyer mumbled, "He that shewed mercy on him."

Then came the final thrust: "Go, and do thou likewise."

James heartily agreed: "Fulfil the royal law," he said. The royal law was not the one that gave commandment concerning circumcision; it was not the law sanctifying the Sabbath; it was not the law enforcing dietary discrimination—as dear as these laws were to the Jews, even Christian Jews. The royal law commands believers to love other people without regard to class, condition, country, or creed.

Paul would agree with James. "Love one another," he said, "for he that loveth another hath fulfilled the law. For this, Thou shalt not commit adultery, Thou shalt not kill, Thou shalt not steal, Thou shalt not bear false witness, Thou shalt not covet; and if there be any other commandment, it is briefly comprehended in this saying, namely, Thou shalt love thy neighbour as thyself. Love worketh no ill to his neighbour: therefore love is the fulfilling of the law" (Rom. 13:8–10).

The spirit of this "royal law" runs very deep. Here you are, coming home from work one day when, on alighting from the bus, you notice that the sky ahead is black with smoke. "Hello!" you say. "It looks as though there is a house on fire." Just then, with sirens blaring, the fire truck roars by. You hurry your steps and turn a corner. Now you can see a crowd of people up ahead, and the fire truck is unloading its men and equipment. "It's on my block!" you say, as you break into a run. Then you notice that it is your *house* that's on fire. "Praise the Lord!" you exclaim. "I'm so glad it's not my neighbor's house."

So a person would react if he were motivated by the royal law. That is a rare person indeed.

    2. The royal law defied (2:9–13)
       a. A very great principle (2:9–11)
          (1) An example (2:9)

"But if ye have respect of persons, ye commit sin, and are convinced [convicted] of the law as transgressors."

So, there it is, out in the open. To discriminate against people is sin. The word here for "transgressors" means literally "one who oversteps." A transgressor breaks through a boundary. He goes too far. He breaks God's law. God does not want cliques in His church. Those who belong to cliques go too far.

This is one advantage that the church had over the synagogue: it was able to start with a clean slate. In his book *The Source,* James Michener tells of a Jewish boy who grew up ostracized by society because he was an illegitimate child. The Law of Moses was explicit: "A bastard shall not enter into the congregation of the LORD; even to his tenth generation shall he not enter into the congregation of the LORD" (Deut. 23:2). It was a law that was intended to secure the sanctity of sex and the strength of family life.

The rabbis went to work on this prohibition, expounded it, amplified it, and probed all of its nuances and ramifications. They came up with a thousand ways to make life intolerable for the victim and invented extraordinary measures for getting around them.

As long as the young man in Michener's story was small, it was not so bad, although the stigma of his birth clung to him. But as he grew older, he was forced to shoulder an increasingly intolerable burden. The full horror of his situation dawned upon him when he faced the fact that, as a bastard and a social outlaw, he could not marry a respectable Jewish girl. The parents of the girl, the rabbis, and the community as a whole militated against any such unthinkable arrangement. Then, in the midst of his grief and bitterness, he found the church! Here was a group of people, emancipated from the law, both able and willing to receive even a person such as him heartily and without reservation into its fellowship. It opened up a new life.

James is at pains, through thirteen verses of his epistle, to see that the church remained that way—free from prejudice, discrimination, and partiality. Such attitudes are sinful in the sight of God.

(2) An explanation (2:10–11)

James now confronts his readers with a revealing fact. First, *the fact is declared:* "For whosoever shall keep the whole law, and yet offend in one point, he is guilty of all" (2:10). He becomes a lawbreaker. A chain is only as strong as its weakest link.

Then *the fact is demonstrated:* "For he that said, Do not commit adultery, said also, Do not kill. Now if thou commit no adultery, yet if thou kill, thou art become a transgressor of the law" (2:11).

Indeed, a weak point exists in all of our efforts to live the kind of life that God demands. Each of us has our "besetting" (prevailing) sin. Solomon had a prevailing sin. In his case, it was women. He never did show any sense in the women he married. Moses had a prevailing sin, although it rarely showed—his temper. Ultimately, it kept him out of the Promised Land. Shimei had a prevailing sin—his foul mouth. Demas had a prevailing sin—his love for this present, evil world. Ananias and Sapphira had a deadly sin—the desire to keep up appearances. Judas had a fatal weakness—love of money. Pilate had an Achilles' heel—his love of power. Aachan had a fatal flaw—covetousness. Even James had his weak spot—his infatuation with the Mosaic Law and his inability to get beyond it. We would do well to find the chink in our armor, the weak link in our own chain of morality and spirituality.

Our weak spot! James put his finger right on the problem. A person might not be tempted along a dozen different lines. But just let him succumb to his weakness, and he is an instant sinner and a lawbreaker.

The apostle Paul confessed as much. He could run his eye down the Decalogue. Commandment after commandment passed before his conscience. Thou shalt have no other gods but God. Thou shalt have nothing to do with idolatry. Thou shalt not take God's name in vain. Thou shalt keep the Sabbath holy. Thou shalt honor thy father and mother. Thou shalt not kill or commit adultery or steal. Thou shalt not bear false witness against thy neighbor. Paul could look complaisantly at each of them. In his mind, he thought that he had kept all of these commandments. Then came the tenth commandment: "Thou shalt not covet," that is "Thou shalt have no evil desire," and Paul collapsed. "I had not known lust," he confessed, "except the law had said, Thou shalt not covet." That was the one weak link in his chain of morality and religion, the rock upon which he made shipwreck. "When the commandment came, sin revived, and I died," he said (Rom. 7:7–9).

It was the same with the rich young ruler. He wanted to know what to do to inherit eternal life. "Keep the commandments," Jesus said, putting the answer on the same ground as the question: "Thou shalt do no murder, Thou shalt not commit adultery, Thou shalt not steal, Thou shalt not bear false witness, Honour thy father and thy mother: and [summarizing them all], Thou shalt love thy neighbour as thyself." He quoted just the commandments that had to do with man's duty to man.

The young man said that he had kept all of those commandments from his youth up, but still he sensed that something was lacking in his life.

Jesus understood. He said, "If thou wilt be perfect, go and sell that thou hast, and give to the poor, and thou shalt have treasure in heaven." That answer confronted the young man with a practical way to prove that he loved his neighbor as himself. "And come and follow me," Jesus added, confronting him with a practical way to show that he loved God with all of his heart. The rich young ruler backed off at once (Matt. 19:16–22).

We have the same problem. Certain sins do not tempt us at all. But we all have at least one area where we are vulnerable. To break just *one* of God's commandments, just *one* time, is all that it takes to constitute one a sinner and a transgressor. That is why God puts salvation on a different basis altogether than personal merit, law keeping, and good works. We just cannot make it that way. And God knows it. Our failure to *keep* all of the commandments makes us guilty of *breaking* all of the commandments. It takes only one blot on a page to ruin the copy. It takes only one sour note to spoil the tune. It takes only one mistake in working out a mathematical problem to ruin the whole calculation. It takes only one sin to make a person guilty.

b. A very good policy (2:12–13)

James points now to *God's magnanimity:* "So speak ye, and so do, as they that shall be judged by the law of liberty" (2:12). That is, we should speak and act as those who will be judged by the law of liberty, by the fact that God has set us free from sin and free from the legalism that so many people embrace.

In the Gospels, we read of the occasion when the Lord Jesus rode into Jerusalem on a donkey. Three facts are connected with that little animal. First, it had to be *redeemed.* The Law of Moses commanded that the firstborn of an ass had to be redeemed by a lamb, or its neck had to be broken. So, this little donkey was born under the sentence of death. Either the donkey had to die or a lamb had to die in its stead (Exod. 13:13).

It was redeemed, it had life, but it was tied to a post. It had life, but it did not have liberty. It needed to be *released* (Matt. 21:1–9). That is the condition that James has in mind. We are set free.

But, then, that donkey had to be *ruled*. It was not set free so that it could kick its heels in the air and gallop off wherever it pleased, over the hills and far away. It was brought to Christ and put under His authority and restraint. That illustrates the perfect law of liberty.

Jesus said, "If the Son therefore shall make you free, ye shall be free indeed" (John 8:36). "Take my yoke upon you," He said, "and learn of me. . . . for my yoke is easy, and my burden is light" (Matt. 11:29–30). Once that donkey was brought into obedience to Christ, it was able to serve Him. All it had to do was to lift Christ up where people could see Him. The little donkey thus carried the Christ of God into the city amid the hosannas of the multitude. It had learned the true meaning of liberty.

We are now free. Free from servitude of the law! Free to serve the Lord! Free to be under His authority! Free to lift Him up before men! Thus shall we anticipate with joyful expectation the day when we shall be judged by the law of liberty. What have we done with that liberty? That will be the question.

James concludes this section by pointing to *God's mercy:* "For he shall have judgment without mercy, that hath shewed no mercy; and mercy rejoiceth against judgment" (2:13).

Mercy! What a tremendous word! It reminds us of the person who had his photograph taken and was not satisfied with the result. He complained to the photographer, "This picture doesn't do me justice."

The photographer replied, "Sir, what you need is not justice but mercy!"

That is what we all need all of the time. God offers us a choice between a fair trial or a free pardon. We would be wise to settle for His mercy.

Mercy! It is the word of a guilty and suffering man. It is the word of someone who is in the hands of another, one who has the power to do what is requested—provide mercy.

God's mercy was what opened first the eyes and then the mouth of Balaam's donkey. Had that little creature not seen the threatening angel and acted accordingly, Balaam would have ridden on to judgment.

Mercy was what twice held back the hand of David from slaying the foul-mouthed Shimei who cursed him with such venom. Abishai, one of David's mighty men, had his sword out in a flash as soon as he heard Shimei's words.

"Why should this dead dog curse my lord the king?" he asked. "Let me go over, I pray thee, and take off his head" (2 Sam. 16:9; 19:21). David restrained Abishai. Little did Shimei know that nothing but David's mercy and grace saved him from immediate execution. David was all too aware of how much he himself owed to God's mercy.

Mercy was what moved the heart of the Lord Jesus to take up the cause of the woman taken in adultery (John 8:1–11). The scribes and the Pharisees were implacable. Had it been up to them, they would have executed the woman as the law decreed. But Jesus read their hearts. He knew their secret sins. He extended mercy—to them. He could have slain them where they stood. Then, without condoning or condemning her sin, He extended His mercy to the woman as well.

Without mercy! What a terrible thing! In the end, Shimei died without mercy (1 Kings 2:36–46). So did Joab, David's former brilliant but murderous general (1 Kings 2:28–35). What must it be to face the Great White Throne judgment, knowing that, when all of the facts are bared, there can be no mercy? "He that despised Moses' law died without mercy under two or three witnesses: of how much sorer punishment, suppose ye, shall he be thought worthy, who hath trodden under foot the Son of God, and hath counted the blood of the covenant, wherewith he was sanctified, an unholy thing, and hath done despite unto the Spirit of grace?" (Heb. 10:28–29). It is a terrible prospect indeed.

So James sets the alternatives before us—mercy or no mercy. Judgment or mercy smiling in the very face of judgment. If we want to have mercy, we must show mercy.

The Lord said so Himself. He told the story of the king who demanded an accounting from his stewards. One man was arraigned before him who owed him ten thousand talents, an enormous sum. The king commanded that the man's property be liquidated and the man and all of his family be sold into slavery to pay off his debt. The servant pleaded for mercy and begged for time to pay off his debt. He received mercy. The king, moved to compassion, canceled the man's entire indebtedness.

The steward left the palace and sought out one of his fellow servants who owed him an insignificant sum. He seized the man violently and demanded instant payment. He brushed aside the man's pleas for mercy and time and threw him into a debtors' prison. This action was reported to the king, who immediately summoned the steward and passed a fresh sentence upon him: "Oh thou wicked servant, I forgave thee all that debt, because thou desirest me: shouldest not thou also have had compassion on thy fellowservant, even as I had pity on thee?" The king immediately withdrew his pardon and delivered the man to the jailers until he should pay all that he owed (Matt. 18:21–35).

If God's mercy does not touch our hearts and transform our lives, then His mercy and forgiveness might very well be withdrawn. The principle, as set forth by James, is that the person who makes no allowances for others will find that no allowance will be made for him either. God expects that recipients of His mercy will have a change of heart toward others. Such is James's final offering on the altar of truth regarding prejudice and partiality among God's people. Forgiveness is not the same as justification. A justified person is declared righteous. Justification is unconditional. It is based on justice, not mercy. It is the great theme of Paul's epistle to the Romans.

PART 5

The Christian and His Beliefs

James 2:14–26

A. The approach (2:14)
   1. The false claim is quoted (2:14a)

James now turns to the question of right and wrong in the matter of our beliefs. He begins with the question of faith and works. "What doth it profit, my brethren, though a man say he hath faith, and have not works? Can faith save him?" That is the question: can we divorce faith from works?

   2. The false claim is questioned (2:14b)

Some people see James as a champion of works against Paul, who stood for salvation by faith alone. Martin Luther, whose whole mighty ministry was based on Habakkuk's famous statement "The just shall live by *faith*" (Hab. 2:4, emphasis added), thought that the epistle of James was "a veritable epistle of straw." He misunderstood James's emphasis on works.

We have here the swing of the pendulum away from rabbinical Judaism. The Jews placed all of the emphasis on works, on a rigid observance of the rites and rules of religion. Some Christians went along with all of that. Others went to the other extreme, insisting on no works at all. Such a view turned liberty into license. James brings things back into balance.

James uses the concepts of righteousness and justification in the sense of actual, measurable, perceivable goodness—just as Jesus used it in the Sermon on the Mount. James did not have in mind the "imputed righteousness" that Paul taught (Rom. 3–4; Gal. 3). It is doubtful whether this doctrinal concept ever entered his mind when he appealed to Genesis 15:6. James had a practical, not a theological, application in mind. He was not discussing the question of *how* Abraham was set right with God or *how* faith was "reckoned" as righteousness. Paul seized on that aspect of things. James quoted the whole verse, as Paul did, but James was concerned with it as proof that Abraham, when put to the test, lived up to his faith.

We have all met people who say that they believe but whose lives contradict the claim. This was James's concern.

B. The appraisal (2:15–18)
   1. A case to consider (2:15–16)

James cites a case. First, *the need is discerned:* "If a brother or sister be naked, and destitute of daily food" (2:15). James had in mind real need. The Jerusalem church was full of poor people. The noble experiment of the infant, Pentecostal church of having all things in common had not worked out in practice. It was in trouble right from the start (Acts 2:45). Cases of fraud occurred on the one hand (Acts 5:1–11), and instances of great generosity occurred on the other (Acts 4:36–37). The first major squabble in the church was related to this practice of communal living (Acts 6:1–6). Because human nature is what it is, the system broke down, and the church was left with large numbers of poor people on its hands. The situation had been aggravated by the persecution of the Jerusalem church by Saul of Tarsus. He had left many widows and orphans behind him. The situation was so critical that, by the time of the Jerusalem conference, the Jerusalem church urged on Paul the importance of remembering the poor. James was one of the people who advanced this proposal (Gal. 2:9–10)—not that Paul needed urging by James or anyone else to be concerned about the poor.

So a need is discerned. But *the need is dismissed:* "And one of you say unto them, Depart in peace, be ye warmed and filled; notwithstanding ye give them not those things which are needful to the body; what doth it profit?" (2:16). To this day, some believers pray for the world's starving millions, but all of their concern ceases with the "Amen" at the end of the prayer. Such prayers are worthless.

We are reminded of the situation that Moses faced at the time of the Exodus. The Egyptian army was closing in on the fleeing people, and the Red Sea was just ahead. Evidently, Moses stood there and wrung his hands over the situation. God said to him, "Wherefore criest thou unto me? speak unto the children of Israel, that they go forward" (Exod. 14:15). It was a time for action, not prayer. It was the same when Israel suffered defeat at the hands of the people of Ai. Joshua was bemoaning the situation when God broke into his prayers and lamentations: "Get thee up; wherefore liest thou thus upon thy face? Israel hath sinned . . ." (Josh. 7:10–11).

A time comes when God expects us to *do* something about things that cry out for action. Poverty is one of those things. It is all about us. God expects us to do something about it. Pious words are worse than useless. They reveal a cold and callous heart. Jesus never failed to help those in need.

2. A conclusion to consider (2:17–18)

James gives us what we would today call "the bottom line" on the issue. He gives, first, *a pontifical conclusion:* "Even so faith, if it hath not works, is dead, being alone" (2:17). Paul warns against *dead works* (Heb. 6:1; 9:14); James warns against *dead faith.* He insists that we must have a belief that behaves. What James deplores is the kind of "faith" that merely gives intellectual assent to various doctrines of the Bible—the kind of "faith" that claims to believe in the Lord Jesus, who "went about doing good" (Acts 10:38), and who was indefatigable in the service of hurting people—but at the same time ignores the needs of those all around them. *That,* according to James and the Holy Spirit, who inspired James to write, is dead faith.

He gives us, also, *a pragmatical conclusion:* "Yea, a man may say, Thou hast faith, and I have works: show me thy faith without thy works, and I will show thee my faith by my works" (2:18). In effect, James says, "All some people do is *say* that they have faith with nothing tangible to back it up. But I," he continues, "can show by what I do that my faith is real."

When I first joined the staff of Moody Bible Institute, a student on campus believed in demonstrating faith by works. His name was George Verwer. Even in his student days, it was evident that the world was going to hear from him. He was a committed soul winner and a successful motivator, and he had a world vision. He was able to get many of his fellow students to blitz various target zones in the Chicago area with tracts and intensive soul-winning efforts.

From the start, he had a vision of the "untold millions still untold." He began, as a student, by setting his sights on Mexico. He mobilized a number of students to join him one Christmas in an effort to distribute thousands of tracts and testaments throughout Mexico. He secured a large amount of Spanish literature, mobilized a number of students, and set forth on his mission. Some Christian leaders told him bluntly, "George, you cannot do it in Mexico."

Those were the days when Rome still ruled Latin America with an iron hand. In Mexico it was both difficult and dangerous, if not actually illegal, to do what George proposed. George, however, had a life text: "Nothing shall be impossible unto you" (Matt. 17:20). His was the kind of faith that moves mountains, the kind of faith that believes that God says what He means and means what He says. Someone told him that he would never get past the Mexican customs with his gospel books and tracts, but he remained undaunted. He and his friends prayed all of the way to the Mexican border. When they arrived at the customs barrier, the Mexican customs officials were all dead drunk! The missionaries rode through triumphantly. It was the beginning.

Before long, George had not only begun regular invasions of Mexico during school recesses but also had established a number of Christian bookstores in key Mexican cities. Then he decided to get on Mexican radio with the gospel. Again someone told him, "You can't do that in Mexico." Again he fell back on his text: "Nothing is impossible!" George not only had a faith that works but also was blessed with a large amount of common sense. He approached the radio stations on a business basis. He said, "I have a series of bookstores. I would like to buy time to tell people about books that we have on sale." It worked! Soon, he or his Mexican partners were on the air: "Ladies and gentlemen, we have a special offer this week. We have secured some copies of Billy Graham's book *Peace with God.* Do you have peace with God? Let me read you a paragraph from this book. . . ."

George graduated from Moody Bible Institute and went off to Spain. Spain was still virtually a closed field to missionaries. Someone told George, "You might have gotten away with it in Mexico, but you'll end up in prison in Spain." George simply leaned a little harder on his text.

Again, he used common sense. He did not apply to go to Spain as a missionary but as a student! He enrolled in the University of Madrid. He signed up for the minimum number of courses that would enable him to be a *bona fide* student— and devoted the rest of his time to evangelism. He scoured the writings of the early church fathers, writings endorsed by Rome. He compiled from the writings those passages that were sound. He published them as tracts—all quotations from the church fathers that Rome revered! He also found an edition of the Spanish New Testament that was free of Romish annotations, one that had the imprimatur of Rome. He was in business! These were the materials that he distributed whole-sale! How could the Roman Catholic Church attack him? He was distributing the writings of its own fathers!

Then he went to Russia! That was in the days when the Iron Curtain was solidly in place and when atheistic Communism controlled the lives and destinies of millions. George and some friends made it past the Soviet customs and headed toward Moscow. Along the way, they left a trail of Bibles and tracts. Then they were stopped, searched, arrested, and put in prison. They were interrogated, but George was unperturbed. He was in God's hands. He and his friends witnessed boldly to their jailers. They told them, quite frankly, that they had come to give the gospel to the Russian people.

"You say the Bible is full of lies," George said. "Then why are you so afraid of it?"

In the end, they were given an armed escort out of the country, and all of their books, Bibles, and tracts were confiscated. "Good!" was George's cheerful comment. "You can be quite sure that those guards will read the Bibles and literature—if only out of curiosity!"

By this time, George had begun praying for a ship! While he was looking at his atlas, it had dawned on him that nearly all of the world's great cities are located on the seacoasts and great rivers of the world. What better way to reach them than by the sea? As he was praying one day about his vision, the Lord spoke to him: "George, if I gave you a ship tomorrow, what would you do with it?"

George had his answer ready. Onboard the ship would be Bible teachers, counselors, and foot soldiers to knock on doors and give out tracts. He would have onboard printing presses to turn out tracts by the thousands. He would have onboard books by the hundreds for sale, including textbooks and reference books, so badly needed in Third World countries—an incentive to get people on board. He would have teams who would deal with officials and dock authorities in advance and make arrangements for the arrival of the ship. He would have people to mobilize the local churches and pastors for a major, cooperative evangelistic effort once the ship docked. He would invite the local people, including officials and dignitaries, to come on board. He would offer seminars, Bible classes, and gospel meetings on the ship. People who queued up outside, waiting to get on board, would be shown gospel films. The white sides of the ship could be used for a screen.

So George told the Lord all of this. The Lord said to him, "George, if I gave you a ship tomorrow, you would do none of those things." George protested, affirming his sincerity.

"No, George," the Lord said, "you would do none of those things because you do not have a captain, and you do not have a crew. If I gave you a ship, you would have to tie it up in port, and you'd go bankrupt paying docking fees. You would not be able to move that ship a single sea mile."

"You're right, Lord," George said, "so give me a captain, and give me a crew—and then give me a ship."

One by one, George prayed in his crew. But he still needed a captain. About that time, George invited me to come over to Brussels and participate in a Bible conference. By this time, he had organized a mission called Operation Mobilization. Every summer, he mobilized hundreds of young people from the United States, Europe, and Latin America to come to Europe to do mass door-to-door evangelism. They converged on Brussels for a week's orientation and Bible teaching. Then they fanned out in teams all over the continent to tell people about Christ.

During that conference, George introduced me to a young Englishman named Graham Scott. In the course of our conversation, Graham asked me what I knew about George Verwer and Operation Mobilization. I told him what I knew and how George was now asking God for a ship's captain. "Can you imagine," I said, "the spiritual audacity of the man! He is expecting a man who has spent his life climbing the professional ladder, and who has achieved the rank of ship's captain, to give it all up to come live like this?" I pointed to the hundreds of young people all around us, willing to sleep on the floor and eat peanut butter sandwiches in a self-denying lifestyle.

Graham looked at me, and a smile slowly lit up his face. "I know," he said, "I'm him!"

George was given his boat, and he called it the *Logos* and sent it out to be a new venture in global evangelism. Then he asked God for another ship! He got that one too! He called it the *Doulos*. That was many years ago. The story of Operation Mobilization from then until now has been the story of one miracle after another. Some years ago, the mission stated that its teams had encountered some 250 million people face-to-face (not counting its radio and other outreaches) and that, during this same period, it had reached 150 million Indian nationals with the gospel.

Nobody would accuse George Verwer of having a dead faith! There you are, James! What do you think of *that?*

C.   The application (2:19–20)

James continues. First, he cites an instance of *faith displayed:* "Thou believest that there is one God; thou doest well: the devils also believe, and tremble" (2:19).

Anyone can say that he believes. James puts it thus: "So! You say that you believe! So what? The demons believe. More! They believe and tremble!" The word for "tremble" means "to bristle," and then "to shudder" or "shiver." They believe in God and are terrified. Theirs is no mere intellectual assent to a theological proposition. They are very well aware of the doom that awaits them (Matt. 8:29). Throughout the Gospels, when Jesus confronted demons, they recognized Him at once as the Son of God and confessed Him as such. The Lord invariably silenced them; their belief in Him did not change them. Their belief was not the kind of belief that saves. So far as their belief in God was concerned, however, it was very much alive indeed. They believed and were filled with horror. James wanted to see in believers something equally real—a faith that expressed itself in observable good works.

James moves on to the case of *faith disputed:* "But wilt thou know, O vain man, that faith without works is dead?" (2:20). The word for "vain" here can be translated "empty." James has already said that "faith without works is dead" (v. 17). Previously, it was more or less an exclamation; here, however, it is an interrogation, as though to say, "God said it! Did you get it?"

Two main words are used for "will" in the New Testament. The word *thelō* means "to wish" or "to desire." This word embodies the emotional element, emphasizing desire that leads to resulting action. The other word is *boulomai,* which conveys the idea of deliberate determination. This determination might be in accordance with the original wish or impulse, or it might be quite contrary to it.

In any case, *thelō* is a stronger world than *boulomai* because the natural impulse is frequently stronger than the reasoned resolve.[1]

James uses the word *thelō*. In effect, he says, "Faith without works is dead and useless. Has that registered? Are you willing to make a decision based on that fact?" James was not asking his readers to make a decision based on intellectual assent to known truth—to do good because it was the coldly logical thing to do. What he wanted was for them to respond because they had a natural, emotional, impulsive realization that faith without works was dead. In other words, the person who truly believes the gospel will instinctively reach out to others.

    D. The appeal (2:21–26)
        1. The proof of the contention (2:21–25)
           a. The case of Abraham the Hebrew (2:21–24)

James now produces two witnesses, one a man, the other a woman; one the Hebrew from Ur of the Chaldees, the other the harlot from Jericho. He begins by viewing the remarkable case of Abraham, the founding father of the Hebrew race.

He begins with *a great triumph*: "Was not Abraham our father justified by works, when he had offered Isaac his son upon the altar?" (2:21). Abraham's life was a series of surrenders. God first called upon him to give up his father and his old way of life in Ur. Then he was called upon to give up the well-watered plains of Jordan. Next he was told to give up Hagar and Ishmael. Finally, he was called upon by God to give up his beloved Isaac. All of the other surrenders were designed to prepare him for this one. He had come a long way from the day he gave up his father to the day when he gave up his son.

Abraham was a great believer. He is mentioned with high honor in Hebrews 11, the picture gallery of the great Old Testament heroes of faith. He was Paul's chosen example of justification by faith (Rom. 4:1–3, 9–25). He is the reckoned father of all them that believe (Rom. 4:16).

James takes us straight to Mount Moriah, the high point in Abraham's pilgrimage. There, Abraham's faith was put to the test—to the uttermost, even to the point where the poised blade was about to be plunged into the heart of his "only begotten son," in whom was all of his delight, the one who was his only link to the promised seed.

Next comes *a great truth*: "Seest thou how faith wrought with his works, and by works was faith made perfect?" (2:22). Faith and works worked together as

----

1. E. W. Bullinger, *The Companion Bible* (reprint, Grand Rapids: Kregel, 1990), app. 102.1.

partners. We see Abraham's works in action all through the story. He rose up early in the morning because he had work to do. He saddled his ass, and he summoned two of his men. He clave the wood. He took the fire. Then he called Isaac and stepped out resolutely along the appointed path. At last, he saw the place afar off. He halted his servants. He took the wood from them and gave it to Isaac to bear. Then he moved on, taking Isaac with him. He listened to Isaac and pointed him to God. At last, he arrived at the place. He built an altar, laid the wood in order, and turned to his son. He placed him on the altar, took the knife, and he raised his arm.

And faith wrought with his works! All that he had left was his faith. "By faith Abraham, when he was tried, offered up Isaac: and he that had received the promises offered up his only begotten son, of whom it was said, That in Isaac shall thy seed be called: accounting that God was able to raise him up, even from the dead; from whence also he received him in a figure" (Heb. 11:17–19). So faith and works went hand in hand. Without that *faith,* Abraham never could have done it. Without those *works,* it would never have been done. The faith without the works would be hypocrisy; the works without the faith would be horrendous.

Then comes *a great trust:* "And the scripture was fulfilled which saith, Abraham believed God, and it was imputed unto him for righteousness" (2:23a). This is a quotation from Genesis 15:6. James now goes back to that time in the life of Abraham before Isaac, the promised "seed," was born, and before Ishmael, the carnal seed, was born. The event to which James now refers had occurred some fifteen years before the birth of Isaac and some forty-eight years before the offering of Isaac on Mount Moriah. The setting is full of interest.

Abraham had just won a resounding victory over the kings of the East. He had rescued Lot from slavery, met with the king of Salem (Melchizedek), had learned a new name for God, and refused all dealings with the king of Sodom. And, sad indeed, Lot had gone back to his backsliding. Once the excitement had died down and the chatter of Lot's children no longer rang in his ears, Abraham felt his own childlessness more keenly than ever.

That was when God reappeared to renew and enlarge the Abrahamic covenant. He pointed Abraham to the stars. "Count them!" He said, "So shall thy seed be" (Gen. 15). At this point, Abraham "believed God and it was counted unto him for righteousness" (Gen. 15:6). That great statement crystallizes the great biblical truth of imputed righteousness.

Then, instead of waiting for God to make good His promise, Abraham tried to hurry things up and help God out. He listened to Sarah's advice and married Hagar. It was a terrible mistake. Hagar gave him a son, sure enough, but it was

Ishmael whom he got, not Isaac. Abraham's faith soared, and then it faltered. After that, God had no more to say to Abraham for thirteen long years. When God finally broke the silence, it was to give Abraham an even greater promise and an even grander covenant.

James takes up the Genesis 15 incident. To him, it was a perfect example of faith going hand in glove with works. There is a sense, of course, in which even the unfortunate affair with Hagar was proof that Abraham believed that God was going to give him a son. God had not actually stated, at that time, that the promised seed would come through Sarah.

Paul writes off the Hagar incident altogether. He leaps ahead to Abraham's complete restoration to unadulterated faith (Rom. 4:16–23) as a result of the more detailed promise of Genesis 17.

Now comes *a great testimony:* James reminds us that Abraham was called "the Friend of God" (2:23b). He is called this in 2 Chronicles 20:7 and in Isaiah 41:8. What is meant by this wonderful title can be gathered from the Lord's word about Moses: "And the LORD spake unto Moses face to face, as a man speaketh unto his friend" (Exod. 33:11). The background of this statement was the sin of the golden calf and the total, corporate failure of God's chosen people from Aaron on down. There was still one man, however, with whom God could have communion, a man whom He could still regard as His friend—Moses.

Abraham was God's friend. It is extraordinary, when we come to think about it, that God needs those whom He can call His friends. He has many children, but He does not have many friends. How amazing that in the heart of God is that which causes Him to look for friends! We can picture God in heaven pointing out Abraham to the angels: "Do you see that old man down there, the one with the staff in his hand? That's Abraham. He's my friend." And, because Abraham was God's friend, God was in the habit of dropping in on him from time to time to visit him and to talk to him. On one occasion, He took two angels with Him (Gen. 18:1–2).

Anyone can be God's friend. The Lord Jesus tells us how: "Greater love hath no man than this," He said, "that a man lay down his life for his friends. Ye are my friends, if ye do whatsoever I command you" (John 15:13–14).

Finally, there comes *a great test:* "Ye see then how that by works a man is justified, and not by faith only" (2:24). It is when faith is married to works that new life is conceived. James does not advocate works as a means of salvation. He does say that works are a proof of salvation. More than that, he points out that "works" are the practical response of the believing heart to the great mandates of the gospel.

The great truth of justification is presented to us in various ways in the Old Testament. Helen H. Shaw has captured the truth of it in a hymn seldom sung these days:

> God's sovereign grace selected me
> To have in heaven a place;
> 'Twas the good pleasure of His will
> I'm justified *by grace.*

> In due time Christ on Calvary died;
> Flowed that crimson flood
> Which makes the foulest white as snow;
> I'm justified *by blood.*

> God raised Him up; this is the pledge,
> Should evil doubtings low'r,
> His resurrection quells each fear;
> I'm justified *by power.*

> The Holy Spirit guided me
> To what the Scripture saith;
> I grasped the truth; Christ died for me!
> I'm justified *by faith.*

> Now if you doubt that I am Christ's
> If one suspicion lurks,
> I'll show by deed that I am His,
> I'm justified *by works.*

> I praise the Lord, 'tis all of Him,
> The grace, the faith, the blood,
> The resurrection power, the works
> I'm justified *by God.*[2]

---

2. Helen H. Shaw, "I'm Justified," *Choice Hymns of the Faith* (Fort Dodge, Iowa: Gospel Perpetuating Fund, 1952), no. 275.

b. The case of Rahab the harlot (2:25)

"Likewise also was not Rahab the harlot justified by works, when she had received the messengers, and had sent them out another way?" At first sight, Rahab seems to be unpromising material for justification on any grounds. The poor soul was a pagan prostitute—without God, without Christ, and without hope—under the sentence of death and with no prospect of escape.

Then the two Hebrew spies came, and Rahab seized with both hands her one chance of salvation. The two men took refuge in her house from the Jericho military police who were scouring the city for them. When the police knocked at her door, she concealed the fact that she had hidden them and brazenly outfaced them.

"Sure, they came here, but they left as soon as it got dark. They're probably out of town and heading for the hills by now."

As to the ethic of Rahab's telling lies, it was a time of war, and a different ethic prevails in wartime than in peacetime. Besides, it was the lesser of two evils. To have told the truth would have meant the betrayal of the two men. Also, it was a daring thing for her to do, for had the police searched her house and found the men, she would have been executed as a traitor. Moreover, her act was an expression of her belief in the power of Israel's God, both to doom and to save.

Once the police were gone, Rahab sought out the spies. She had put two and two together. The exploits of Israel's God in shattering the power of Egypt and the miracles that had followed the Israelites as they went from place to place in the wilderness over the past forty years were all well known in the city. The recent destruction of the Canaanite kings, Sihon and Og, had brought fear of Israel's living God upon the people of Jericho.

Only Rahab, however, did anything about it. She not only believed but also acted. She pleaded that salvation might be extended to her and her family. Then she helped the spies escape over the wall on a scarlet rope. That rope, in turn, became the token of her promised salvation. She was to bind it in the window of her house, which stood on the city wall. She was to shelter, with all of her family, inside that house—the one house protected by the scarlet line. And she was to hold her tongue! Rahab did all of that.

Jericho fell, but Rahab's house remained standing. All of those people within were saved from the avenging sword. Thus, she was justified by works, the point that James makes—just as she was justified by faith, the point that Paul makes (Heb. 11:31). More! She married Salmon, one of the two spies, and gave birth to Boaz and thus became a human ancestress of the Lord Jesus Himself (Matt. 1:5)! Powerful faith! Powerful works!

So then, James has demonstrated the *proof* of his contention that faith without works is dead. He concludes with the point of contention.

2. The point of the contention (2:26)

James sets before us a *dead body* and *a dead belief:* "For as the body without the spirit is dead, so faith without works is dead also." A corpse, after all, is only a corpse once; the spirit has departed. All that is left is dead clay. You can cleanse that corpse, clothe it, and compose it in its coffin. You can curse it, command it, or caress it. There is no response at all from the corpse. It has no soul or spirit. We can write *Ichabod* across it—"the glory is departed."

James makes the obvious application: faith without works is dead. The Spirit of God is not in *that* kind of "faith." That is not "a belief that behaves." The sooner it is buried, the better.

PART 6

The Christian and His Behavior
James 3:1–4:12

A. Sin in the life revealed (3:1–4:5)
1. Sin in the mouth (3:1–12)
a. A word about the teachers (3:1)

Ever practical, James turns now to a thorough discussion of the believer's behavior. He begins with sins of the tongue, and, because teachers do a great deal of talking, he begins with them. He has two observations—*don't multiply teachers:* "My brethren, be not many masters" (3:1a), and *don't misunderstand teaching:* "knowing that we shall receive the greater condemnation" (3:1b). The word for "masters" is *didaskalos,* meaning a teacher or "a doctor." The word occurs some fifty-eight times in the New Testament. The Lord was addressed by this title thirty-one times and used this title of Himself eight times.

Teachers are under a special obligation not only to practice what they preach but also to ensure that what they teach is true. To lead people astray with wrong information is a solemn thing. Teachers will be held accountable for their doctrines. Sincerity is not enough; we must also be *right.* James may have had in mind, here, controversies among teachers about the relative merits of faith and works. Or perhaps he is targeting those teachers who substitute words for works.

Teachers are necessary, but we do not need the kind against whom Paul warns. He knew people who had "itching ears," who surrounded themselves with teachers who pandered to their lusts (2 Tim. 4:3). James, with his strong ties to the synagogue, probably had in mind "the open platform" policy common in the synagogues. This custom made room for visitors and others to speak to the congregation. Both the Lord Jesus (Matt. 12:9; Mark 1:39; Luke 6:6) and Paul (Acts 13:15, 45; 18:6) took advantage of this feature of synagogue worship. Much profitable teaching, no doubt, did result from this system, but it also tended to proliferate a great deal of mediocre teaching and also an abundance of self-appointed "teachers"—people who only *thought* that they had the gift of teaching. God holds all of us—especially teachers, as James warns—accountable for what we say (Matt. 12:36).

b. A word about the tongue (3:2–12)
(1) A divine standard (3:2)

"For in many things we offend all. If any man offend not in word, the same is a perfect man, and able also to bridle the whole body." How true! The person who can honestly claim that he never says anything wrong or out of place, James says, can consider himself perfect. A person who can control his tongue can control his entire being.

Surely James wrote that as his personal tribute to the Lord Jesus. That wondrous Person had lived with him in the same home in Nazareth for many years. He had attended the same school and synagogue and had worked beside him at the carpenter's bench. Then, for three and one-half years, He had traversed the length and breadth of the Promised Land teaching, encouraging, debating, rebuking, and warning. How well James knew it. He and Jesus had grown up together.

Looking back on that experience, James pondered the significance of it all. He had never heard Jesus speak a cross word or tell a lie. He had never heard Him answer back. He had never heard Him say anything suggestive or vulgar or say anything of which, afterward, He would have felt ashamed. He had never heard Him speak angrily in a fit of temper or say anything that called for an apology. On the contrary, everything that Jesus ever said had been wise, loving, kind, and true.

Looking back over the Nazareth years, James could think of no better definition of perfection: "The man who can claim that he never says anything wrong is perfect!" Jesus was perfect. His control of His tongue demonstrates the fact.

(2) A devastating statement (3:3–12)
(a) The unbridled tongue (3:3–5a)

James now parades an array of illustrations to prove his point. This is one of the great passages in Scripture in which the Holy Spirit makes a full statement on a subject. Similar passages are 1 Corinthians 12–14 on the gifts, Matthew 24–25 on prophecy, and Hebrews 11 on faith. After reading such passages, one thinks that little more remains to be said.

James begins with *an illustration* (3:3–4). First, he draws an illustration from *nature,* and then he draws an illustration from *navigation.* He reminds us *how a beast is controlled:* "Behold, we put bits in the horses' mouths, that they may obey us; and we turn about their whole body" (3:3). It is an evidence of man's lordship over nature that he has been able to tame and harness the mighty horse, a creature bigger and stronger and swifter than he.

In one of his stories, Jeffrey Farnol tells how his hero, Barnabas Beverley, bought and subdued a fierce and ungovernable horse. The horse had just thrown its owner, Captain Slingsby of the guards. In his rage, the bruised and battered captain decided to auction off the intractable steed to the highest bidder. He described it as an ugly, vicious beast that nobody could hope to ride, a regular terror that had already killed one groom and would doubtless kill another. Barnabas bought him.

While Barnabas was settling his accounts, "the great black horse, tired of comparative inaction, began again to snort and rear, and jerk his proud head viciously," a proceeding that alarmed the two hostlers who were holding it. Having finished his business, Barnabas proposed to ride the black fiend.

"In that moment the powerful animal reared suddenly, broke from the grip of one hostler, and swinging the other aside, stood free, and all was confusion." A groom sprang for the horse's head, but Barnabas was ahead of him. He caught the hanging reins and swung himself into the saddle.

"For a moment the horse stood rigid, then reared again, up and up, his teeth bared, his forefeet lashing." Barnabas brought down the heavy stick he was holding between the flattened ears, once, twice, and brought the animal back to earth again. The struggle for mastery began.

In the end, Barnabas won. He dropped the stick, leaned over, and patted that proud head. Now his hand was gentle. He spoke to the horse softly and eased his tight grip on the reins. He sat back and waited. The battle was over. The horse gave in. Now all that was needed was for Barnabas to indicate his will by means of the bit and bridle.[1]

James's point is well taken: if man can so subdue a fierce horse and make him obedient to the pressure of a bit, a small piece of metal, in his mouth, why cannot man thus curb and control his tongue?

Next, James reminds us *how a boat is controlled:* "Behold also the ships, which though they be so great, and are driven of fierce winds, yet are they turned about with a very small helm, whithersoever the governor listeth" (3:4). It was so with the battle cruiser *Bismarck.* She was the pride of the German navy, the newest and most powerful ship afloat. She could make short work of convoys. Britain's two biggest and fastest luxury liners, the *Queen Elizabeth* and the *Queen Mary,* were racing back and forth across the Atlantic, relying on their speed to out sail the U-boats. The *Bismarck,* however, was faster than they. Moreover, no ship in the British navy could face her alone.

When news was received that the *Bismarck* was at sea, the Admiralty sent the battleship *Hood* and the carrier *Prince of Wales* to intercept and sink her. *Hood* was England's largest and most powerful battleship, served by two thousand officers

---

1. Jeffrey Farnol, *The Amateur Gentleman* (Toronto: Musson Book Co., n.d.), 176-87.

and men, but she was twenty years older than the *Bismarck*. As for the *Prince of Wales*, she was brand new and was still not completely finished. Civilian workers still were on board when she put to sea to fight.

The first encounter was disastrous. The *Hood* was blown up and sunk with all hands, and the *Prince of Wales* was hit and broke off the engagement. All that the *Bismarck* suffered was a hit by one shell that damaged a fuel tank and caused the ship to slowly lose oil. She was now footloose and fancy-free. The oceans were before her. She could play havoc with British shipping. The situation was desperate. The sea-lanes were Britain's lifeline for survival. The war would be over if the *Bismarck* could sink enough ships.

The British admiralty scraped together a small fleet in hopes of catching the *Bismarck* before she could get back into port. One of the ships was the aircraft carrier *Ark Royal*, an experienced ship but ill equipped with only antiquated sword-fish aircraft to send against the powerful foe. The aircraft took off. One came in for the attack, swooping at the stern as she swung low. The wake of a torpedo could be seen. On board the *Bismarck*, the captain tried to swerve out of the way, but it was too late. The torpedo struck, and the *Bismarck's* rudder was jammed.

The *Bismarck* was now almost within sight of France. A few more leagues, and she would be safe. The Luftwaffe would be able to protect her from her foes. But the *Bismarck* was doomed. With a jammed rudder, all she could do was steam in a big circle. Admiral Lutjens put a brave face on to his crew. He spoke of the two British ships now closing in. "We can sink the *King George V*," he boasted. "We can make the *Rodney* run away, as we did the *Prince of Wales*. By noon tomorrow, we'll be surrounded by U-boats, and then no one will dare attack us."

Darkness descended, and five British destroyers took up their positions and began to torment the foe. Then the *King George V* arrived, all thirty-five thousand tons of her, with her massive sixteen-inch guns and her speed of twenty-four knots. She began to fire, and still the *Bismarck* steamed in her doomed circle on the sea. Shells began to explode as hit after hit was registered. Her hull was reduced to a shapeless ruin, and smoke poured out from everywhere. She became a floating wreck; and then, ships with torpedoes were sent in to finish her off.

All because of the rudder! Once the rudder got out of control, the great ship was lost. James knew about that kind of thing. On his native Sea of Galilee, he had seen vessels turn this way and that by means of a rudder and a helm. He applied his illustration to the tongue. A helm, after all, is not very big in relation to the size of a great ship. But woe betide those who cannot control it. Just so, the tongue!

James concludes with *an application:* "Even so the tongue is a little member, and boasteth great things" (3:5a). We must get hold of our tongue if we are to escape shipwreck. The tongue has often been used to goad someone to destruction. James's expression "boasteth great things" comes from *megalaucheō*—"to lift up the neck." The idea signified is that of boasting, haughty speech, or provocative language.

b. The untrammeled tongue (3:5b–6)

Again, James has *an illustration:* "Behold, how great a matter a little fire kindleth!" (3:5b). The word for "great" here denotes a forest; a whole forest can be set ablaze by a very small fire.

The story is told about four men who decided to share their personal weaknesses one with another. The first man confessed that his one, fatal weakness was kleptomania. He was a compulsive thief. Usually, he pilfered only small items, but the fact remained that he stole things.

The second man confided that he was an alcoholic, a secret drinker. He managed to hide his weakness, but there it was—he drank.

The third man admitted that he had a weakness for women. He, too, had been able to conceal it so far. He was ashamed of it, but, sad to say, he had indulged in numerous clandestine affairs.

Then came the turn of the fourth man. The others looked at him expectantly. What was his secret vice?

"Well, I'll tell you how it is, fellows," he said. "I don't steal, drink, cheat on my wife, or anything like that. I'm a terrible gossip—and I can't wait to get out of here!"

Let all gossips beware!

The tongue! What an incendiary it is, what an arsonist! Take, for instance, the history of the Second World War. The Third Reich lasted twelve years and four months, but it caused a holocaust of destruction on this planet more violent and earthshaking than anything that the world had ever experienced. At one point, the Germans reigned supreme from the Atlantic to the Volga, from Norway to the Mediterranean. But then the tide turned, and the German people were thrust down to the uttermost depths of destruction, desolation, and despair. During the days of their power, the Germans instituted a far-flung reign of terror that outdid in savagery all of the oppressions of the past.

By the end of September 1944, the Germans had seven and one-half million slaves to do their will. Most of those people had been dragged from their homes and transported to Germany in boxcars from all over occupied Europe. They were put to work in the factories, the mines, and the fields. They were beaten, starved, and deprived of proper clothes and shelter. Families were savagely broken up as a matter of course. Children were beaten, brutalized, put to work, or killed. Jews and Slavs were looked upon as subhumans who were unfit to live and exterminated by the millions. Prisoners of war, especially Russians, died in captivity in vast numbers. The Germans retaliated for acts of sabotage by freedom fighters. The formula was one hundred to one—one hundred hostages rounded up at random and shot for every German life lost. The fate of Jews was death in the extermination camps. At Auschwitz alone, at the peak of operations, six thousand Jews were gassed every day. The joke among the German exterminators was that Jews came in by way of the gate and left by way of the chimney. Atrocious medical experiments, barbarously conducted with great cruelty, were routine. And millions of people died on the battlefields as a matter of course. The whole world became engulfed in the carnage.

The human cost of Hitler's attempt to seize world power staggers the imagination. Thirty-five million lives were lost. On the battlefields, one out of every twenty-two Russians was killed, one out of every twenty-five Germans, and one out of every 150 Britons. The toll on the Jews was even higher—two out of every three European Jews perished in Hitler's attempt to rid Europe of all of its Jews.

This vast conflagration was kindled *by one man's tongue.* Adolph Hitler was an orator, a master at whipping his audience into a frenzy. He could mobilize men by the millions at a word. His rages cowed visiting statesmen, and his tirades paralyzed his top generals. And his countrymen, urged on by the lash of his tongue and mesmerized by the power of his words, fought on and on, long after the war was lost, until all of Germany was reduced to rubble.

James was right! How great a forest can be set ablaze by a mere match. Europe was the forest. Hitler was the match.

Now comes *the application* (3:6). James gives us a fourfold description of the tongue. He tells us *how decadent it is:* "And the tongue is a fire, a world of iniquity" (3:6a). The word for "world" here is *kosmos.* It denotes the world as created and set in order. Here it stands for the sum total of iniquity. The word for "iniquity" is *adikia,* the word for unrighteousness and wrongdoing. The tongue is as dangerous as any fire. It has a vast potential for evil. It can speak falsehood and filth. It can be smooth as butter or as sharp as a knife. It can curse or cajole. It can criticize and complain. It can castigate and corrupt. There is no evil to which the unregenerate heart of man is heir that the tongue cannot promote. Sin entered this world, in the first place, by means of a forked tongue, the tongue of "that old serpent." The moment that Adam was confronted with his sin, he used his tongue to blame God and accuse Eve. When Eve was faced with her sin, she employed her tongue to blame the Evil One and his beguiling words. Adam blamed both Eve and God for what he, himself, had done. The first recorded words of Cain were insolent words wrapped around a lie and addressed to God: "I know not: [where he is]: Am I my brother's keeper?"

The first recorded words of an organized human society were words of rebellion against God, humanistic and self-centered: "Let us . . . Let us . . . Let us" (Gen. 11:3–4). Thus, the building of the Tower of Babel and a world capital city was begun. God's response was to confound human speech so that every man spoke to his neighbor in a foreign tongue. The proliferation of tongues has continued down the centuries so that now, according to the Wycliffe Bible Translators International Linguistic Center in Dallas, Texas, there are more than five thousand language groups known to exist in the world.

Even some of God's greatest saints have revealed the evil power of the tongue. Abraham lied about his wife twice (Gen. 2:10–20; 20:1–7). In a fit of temper, Moses called God's people rebels (Num. 20:10), and, for so doing, God kept him out of the Promised Land. David lied to Ahimelech the priest and occasioned his murder by King Saul (1 Sam. 21:1–10; 22:9–23).

James continues. *How defiling it is,* he says: "So is the tongue among our members, that it defileth the whole body" (3:6b). The word for "defileth" refers to a spot or stain. James uses the word to underline the defiling effects of an evil use of the tongue.

Fallout! It is a comparatively new word in our vocabulary. The word began to take root when the nuclear age dawned. The two atomic bombs dropped on Japan in 1945 not only wiped out the cities of Hiroshima and Nagasaki but also set everything ablaze for miles around. Not only were one hundred thousand people killed but also deadly radiation threatened everyone who survived. Testing of atomic and hydrogen bombs in the Marshall Islands thoroughly contaminated Eniwetok and Bikini in 1946 and 1958. Fallout!

The Persian Gulf War also taught us afresh the risks of fallout. An estimated one million to six million barrels (a barrel equals forty-five gallons) of oil were released into the Gulf (as compared with 250,000 barrels spilled by the tanker *Exxon Valdez* off the coast of Alaska). At one point, the Iraqis deliberately brought in loaded tankers and dumped their contents into the Gulf. About three hundred miles of the shoreline waters were contaminated, and wildlife was killed in a wide swath along the coastline. Then the Iraqis set fire to more than six hundred Kuwaiti oil wells, sending black plumes of smoke, soot, carbon dioxide, and toxic gases into the air. This pall of doom was carried downwind for some five hundred miles. One estimate was that one hundred thousand tons of carbon, in the form of soot, and fifty thousand tons of sulfur dioxide were released into the air every day by this wholesale act of vandalism. Acid rain was one result. Also, black rain, caused by the enormous amounts of soot in the air, fell.

Fallout! That is what James is talking about. But he is talking about even more deadly fallout—the contamination that results from a defiling tongue.

James also reminds us of the unruly tongue, *how destructive it is:* "And setteth on fire the course of nature" (3:6c). The expression "setteth on fire" comes from a word that means "to burn up." It refers to the disastrous effects that a wicked tongue can have on all of the circumstances of life. The word for "course" (of nature) is *trochos.* It means literally "a wheel" and has to do with the whole round of human activity. The word for "nature" is *genesis,* referring to the sphere of our earthly life. James sees life as a great revolving wheel of circumstances. The tongue is capable of disrupting everything. The tongue can ignite all of our worst passions of lust, envy, hatred, malice, and murder and give reign to all kinds of resulting evils.

The unsung heroine of Dickens's novel *Oliver Twist* is Nancy, one of Fagin's female accomplices. Her live-in partner, Bill Sikes, is the villain of the story. Sikes was a burglar, a man with a violent, murderous temper.

In time, Nancy overheard something that was vital to the well-being of the poor orphan Oliver Twist. A man named Monks had bargained with Fagin to have Oliver abducted and turned into a thief. The scheme was then to drive Oliver through every jail in London and end by having him accused of some capital offense and hanged.

Nancy managed to get an interview at the home where Oliver was staying, but to do so, she had to drug the suspicious Bill Sikes before she could get away. She promised Oliver's guardians that she would come back with more information the next Sunday.

Meanwhile, Fagin had grown suspicious of Nancy. She knew too many of his secrets. He suspected that she was planning to defect, so he sent a spy named Noah to watch her and follow her. Nancy met with Oliver's friends and warned them what was afoot. She declined their offer to help her escape to a new life and went back to her sad, soiled life. The spy reported the meeting and the conversation to Fagin.

Fagin wasted no time. He would see Bill Sikes. He would use the power of his tongue to incite the violent man to murder. His opportunity came when Sikes turned up at Fagin's den with some stolen loot. Fagin went to work:

> "Suppose that lad that's lying there—" Fagin began. Sikes turned round to where Noah was sleeping, as if he had not previously observed him. "Well!" he said, resuming his former position.

"Suppose that lad," pursued Fagin, "was to peach—o blow upon us all—first seeking out the right folks for the purpose, and then having a meeting with 'em in the street to paint our likenesses, describe every mark that they might know us by, and the crib where we might be most easily taken. Suppose he was to do all this, and besides to blow upon a scheme we've all been in, more or less—of his own fancy, to please his own taste; stealing out at nights to find those most interested against us, and preaching to them. Do you hear me?" cried the Jew, his eyes flashing with rage. "Suppose he did all this, what then?"

"What then!" replied Sikes; with a tremendous oath. "If he was left alive till I came, I'd grind his skull under the iron heel of my boot into as many grains as there are hairs upon his head. . . ."

Fagin looked hard at the robber; and, notioning him to be silent, stooped over the bed upon the floor, and shook the sleeper to rouse him. Sikes leant forward in his chair; looking on with his hands upon his knees, as if wondering much what all this questioning and preparation was to end in.

"Poor lad!" said Fagin, looking up with an expression of devilish anticipation, and speaking slowly and with marked emphasis. "He's tired—tired with watching for *her* so long,—watching for *her*, Bill."

"Wot d'ye mean?" asked Sikes, drawing back.

Fagin made no answer, but bending over the sleeper again, hauled him into a sitting posture. When his assumed name had been repeated several times, Noah rubbed his eyes, and, giving a heavy yawn, looked sleepily about him.

"Tell me that again—once again, just for him to hear," said the Jew, pointing to Sikes as he spoke.

"Tell yer what?" asked the sleepy Noah, shaking himself pettishly.

"That about—Nancy," said Fagin, clutching Sikes by the wrist, as if to prevent his leaving the house before he had heard enough.

"A gentleman and a lady that she had gone to of her own accord before, who asked her to give up all her pals, and Monks first, which she did—and to describe him, which she did—and to tell her what house it was that we meet at, and go to, which she did—and where it could be best watched from, which she did—and what time the people went there, which she did. She did all this. She told it all every word without a threat, without a murmur—she did—did she not?" cried Fagin, half mad with fury.

"All right," replied Noah, scratching his head. "That's just what it was!"

"What did they say, about last Sunday?"

"They asked her," said Noah, as he grew more wakeful, seemed to have a dawning perception who Sikes was, "they asked her why she didn't come, last Sunday, as she promised. She said she couldn't."

"Why—why? Tell him that."

"Because she was forcibly kept at home by Bill, the man she had told them of before," replied Noah.

"What more of him?" cried Fagin. "What more of the man she had told them of before? Tell him that, tell him that."

"Why, that she couldn't very easily get out of doors unless he knew where she was going to," said Noah; "and so the first time she went to see the lady, she—ha! ha! ha! It made me laugh when she said it, that it did—she gave him a drink of laudanum."

Sikes swore and broke away fiercely from the Jew. "Let me go!"

The day was breaking, and there was light enough for the men to see each other's faces. They exchanged one brief glance; there was fire in the eyes of both, which could not be mistaken.

"I mean," said Fagin, showing that he felt all disguise was now useless, "not too violent for safety. Be crafty, Bill, and not too bold."

Sikes made no reply; but, pulling open the door, of which Fagin had turned the lock, dashed into the silent streets.

He went home. He dragged Nancy from her bed. He smashed her twice in her upturned face with his pistol, then beat her brains out with a heavy club.[2]

Such is the power of the tongue. That is how destructive it is.

James tells us, too, *how devilish it is:* "And it is set on fire of hell," he says (3:6d). Some of the lies that the tongue tells are diabolically wicked. Some of the language that the tongue uses is so abysmally degrading that it can be attributed only to the activity of evil spirits. The Bible abounds with illustrations of such use. We think of the curses that Shimei directed against David, the Lord's anointed (2 Sam. 16:5–7). We think of the depraved advice that Ahitholphel gave to Absalom (2 Sam. 16:20–23). We think of the wicked lie that the backslidden old prophet of Bethel told to the bright, young prophet from Judah (1 Kings 13:1–32).

---

2. Charles Dickens, *The Adventures of Oliver Twist* (reprint, New York: Oxford University Press, 1998), n.p.

The devilish work of the tongue, however, is best seen at the time of the Lord's trial and death. There was Caiaphas, for instance, Israel's reigning high priest. When all of his other tricks failed, he wrapped his tongue around the most solemn oath in the Jewish legal code and said, "I adjure thee by the living God, that thou tell us whether thou be the Christ, the Son of God" (Matt. 26:63). He knew that he could use the Lord's answer to that question against Him. When Jesus at once affirmed His deity, Caiaphas sentenced Him to death with a tongue set on fire of hell.

And what about the many false witnesses who were subpoenaed to testify against the Lord? How their lying tongues must burn with torment now (Matt. 26:59–62)!

Then there were those who, having blindfolded Him, slapped Him in the face and said, "Prophesy unto us, thou Christ, Who is he that smote thee?" (Matt. 26:68). Theirs were tongues set on fire of hell.

And what about Herod Antipas? When Jesus refused to speak to him, much less perform a miracle to satisfy his curiosity, he set Him at nought and mocked Him (Luke 23:7–11).

The chief priests and scribes, too, lent their flaming tongues to accusing Him vehemently (Luke 23:10). The chief priests joined with the elders to persuade the Jerusalem mob to choose Barabbas over Jesus and to demand that Pilate crucify Christ (Matt. 27:20–22).

It was the same at Calvary. The chief priests mocked Him as He hung on the cross: "He saved others," they sneered, "himself he cannot save. If he be the King of Israel, let him now come down from the cross, and we will believe him. He trusted in God; let him deliver him now, if he will have him: for he said, I am the Son of God" (Matt. 27:41–43). All that can be said of these benighted religious leaders is that their tongues were devilish.

(c) The untamed tongue (3:7–10)

Again, James begins with *an illustration:* "For every kind of beasts, and of birds, and of serpents, and of things in the sea, is tamed, and hath been tamed of mankind" (3:7). Apart from domesticated animals, some of which have long since been trained and harnessed to do our work, are our household pets. These quickly become our companions and friends. And who has never been to a circus and watched great animals performing astounding feats?

Man has trained many varieties of birds to do his will. The carrier pigeons fly with his messages. Parrots can be trained to talk. In days gone by, no noble was worth his salt if he did not have a falcon trained to catch prey for him.

As for the denizens of the deep, dolphins and killer whales now entertain us and evidently grow attached to their trainers.

We have a dog, a toy poodle that is not much more than a foot long, but it is all frolic and fun. We call her "Missie," and there's not much that she doesn't know. When I get dressed in the morning, Missie comes over to check things out. She always sniffs the cuffs of my pants. She knows at once what kind of a day it's going to be. If I put on one of my good suits, she walks away in disgust. It's Sunday. For some mysterious reason, she will spend much of the day alone. If I put on my everyday clothes, she knows that I'll be spending much of the day in my study and resigns herself to taking up her position near my desk. If I put on my gardening clothes, off she goes to tell the good news to Rainbow, her stuffed toy, to which she confides both her gladness and her gloom.

Missie hates getting a bath. She knows where we keep her towels and the bath soap. When she sees me heading for that cupboard, off she goes—to hide! She'll find some dark corner, where she'll curl up and make herself as small and as inconspicuous as possible, hoping that I'll forget!

She dislikes bedtime and will prolong and postpone her coming fate as long as possible, running all over the house, Rainbow in her mouth, hoping to be chased and played with one more time.

Her favorite words are *Go outside?* and *Go for a ride?* She will "speak" when asked if she wants to go in the car.

She knows when I'm going away, a regular occurrence for a traveling preacher. She watches me pack garment bag, suitcase, and shoulder bag with big, sad eyes.

She even knows what to do when we pray! She curls up beside us and puts her head on her paws. She waits patiently while the petitions proceed. When we come to the phrase "in Jesus' name," up goes her head. With the "Amen!" she's off!

But, after all, Missie is only a dog, one of the "beasts" to which James alludes, a descendant, through many generations, of the wild dog and the wolf. But she has been tamed. "So," James says, "if you can tame a dog, why can't you tame your tongue?"

Now comes *the application* (3:8–10). James has three points. He reminds us of *the tongue and its disloyalty:* "But the tongue can no man tame; it is an unruly evil, full of deadly poison" (3:8). The tongue is *pugnacious.* Try as we might, we cannot prevent the tongue from lashing out at times. Even the greatest and most gifted and gracious of men have said things that they later regretted. They could have bitten their tongue the moment they said them. No apology can undo the damage. The innermost secret thought has been bared. Sometimes we, ourselves, do not know what made us say such things.

The tongue is not only pugnacious but also *poisonous*. Years ago, Alexander Whyte preached a series of sermons on the various characters that appear in Bunyan's *Pilgrim's Progress*. One of those characters was a man named Talkative. Faithful, a brother beloved by Christian, was at first quite taken with the man, but Christian knew Talkative of old. He was a resident of the City of Destruction. He warned his fellow pilgrim, "This man," he said, "will beguile, with this tongue of his, twenty of them that know him not." He continued, "He talketh of prayer, of repentance, of faith, and of the new birth: but he knows only to talk of them." Christian knew him to have been the ruin, with his tongue, of many. And so Faithful found him to be when he tried to get beyond the man's talk to his walk.

In commenting on this man, Talkative, Alexander Whyte wrote the following.

> Take detraction, for an example, one of the commonest, and, surely, one of the most detestable of the sins of the tongue. And the etymology here, as in this whole region, is most instructive and most impressive. In detraction you *draw away* something from your neighbour that is most precious and most dear to him. In detraction you are a thief, and a thief of the falsest and wickedest kind. For your neighbour's purse is trash, while his good name is far more precious to him than all his gold. Some one praises your neighbour in your hearing, his talents, his performances, his character, his motives, or something else that belongs to your neighbour. Some one does that in your hearing who either does not know you, or who wishes to torture and expose you, and you fall straight into the snare thus set for you, and begin at once to belittle, depreciate, detract from, and run down your neighbour, who has been too much praised for your peace of mind and your self-control. You insinuate something to his disadvantage and dishonour. You quote some authority you have heard to his hurt. And so on past all our power to picture you. For detraction has a thousand devices taught to it by the master of all such devices, wherewith to drag down and defile the great and the good. But with all you can say or do, you cannot for many days get out of your mind the heart-poisoning praise you heard spoken of your envied neighbour.
>
> Never praise any potter's pots in the hearing of another potter, said the author of the *Nicomachean Ethics*. Aristotle said potter's pots, but he really all the time was thinking of a philosopher's books; only he said potter's pots to draw off his readers' attention from himself. Now, always remember that ancient and wise advice. Take care how you praise a potter's pots, a philosopher's books, a woman's beauty, a speaker's speech, a

preacher's sermon to another potter, philosopher, woman, speaker, or preacher; unless, indeed, you maliciously wish secretly to torture them, or publicly to expose them, or, if their sanctification is begun, to sanctify them to their most inward and spiritual sanctification.

Backbiting, again, would seem at first sight to be a sin of the teeth rather than of the tongue, only, no sharpest tooth can tear you when your back is turned like your neighbour's evil tongue. Pascal has many dreadful things about the corruption and misery of man, but he has nothing that strikes its terrible barb deeper into all our consciences than this, that if all our friends only knew what we have said about them behind their back, we would not have four friends in all the world. Neither we would. I know I would not have one. How many would you have? And who would they be? You cannot name them. I defy you to name them. They do not exist. The tongue can no man tame.[3]

James speaks, too, of *the tongue and its dichotomy.* There is, for instance, its *ability to bless God:* "Therewith bless we God," and its equal *ability to berate men:* "And therewith curse we men, which are made after the similitude of God" (3:9). Those who have attended a Welsh soccer match, especially a championship game, sometimes tell of having had this experience. While the people wait for the event to begin, they fill the vast stadium with harmonious song. The Welsh love to sing! It is their natural pastime. They instinctively take their parts. The great hymns of the faith come readily to their lips, and their tongues sound out the great anthems of the church. You would think that it was a Billy Graham crusade, not a soccer match, to which the crowds have come. The whole arena rings and rings again with hymn after hymn, all in majestic four-part harmony, and God's name is exalted in resounding songs of praise.

Then the teams come in, and the fans forget the hymns. They watch each play. Just let a player fumble the ball, the goalie fail to block a play, or an umpire make an unpopular call, and fans will explode with oaths and curses. One would think that the destiny of nations rather than the outcome of a mere game hung in the balance. The same tongues that a short while before sang the praises of the living God now curse the unfortunate player whose mistake cost the Welsh team a goal.

We see the same thing in our own lives. One moment we are singing hymns in church, lifting our voices in praise and uttering a fervent, "Amen!" Within the

---

3. Alexander Whyte, *Bunyan's Characters* (London: Oliphant, Anderson and Ferrier, 1893), 182–84.

hour, we are outside the church and a child misbehaves or a car cuts us off on the highway or the line at the restaurant is too long or we learn that an investment has turned sour—and we discover afresh the treachery of the tongue.

James speaks, moreover, of *the tongue and its duplicity.* First, we have *repetition* (*exerchomai,* the idea here is that of "coming and going"): "Out of the same mouth proceedeth blessing and cursing," and then *repudiation:* "My brethren, these things ought not so to be" (3:10). Repetition is not a bad thing. It is an important principle of sound pedagogy. That is how we learn the multiplication table, by saying it over and over again. The Holy Spirit does not scorn to use this teaching device to deepen in our minds the groove of this truth—the tongue is a treacherous matter.

"This kind of thing," James says, "ought not to happen." Of course not! But it is much easier to state the problem than it is to solve it. James did not have a well-developed theology of the cross. Paul spells out the way of victory "through Jesus Christ our Lord," especially in his epistle to the Romans (chaps. 6–8). Still, being aware of the problem is a good start. At least we can recognize the problem for what it is—part of the great problem of original, inherited, and universal sin.

(d) The unredeemed tongue (3:11–12)

James comes to his final point. Again he has *an illustration:* "Doth a fountain send forth at the same place sweet water and bitter?" (3:11). We are reminded of Elisha's second miracle. The people of Jericho appealed to him because, although the situation of the city was pleasant, the water was bad and the ground was barren. The whole process that follows, of changing the effects of the curse that rested on Jericho (Josh. 6:26), is full of interest and instruction. Involved was a man, a cruse, some salt, and a word.

A *vision* was connected with that man. He was a man who had his eye on heaven (2 Kings 2:9–12). *Value* was connected with the cruse. It was new. That new earthen cruse spoke of the incarnate Christ, who came from heaven to inhabit a body of clay. *Virtue* was connected with the salt. Our Lord's humanity was not merely sinless; it was holy. Salt had to be added to all of the sacrifices (Lev. 2:13). It was that which made them acceptable. *Vitality* was connected with the word. It was a word from God. "I have healed!" That was it!

It was all very well for Elisha to know that there was a man (Elijah) in heaven. It was all very well to know that the man in glory inhabited a human body in which he had exhibited on earth a life of obedience. Elisha had to act on his knowledge. The river still ran from an unchanged spring.

It is the same with us. We know that a Man is in heaven in a glorified human body. We know that He once lived down here a sinless life. But somehow our hearts remain deceitful and desperately wicked—as evidenced by our tongue. There has to be a word from God. It was not the word of Elisha that regenerated the fountain; it was the word from God. Just so, we have to get to the source with the gospel.

"So the waters were healed unto this day," God says, commenting on the transforming word of power in Elisha's day. It took a miracle. It still does. The miracle performed at Jericho changed the nature of the water totally and permanently. It did not taste sometimes bad and other times good. James is right; that is not God's way. It has to be "one thing or the other," James contends. It is the counsel of perfection. The Sermon on the Mount preaches the same uncompromising position, a piece of divine legislation on which James always rests his case.

Finally, James has *an application:* "Can the fig tree, my brethren, bear olive berries? either a vine, figs? so can no fountain both yield salt water and fresh" (3:12). The problem is that we do have a divided heart, as Paul so clearly teaches in Romans 7. We have two natures. We were born with a nature that can do nothing right (Rom. 7:18), and we have been born again, heirs to a nature that can do nothing wrong (1 John 3:9). All of our conduct and conversation stems from either the one nature or the other. We either exhibit the works of the flesh or display the fruit of the Spirit (Gal. 5:16–26). Paul tells us to crucify the flesh and to walk in the Spirit.

The tongue does not have a life of its own, even though James uses the figure of speech of personification to describe its activities. It is controlled by either the flesh—by the old, fallen Adamic nature—or the indwelling Spirit of God. It cannot be controlled by both at the same time. If the flesh is reigning, then out comes bitter water. If the Holy Spirit is on the throne, then out of our innermost being flows that river of living water of which the Lord Himself spoke (John 7:37–39).

2. Sin in the mind (3:13–18)
   a. Wisdom and its course (3:13–14)
      (1) The main stream of wise behavior (3:13)

James moves now from words to wisdom. The two concepts are, of course, closely related. Even an unregenerate man can hold his tongue when it is in his interest to do so. We have all known foul-spoken men who have refrained from cursing and obscenity when they are in the presence of a high-principled employer whom they know will not tolerate use of bad language. Wisdom controlled their words. They knew well enough that if they spoke to their boss the way they spoke to others, they would lose their job.

So James points first to the mainstream of wise behavior: "Who is a wise man and endued with knowledge among you? Let him show out of a good conversation his works with meekness of wisdom." A wise man does not need to boast. The old-fashioned word *conversation* here refers to a lifestyle and everyday behavior. *Endued with knowledge* comes from a word that means to have skill and under-standing. It also means to know something well. The word for "meekness" is one that James has already used—we must "receive with meekness the engrafted word" (1:21).

Jesus exemplified all of these characteristics even as a boy (Luke 2:40, 52). James was blind to the wonder of Christ's life until he met the risen Lord after His resurrection. He had sat at table with incarnate Wisdom. He had walked to and from school with Him. He had heard His answers to all kinds of questions. A greater than Solomon resided in that home in Nazareth, worked at that carpenter's bench, and took the scroll in the synagogue to read and expound the Scriptures.

James calls on the people in the church who professed to be wise to "show" it. The word is emphatic. Thinking back over the years in Nazareth and the years of the Lord's public ministry, and dwelling on His teaching, especially as enshrined in the Sermon on the Mount, James could have confessed that no one had ever shown wisdom more clearly and wonderfully than did Jesus.

(2) The muddy stream of wicked behavior (3:14)

Sometimes the negative accentuates the positive. A dark piece of velvet best reveals the glory of the diamond. The bad behavior of Judah enhances the good behavior of Joseph (Gen. 38–39). Similarly, James produces four exhibits of things that negate wisdom.

Take, for instance, the man with a *bitter spirit:* "But if ye have bitter envy-ing . . ." (3:14a). The word for "envying" is *zēlos,* the word for "jealousy." James has just used the word in relation to bitter water (3:11). Undoubtedly, jealousy makes a person bitter. This double use of *zēlos,* one use connected with bitter water and the other use connected with bitter jealousy, might indicate that James had in mind the Mosaic Law. God required that bitterness and jealousy be dealt with in accordance with the law (Num. 5:12–31).

To have "bitter envying" in one's heart toward a wiser, more gifted, and more successful brother is the very opposite of wisdom. It leads the envious person to do and say things that are mean-spirited and contrary to the Spirit of the Lord Jesus.

Then consider the man with *a belligerent spirit:* "if ye have . . . strife in your hearts" (3:14b). The word for "strife" here contains the ideas of ambition, self-seeking, and rivalry. Self is on the throne, and factions are the result. Paul had to face this problem with the Corinthian church (2 Cor. 12:20). Even the Philippian church was not altogether free of it (Phil. 2:3; 4:2). Indeed, during his first imprisonment at Rome, Paul knew of some people at Philippi who were actually preaching Christ in an acrimonious spirit, hoping to get a rise out of Paul (Phil. 1:16).

James was familiar with the problem right there in the Jerusalem church over which he presided. In the very early days, that church had experimented with communal living. The practice soon died out, however. It had to face too many problems arising from human nature. Indeed, it did not take long for problems to arise. The Hellenist Jews in the infant church complained that the Hebraist Jews were getting more than their fair share of the communal handouts. The apostles heard about the resulting strife. Their solution was to appoint godly, gracious, and gifted men to administer the program. One of the required qualifications for such men was wisdom (Acts 6:1–6). James warns the believers scattered throughout the Roman world that the spirit of strife was the opposite of wisdom. It denoted a carnal spirit, not a Christian spirit.

There was also *a boastful spirit:* "glory not," he says (3:14c). The word he uses is *katakauchaomai,* which means "to boast," or "to exult." Some people in Jerusalem had fostered a party spirit and promoted themselves and their faction. James had no use for that kind of thing. But James himself, as a matter of fact, might have been suspected of promoting, or at least of protecting, the legalistic, Jewish faction in the church. But he did not do so out of a spirit of contention and strife. He truly believed himself to be standing for the truth. Moreover, he was prepared to be as accommodating as his stern principles would allow him to be of others who were not of his persuasion, notably the apostle Paul.

Other people, however, did not have the high principles of James. They were out for partisan triumph and were prepared to use underhanded methods to promote their faction. Such Jewish teachers dogged Paul's footsteps, seeking to subvert his churches and glorying in their successes. They were not above using forged credentials, posing as authentic delegates from the Jerusalem church. James had only contempt for such people.

But there was also *a blind spirit:* "and lie not against the truth" (3:14d) is James's final offering on the altar of wisdom. Wisdom never parts company with truth. To imagine that one can use lies, half-truths, and trickery to promote the cause of Christ is to reveal a heart that is a stranger to true wisdom. Lies may often produce quick results, but they are counterproductive in the end—and they tend to come home to roost.

The classic biblical example of this fact is that of the wandering Amalekite who brought King Saul's crown and ornaments to David, claiming that he had killed Saul, David's bitterest enemy. Doubtless, the man hoped to be rewarded by David. His lie was glib enough: "As I happened by chance upon mount Gilboa, behold, Saul leaned upon his spear . . ." (2 Sam. 1:6). Saul was attempting to commit suicide.

The Amalekite continued, "When he [Saul] saw me," he "called . . . me. . . . He said . . . , Stand, I pray thee, upon me, and slay me: for anguish is come upon me, because my life is yet whole in me. So I stood upon him, and slew him, because I was sure that he could not live after that he was fallen: and I took the crown that was upon his head, and the bracelet that was on his arm, and have brought them hither unto my lord" (2 Sam. 1:7–10).

It was a lie, and David saw through it the moment the man confessed to being an Amalekite. The Amalekites had no reason to love King Saul (1 Sam. 15:1–9). In fact, Saul committed suicide by falling on his sword in the presence of his armor bearer who, once Saul was dead, committed suicide himself (1 Sam. 31:4–6).

David turned to the Amalekite: "How wast thou not afraid to stretch forth thine hand to destroy the LORD's anointed?" he demanded (2 Sam. 1:14). He sentenced him to death. The man's lies came home to roost. "Thy blood be upon thy head," David said, "for thy mouth hath testified against thee, saying, I have slain the LORD's anointed" (2 Sam. 1:16). A wise man would have known David better than to boast to him of having killed his enemy, Saul. On two separate occasions, Saul had been in David's power, but David had spared him both times (1 Sam. 24:1–22; 26:1–21).

James knew of those people who, professing themselves to be wise, were blind. They were lying against the truth.

> b. Wisdom and its source (3:15–17)
>   (1) The source of human wisdom (3:15–16)
>   (a) Its outflow (3:15)

Two kinds of wisdom exist: the earthly, carnal, and worldly wisdom of unsaved people and the wisdom of God. Paul devotes a considerable amount of space in his epistle to the Corinthians contrasting the two types of wisdom (1 Cor. 1:18–2:16). James summarizes things more tersely. He begins with the threefold source of human wisdom.

James begins with its *secular source:* "This wisdom," the phony wisdom that he has just been denouncing, "descendeth not from above, but is earthly. . . ." It is the wisdom of this world. It expresses itself in various ways. All human philosophy, psychology, science, and religion betray their secular origins.

By the time of Christ the great philosophers of Greece and Rome had come and gone. They had been unable to produce any real answers to life's most profound problems. Modern psychology does no better.

The world's religions (except for Islam, which borrowed extensively from Judaism, Christianity, and the Bible) had all had their day and had been given ample time to demonstrate their essential idolatry and bankruptcy by the time Christ came.

Freud, who hated Christianity and called himself "a completely godless Jew" and "a hopeless pagan," invented modern psychology.[4] He endorsed irresponsible behavior and made it respectable. He gave irresponsible people welcome excuses with which to justify their behavior.

Science has achieved wonders but has created as many problems as it has solved. It has given us nuclear weapons, intercontinental missiles, and revolutionary ways to disseminate information and process data. What horrors it has in store for us through genetic engineering, cloning, and the like remains to be seen. Much of modern science is secular and humanistic. The accepted basic philosophy of most scientists is evolution, a God-dishonoring, soul-destroying, man-debasing religion that gives people a working hypothesis for atheism.

James points us also to the *sensual source* of earthly wisdom. "This wisdom . . . is sensual," he says. The word for sensual is *psuchikos.* It is related to the word *psuchē,* the soul. It speaks of the natural man and has to do with the physical side of man. The way James uses the word here points, perhaps, to the physical part of man, and to wisdom that springs from the corrupt desires and affections of the natural man. It refers to wisdom that has its roots in man's own lower nature.

Greek scholars say that no single English word renders this word properly. Our word *psychic* is a transliteration only, not a translation. The word *sensual* makes it too much a matter of the body. So does the word *fleshly.* The worldly wisdom that James has in mind is that of man in his unsaved state of sin.

The lower nature of the unsaved man has hungers, appetites, lusts, cravings, and desires that he does not wish to, or cannot, control. He finds ways, some of them very sophisticated, to rationalize his lawless indulgence of these inner forces.

---

4. Heinrich Meng and Ernst L. Freud, eds., *Psychoanalysis and Faith: The Letters of Sigmund Freud and Oskar Pfister,* trans. Eric Mosbacher (New York: Basic Books, 1963), 63, 110.

He blames his parents, his environment, his glands, or his genes. He can be clever and sophisticated in his philosophical justification of his sinful behavior.

But something is worse than this. James reminds us that earthly wisdom has a *satanic source:* "This wisdom . . . is devilish," he says. The word for "devilish" can be rendered "demoniacal." It occurs only here in the New Testament. The first time the word *wise* occurs in the Bible is in connection with Satan's temptation of Eve. He directed her attention to the forbidden fruit and let her dwell upon the fact that it was "a tree to be desired to make one wise" (Gen. 3:6).

Satan's greatest cunning, however, is displayed in his invention of hundreds of false religions. These are useful tools to keep his captives in soul-destroying bondage and to lure believers from their fidelity to the simple truths of the gospel.

John Bunyan captured the spirit of such diabolical "wisdom" early in the adventures of Christian, who was fleeing from the City of Destruction and heading for the Celestial City. Christian had just escaped from the miry slough, and his companion, Pliable, had given up the pilgrimage altogether. Christian, still carrying his burden of sin, which was made all the heavier because of his study of God's Word, continued on his way. Bunyan wrote:

> Now, as Christian was walking solitary by himself, he espied one afar off come crossing over the field to meet him; and their hap was to meet just as they were crossing the way of each other. The gentleman's name that met him was Mr. Worldly Wiseman: he dwelt in the town of Carnal Policy, a very great town, and also hard by from whence Christian came. This man, then, meeting with Christian, and having some inkling of him (for Christian's setting forth from the City of Destruction was much noised abroad, not only in the town where he dwelt, but also it began to be the town talk in some other places), Mr. Worldly Wiseman, therefore, having some guess of him, by beholding his laborious going, by observing his sighs and groans, and the like, began thus to enter into some talk with Christian:
>
> World: How now, good fellow! whither away after this burdened manner?
>
> Chris: A burdened manner indeed, as ever I think poor creature had! And whereas you ask me, "Whither away?" I tell you, sir, I am going to yonder wicket gate before me; for there, as I am informed, I shall be put into a way to be rid of my heavy burden.

World:	Hast thou a wife and children?
Chris:	Yes; but I am so laden with this burden, that I cannot take that pleasure in them as formerly; methinks I am as if I had none.
World:	Wilt thou hearken to me, if I give thee counsel?
Chris:	If it be good, I will; for I stand in need of good counsel.
World:	I would advise thee, then, that thou with all speed get thyself rid of thy burden; for thou wilt never be settled in thy mind till then; nor canst thou enjoy the blessings which God hath bestowed upon thee till then.
Chris:	That is that which I seek for, even to be rid of this heavy burden; but get it off myself I cannot; nor is there any man in our country that can take it off my shoulders; therefore am I going this way, as I told you, that I may be rid of my burden.
World:	Who bid thee go this way to be rid of thy burden?
Chris:	A man that appeared to me to be a very great and honorable person; his name, as I remember, is Evangelist.
World:	I beshrew him for his counsel! There is not a more dangerous and troublesome way in the world than is that into which he hath directed thee; and that thou shalt find, if thou wilt be ruled by his counsel. Thou hast met with something, as I perceive, already; for I see the dirt of the Slough of Despond is upon thee; but that slough is the beginning of the sorrows that do attend those that go on in that way. Hear me: I am older than thou: thou art like to meet with, in the way which thou goest, wearisomeness, painfulness, hunger, perils, nakedness, sword, lions, dragons, darkness, and, in a word, death, and what not. These things are certainly true, having been confirmed by many testimonies. And why should a man so carelessly cast away himself, by giving heed to a stranger?
Chris:	Why, sir, this burden upon my back is more terrible to me than all these things which you have mentioned; nay, methinks I care not what I meet with in the way, if so be I can also meet with deliverance from my burden.
World:	How camest thou by the burden at first?
Chris:	By reading this book in my hand.
World:	I thought so. And it has happened unto thee as unto other weak men, who, meddling with things too high for them,

do suddenly fall into thy distractions; which distractions do not only unman men, as thine I perceive have done thee, but they run them upon desperate ventures, to obtain they know not what.

Chris: I know what I would obtain; it is ease from my heavy burden.

World: But why wilt thou seek for ease this way, seeing so many dangers attend it? Especially since (hadst thou but patience to hear me) I could direct thee to the obtaining of what thou desirest without the dangers that thou in this way wilt run thyself into. Yea, and the remedy is at hand. Besides, I will add that, instead of those dangers, thou shalt meet with much safety, friendship, and content.

Chris: Sir, I pray, open this secret to me.

World: Why, in yonder village (the village is named Morality) there dwells a gentleman whose name is Legality, a very judicious man, and a man of very good name, that has skill to help men off with such burdens as thine is from their shoulders; yea, to my knowledge he hath done a great deal of good this way; aye, and besides, he hath skill to cure those that are somewhat crazed in their wits with their burdens. To him, as I said, thou mayest go, and be helped presently. His house is not quite a mile from this place; and if he should not be at home himself, he hath a pretty young man to his son, whose name is Civility, that can do it (to speak on) as well as the old gentleman himself. There, I say, thou mayest be eased of thy burden; and if thou art not minded to go back to thy former habitation (as indeed I would not wish thee), thou mayest send for thy wife and children to thee in this village, where there are houses now standing empty, one of which thou mayest have at a reasonable rate; provision is there also cheap and good; and that which will make thy life the more happy is, to be sure there thou shalt live by honest neighbors, in credit and good fashion.

Now was Christian somewhat at a stand; but presently he concluded, "If this be true which this gentleman hath said, my wisest course is to take his advice"; and with that, he thus further spake:

Chris: Sir, which is my way to this honest man's house?

World: Do you see yonder high hill?

Chris: Yes, very well.

World: By that hill you must go, and the first house you come at is his.[5]

So Christian turned out of his way to go to Mr. Legality's house for help; but, behold, when he was got now hard by the hill, it seemed so high, and also that side of it that was next the wayside did hang so much over, that Christian was afraid to venture farther, lest the hill should fall on his head; wherefore there he stood still, and wotted not what to do. Also his burden now seemed heavier to him than while he was in his way. There came also flashes of fire out of the hill, that made Christian afraid that he should be burnt: here, therefore, he sweat and did quake for fear. And now he began to be sorry that he had taken Mr. Worldly Wiseman's counsel; and with that, he saw Evangelist coming to meet him, at the sight also of whom he began to blush for shame.[6]

Bunyan's pilgrim almost lost his soul, thinking that he could get to heaven by keeping the law or by producing a man-made righteousness. It is one of the Evil One's oldest and most successful wiles. It began with Cain. At the root of all false religion is the idea that salvation has to be earned. But the notion is contrary to the entire body of revealed truth in the Word of God. It is the very opposite of the wisdom of God and is the very essence of the religious wisdom of this world.

(b) Its outcome (3:16)

According to James, the outcome of worldly wisdom is twofold. It results in *unrest*—"For where envying and strife is . . ."—and it results in *ungodliness*—"there is confusion and every evil work." The word for "confusion" is *akatastasia*. The word conveys the idea of disorder and tumult. The Lord used it in describing the "commotions," the unrest, of the last days (Luke 21:9). Paul used the word when he commanded the Corinthians to bring order into their church services. "God," he wrote, "is not the author of *confusion*" (1 Cor. 14:27–35, emphasis added). He also uses the word to describe the "tumults" that he had experienced as a pioneer missionary in dangerous places (2 Cor. 6:5). And he

---

5. John Bunyan, Pilgrim's Progress (Philadelphia: Universal Book and Bible House, n.d.) 1-21.

6. Wilbur M. Smith, *World Crises and the Prophetic Scriptures* (Chicago: Moody, 1951), 111–13.

used it when he warned the Corinthians that the next time he came to visit them he intended to deal with the terrible disorders in their church, including the tumults (2 Cor. 12:20).

The word for "evil" used here by James is *phaolds*. It pictures something being blown about by the wind. It also conveys the idea of something worthless. Such is the Holy Spirit's estimate of worldly wisdom.

The classic biblical example of worldly wisdom is found in the career of King Solomon. He started well. At first, he was distinguished by his possession of the wisdom of God, the wisdom that he so gloriously personified and described in the opening chapters of the book of Proverbs. Solomon's wisdom was so universally applauded, even in his day, that people such as the Queen of Sheba came from the ends of the earth to sample it.

The Lord Jesus warned, however, that the light that is within us can be turned into darkness: ". . . how great is that darkness," He said (Matt. 6:23). That is what happened to Solomon. For years, he wandered in a kind of twilight zone. His decline began early when he chose a pagan woman for his queen. It deepened as he adopted, as a matter of policy, the practice of cementing relations with neighboring pagan kings by marrying their daughters. By the time he was old, Solomon actually did the rounds. He bowed and worshiped first at this pagan altar and then at that one. He had become an old fool. In fact, Solomon did more to destroy the nation of Israel than any other king who sat upon the throne of Israel. By the time he was through, he had turned Jerusalem into Babylon. His wisdom had become earthly, sensual, and devilish. The nation never recovered from the damage that Solomon did to it until after the end of the Babylonian captivity.

(2) The source of heavenly wisdom (3:17)

James now turns to the wisdom that comes down from God. First, he gives us *its basic characteristic:* "But the wisdom that is from above is first pure" (3:17a). The word that James uses is *hagnos,* meaning "free from defilement." The word *chaste* aptly conveys the thought. In his early years, Solomon understood this feature of wisdom. The first nine chapters of the book of Proverbs contrast wisdom with immorality and impurity:

1.   Wisdom's call (1:6–2:15)
      The immoral woman (2:16–22)

2.   Wisdom's call (3:1–4:27)
     The immoral woman (5:1–23)
3   Wisdom's call (6:1–23)
     The immoral woman (6:24–35)
4   Wisdom's call (7:1–4)
     The immoral woman (7:5–27)
5   Wisdom's call (8:1–9:12)
     The immoral woman (9:13–18)

The first and last of these segments dealing with wisdom's call are especially graphic. In them, wisdom is personified as a woman. She stands in the streets and at the great thoroughfares where people congregate, offering herself to the simple, to the unlearned, and to the fool. She offers to make them wise and to lead them in the path of light. She is of old, the companion of the Creator Himself. Thus, cleverly, Solomon contrasts her with the wanton woman, who likewise plies the streets and marketplaces, offering herself and her advertised charms to fools.

Heavenly wisdom is pure. It will never suggest or condone anything unclean or vile. Wisdom never offers a defiling thought. It partakes of the impeccable righteousness and absolute holiness of God.

Next, James gives us wisdom's *benevolent characteristics* (3:17b–d). He mentions wisdom's *motivation*—it is "peaceable" (3:17b); its *moderation*—it is gentle (3:17c); and its *mediation*—it is easy to be intreated (3:17d).

The word for "peaceable" can be rendered "peace loving" or "disposed to peace." Solomon said of wisdom that "all her paths are peace" (Prov. 3:17). Peace was one of the outstanding characteristics of the early years of his reign. This fact had been anticipated. David said to Solomon, "My son, as for me, it was in my mind to build an house unto the name of the LORD my God: but the word of the LORD came to me, saying, Thou hast shed blood abundantly, and hast made great wars: thou shalt not build an house unto my name, because thou hast shed much blood upon the earth in my sight. Behold, a son shall be born to thee, who shall be a man of rest; and I will give him rest from all his enemies round about: for his name shall be Solomon [i.e., 'peace'], and I will give peace and quietness unto Israel in his days" (1 Chron. 22:7–9).

The word for "gentle" here conveys the ideas of moderation and forbearance. It paints the picture of a person who does not stand up for his rights but who is willing to make room for others. It marks the man who is not a stickler for the letter of the law. Paul used the word when he urged his friends at Philippi, "Let your *moderation* be known unto all men" (Phil. 4:5, emphasis added). Paul listed it as a qualifying mark of a church elder. He must be *patient* (the same Greek word), he said (1 Tim. 3:3). The wise man does not insist on getting his pound of flesh.

The word for "easy to be entreated" can be translated "approachable," or "compliant." It is a military word. A good soldier knows how to receive and execute orders. The word also can mean "easily persuaded." That does not mean, however, that the wise man is gullible. On the contrary, he is fully aware of all of the factors in the equation of his decision.

David exemplified this kind of wisdom. Even as a young man, tied to the court by official duties and to King Saul by family relationship, he displayed the spirit of wisdom. Again and again, the Holy Spirit says, "he behaved himself wisely." After he killed Goliath, his name was on everyone's lips, so much so that King Saul was jealous of him and set traps for him. He tried to kill him with his spear. He tried to trap him when he offered to make him his son-in-law. David, however, saw through Saul's snare when he offered him his oldest daughter, Merab, to be his wife, and answered wisely. He saw through Saul's further trap when he offered to make him his son-in-law by marriage to Michal. He saw through Saul's transparent plot to kill him when he demanded a hundred "scalps" (as we would say today) as the dowry for Michal (1 Sam. 18). Yet, for all that, David was "easy to be intreated." On the two occasions when Saul sought to be reconciled with the man he had so wickedly wronged, David responded at once, graciously and like the Lord's anointed.

David was the same with Absalom when the wise woman of Tekoa came to plead his cause (2 Sam. 14). It was the same when the scoundrel Shimei came begging for his life (2 Sam. 19:16–23). Such are the benevolent aspects of the wisdom from above. In such a benevolent fashion has the "Wonderful, Counsellor" (Isa. 9:6) dealt with us. God is peaceable, gentle, and easy to be entreated. We should be the same.

James continues. He reminds us of wisdom's *bountiful characteristics*. He sets before us *the thoughts that wisdom entertains*—it is "full of mercy" (3:17e) and *the things that wisdom espouses*—it is "full of . . . good fruits" (3:17f). What mercy exists in the philosophy of a man such as Nietzsche, who pictured a world based on blood and barbarism and whose ideal superman was Cesare Borgia? Nietzsche said that Christianity was "the one immortal blemish upon the human race."[7] What mercy is there in Darwinism, which Huxley hailed as a working hypothesis for atheism? Evolution says that might is right. It promotes the survival of the

7. Friedrich Nietzsche, *The Antichrist*, trans. H. L. Mencken, Great Literature Online 1997–2003, www.underthesun.cc/classics/Nietzsche/antichrist/(7 Nov. 2003).

fittest. It is a philosophy that gave the world two global wars in one lifetime. What mercy exists in the philosophy of Karl Marx and Friedrich Engels, who sought to abolish great truths common to all society and build a world based on atheism? What mercy did Lenin and his heirs ever have in imposing communism on Russia and much of the rest of the world? What mercy exists in Hitler's *Mein Kampf,* with its strident demand for the extermination of world Jewry?

The wisdom that comes down from heaven is steeped in mercy, mercy for all of Adam's ruined race. The word for "mercy" here is *eleos,* "the outward manifestation of pity," or a "feeling of sympathy with misery." *Eleos* embraces the idea of succor, as distinguished from mere pity. God's mercy responds to a cry of distress. It is a good thing for all of us that God's character includes mercy. "It is of the LORD's mercies that we are not consumed," said Jeremiah (Lam. 3:22).

A story is told about Napoleon's having condemned a man to death. The man's mother appealed to the emperor for a pardon. Napoleon replied that it was the man's second offense and that justice must be done.

The mother persisted. "I am not asking for justice," she said, "but for mercy."

The emperor replied, "He doesn't deserve mercy."

She said, "It would not be mercy if he deserved it. And what I ask for is mercy."

Napoleon gave in.

We do not have to plead thus with God because God does not need to be persuaded. Mercy is not second nature to God; it is His nature. It is the nature, too, of everyone who partakes of His nature.

James points also to *the things that wisdom espouses.* It is "full . . . of good fruits." It is full of kind deeds. Thus did David extend practical grace to poor, lost Mephibosheth. In the first place, the unfortunate fellow was lame in both of his feet. He lived far off in distant Lo-debar. He was born into the family of a man (King Saul) who hated David so much that he tried to kill him on at least two dozen separate occasions. David told Ziba that he wanted to show "the kindness of God" to Mephibosheth. And so he did. He sent the messengers of his grace to find him. He brought him to himself, restored to him all of his lost estates, adopted him into his family, and set him at his own table (2 Sam. 9). What an example of being *full* of good fruit!

That is what God's wisdom teaches that He does for us. As hymn writer Samuel Medley put it in "Awake, My Soul, in Joyful Lays,"

> He saw me ruined in the Fall,
> Yet loved me notwithstanding all;

He saved me from my lost estate
His loving kindness, O how great![8]

The believer who has drunk deeply of that heaven-descended wisdom will be full of good fruits because "the fruit of the Spirit" (Gal. 5:22–23) will be a characteristic of his life.

That's how Joseph treated his brethren. Dying Jacob well understood the goodness and wisdom of his beloved son. "Joseph," he said, "is a fruitful bough, even a fruitful bough by a well; whose branches run over the wall" (Gen. 49:22). Joseph not only proved to be easily entreated and not only frankly and freely forgave his brothers for their terrible sin of selling him into slavery but also settled them in the green pastures of Goshen. He was not ashamed to call them brethren. He presented five of them before the throne in a generous display of wisdom because that action opened for them tremendous doors of opportunity. The fruit of his goodness extended, moreover, to the Egyptian people when they begged him to do something about their bankrupt condition. He provided generously for their future. More still, "all nations came into Egypt to Joseph" (Gen. 41:57), and he dealt with these suppliants from distant and neighboring lands according to the same heavenly wisdom that he showed to one and all.

Finally, James mentions wisdom's *balanced characteristics*. It is *absolutely unbiased*: it is "without partiality" (3:17g); and it is *absolutely unblemished*: it is "without hypocrisy" (3:17h). The expression "without partiality" comes from *adiakritos*. The word occurs only here in the New Testament and seems to have puzzled translators considerably. It is rendered in a variety of ways. It is described as a negative and adjectival form of a word similar to *diakrinō* that is unambiguous enough; it means "to discriminate" or "to make a difference."

James has already discussed the problem of believers showing partiality to the more affluent members of the Christian community. God, in His wisdom, never allows Himself to be swayed by the size of a person's bankbook, the color of his skin, from which side of the tracks he comes, or the number of letters he can put after his name. Nor should we.

The expression "without hypocrisy" comes from *anupokritos*. The idea behind the word is an actor's playing a part on a stage, portraying a character quite different from himself. The great hypocrites of the Gospels were the Pharisees, who pretended to a holiness and a spirituality that they did not possess. Christ roundly

---

8. Samuel Medley, "Awake, My Soul, in Joyful Lays," *Hymns of Worship and Remembrance* (Kansas City: Gospel Perpetuating Publishers, 1960), no. 1.

condemned them in a passage of singular power (Matt. 23). True wisdom will keep us from putting on such airs and graces. Nobody likes a hypocrite.

c. Wisdom and its force (3:18)

"And the fruit of righteousness is sown in peace of them that make peace." So James summarizes this discourse. Those who are truly wise, who are endowed with the wisdom that comes from above, are peacemakers. They sow everywhere a harvest of righteousness. They sow in peace, and their harvest of righteousness is garnered in peace. They exhibit that unique wisdom of the Sermon on the Mount generally and the seventh beatitude particularly: "Blessed are the peacemakers: for they shall be called the children of God" (Matt. 5:9).

All of these characteristics of heavenly wisdom are incarnated and displayed in the Lord Jesus. *He was pure.* He exhibited sinless perfection, absolute holiness, in every thought, every word, and every deed. He could challenge His enemies, who scoured His life for some inconsistency upon which they could seize: "Which of you," He asked, "convinceth me of sin?" (John 8:46). They were unable to find a single flaw in His character, conduct, or conversation. Pilate, after a thorough examination, declared, "I find in him no fault at all" (John 18:38). Even the dying thief realized suddenly the complete and supernatural sinlessness of Christ: "We indeed justly," he said, "for we receive the due reward of our deeds: but this man hath done nothing amiss" (Luke 23:41). God Himself proclaimed Him as His beloved Son, the One in whom He was well pleased (Matt. 3:17). The testimony of the Holy Spirit is that He was "holy, harmless, undefiled, separate from sinners" (Heb. 7:26). No impure thought ever entered His mind. He was the sinless, spotless Lamb of God. Peter, who knew Him as well as anyone, declared Him to be "without blemish and without spot" (1 Peter 1:19).

He was peaceable. That did not mean that He was a pacifist. On two occasions, He forcibly cleansed the temple of those who defiled and debased it. Nor did He hesitate to tell people unpalatable truth in particularly pungent and unforgettable forms. People came to Him with all sorts of troubles; He sent them away in peace (Mark 5:34). As He stilled the storm on the tempestuous Sea of Galilee, so He hushes the winds and waves of our wild passions and gives us peace. After all, His name is "the Prince of Peace" (Isa. 9:6). Solomon—in all of his glory and in the early, palmy days of his empire—was a mere temporary type of Him. Christ could well say "a greater than Solomon is here" (Matt. 12:42).

"Peace!" cried the angel hosts who swarmed down the star road from glory to herald His birth (Luke 2:14).

"Peace!" cried the exulting multitudes as the King came riding into Jerusalem (Luke 19:38).

"Peace!" He said as He burst into their midst on that glorious resurrection day (Luke 24:36). "Peace!" He said a week later when He came back to deal with doubting Thomas (John 20:26).

"Peace!" says Paul, summarizing redemption's story: He had "made peace through the blood of his cross" (Col. 1:20).

He was gentle. How gently He dealt with the woman taken in adultery (John 8:1–11) and with the city woman who wept at His feet in the Pharisee's house (Luke 7:36–50). How gently He dealt with poor, backslidden, broken Peter (John 21:15–22). How gently He dealt with the discerning mothers who brought their little ones to Him (Matt. 19:13–15). As W. M. Hutchings put it in the old children's hymn,

> When Mothers of Salem
> Their children brought to Jesus,
> The stern disciples drove them back
> And bade them all depart;
> But Jesus saw them ere they fled
> And sweetly smiled and kindly said,
> "Suffer little children to come unto Me."[9]

The prophet rightly said of Him, "A bruised reed shall he not break, and the smoking flax shall he not quench" (Isa. 42:3; Matt. 12:20). A bruised reed never was of much use; a smoking flax once served a useful purpose as wick to a lamp, but now it was of no use at all. Jesus is gentle with both types of people.

He was easy to be entreated, the most friendly and approachable of men. He said, "Him that cometh to me I will in no wise cast out" (John 6:37). No one ever appealed to Him in vain. Twice He allowed Himself to be delayed, once when Jairus pleaded with Him to come and heal his little girl (Mark 5:22–43) and once when Martha and Mary urged Him to come and heal His friend Lazarus (John 11:1–46). But in both cases He intended to perform a greater miracle than anything He had done before. He was the Great Physician. He never lost a case, charged a fee, or turned anyone away. When the dying thief, who had been cursing Him, turned to Him at last and said, "Lord, remember me when thou comest into thy kingdom," He responded at once, "Verily I say unto thee, Today shalt thou be with

---

9. W. M. Hutchings, "Mothers of Salem," *Redemption Songs* (London: Pickering and Inglis, n.d.), no. 683.

me in paradise" (Luke 23:42–43). If Judas had taken his sad confession, "I have sinned," to Christ, rather than to Caiaphas, he would have found one "easy to be intreated," rather than a scornful and callous high priest (Matt. 27:4).

He was "full of mercy." It was mercy that brought Him down from heaven's heights and mercy that caused Him to become God incarnate so that He could redeem us with His blood. When the two blind men pleaded, "Thou son of David, have mercy on us," they did not plead in vain (Matt. 9:27–30). Nor did the Syro-Phoenician woman (Matt. 15:21–28), nor did the two blind men of Jericho (Matt. 20:29–34), nor did blind Bartimaeus (Mark 10:46–52). The father of the demon-possessed boy, at the foot of the Mount of Transfiguration, pleaded that the Lord would have mercy on his son. He found a ready response (Matt. 17:14–21). When the ten lepers cried for mercy, He healed them all (Luke 17:11–14). Now, He is enthroned in glory "a merciful and faithful high priest" (Heb. 2:17), One who "remembereth that we are dust" (Ps. 103:14), One who is "touched with the feeling of our infirmities" (Heb. 4:15).

He was "full of good works." Indeed, Peter, after spending three and a half years in His company, could think of no better way to describe Him to the Gentile Cornelius than to say that He "went about doing good" (Acts 10:38). John lost count of how many good works He did. He simply says that if they were all to be recorded, "even the world itself could not contain the books that should be written" (John 21:25).

He was "without partiality." He was as gracious and true with the woman at the well, who had run through some half-dozen husbands, as He was with the religious aristocrat Nicodemus. He was as kind to the woman with the incurable hemorrhage as He was to the ruler of the synagogue. He was as earnest with Judas as He was with Simon Peter. He loved His unbelieving brother James as much as He loved His disciple and cousin James, the son of Zebedee.

And He was "without hypocrisy." He was absolutely transparent, completely, even disconcertingly, honest. He told the religious Nicodemus, a member of the ruling class, that unless he were to be born again, he would not even see the kingdom of God (John 3:1–12). He told the powerful Pharisees bluntly that they were hypocrites, and then He painted their portrait for them in vivid colors (Matt. 23). But there was never any pretense, nothing put on, about the Lord Jesus. He was always Himself, as fair as the morning, and as bright as the day. His life was an open book, a living epistle, known and read of all men. He sowed the fruit of righteousness. He was incarnate wisdom. Nobody put it better than Paul: "In [Him]," he said, "are hid all the treasures of wisdom" (Col. 2:3).

3. Sin in the members (4:1–5)
   a. The first question (4:1–4)
      (1) The question asked (4:1)

"From whence come wars and fightings among you? come they not hence, even of your lusts that war in your members?" James has just mentioned peace twice in one short verse. Now he speaks of war.

The word for "wars" is *polemos*. It is the usual word for war and fighting and is used of literal wars among men (Matt. 24:6). The word for "fightings" is *machē*. It refers to fighting and strife and is always used in the plural in the New Testament. Paul uses the word to describe the unsettled state of his soul when he came to Macedonia after leaving Troas. He had written a sharp letter to the Corinthians and had dispatched it by Titus, his representative. Now he was anxiously awaiting word as to how the church had reacted. Convinced that Titus would not now show up at Troas, he had gone on to Macedonia, hoping to bump into him along the way. Moreover, he had just come through a desperate situation at Ephesus, having endured such perils that he had despaired for his very life (2 Cor. 1:8–10; 2:13; 7:6–7, 13). "Without were fightings," he said, "within were fears" (2 Cor. 7:5). He used the word in warning Timothy to avoid foolish and unlearned questions, "knowing that they do gender strifes" (*machē*), he said (2 Tim. 2:23).

The word for "lusts" here means "pleasure" and includes the idea of gratifying one's natural and sinful desires.

Then James uses a second word for war, referring to the war in our members, the word *strateuomai*. It is derived from *stratos,* the word for an armed camp. Paul uses the word in defending his lifestyle against those at Corinth who were challenging his apostleship: "Who goeth a warfare [serves as a soldier, *strateuomai*] any time at his own charges?" he asks (1 Cor. 9:7). Peter uses the word to describe those "fleshly lusts, which war against the soul" (1 Peter 2:11).

James seems to have had some rather unruly situations in mind when he flung down this question to the scattered congregations of Jewish believers. Some people have expressed surprise that the chaotic conditions that James describes could have arisen so soon in Christian gatherings. Indeed, James paints an appalling picture of moral depravity. He mentions open warfare, lust for pleasure, murder, covetousness, adultery, envy, pride, and slander.

Well, Paul had to contend with the same thing in the churches that he planted; the devil never gives up. In church history, Satan followed the Reformation with the Counter-Reformation. He follows up revival with reaction. The morrow after a great spiritual experience is always a dangerous time in the life of the believer. Churches are no different. The Welsh Revival was followed by a spurious "revival" that caused Evan Roberts's friend, Jesse Pen Lewis, to write her book *War on the Saints*.

"From where do these things come?" James asks. They certainly do not come from Christ. They are not the fruit of the Spirit. They are foreign to that wisdom that is from above. James is not prepared to go to the length of blaming the Devil for these things. He does not see a demon lurking at the heart of every sin. The answer to his question lies closer at hand.

(2) The question answered (4:2–4)
(a) Their fleshly lusts (4:2a–b)

James finds three sources for the bad behavior of some people who, although professing to know Christ, contradicted their testimony by their scandalous lives. One explanation lay in their fleshly lusts. James mentions *their wants:* "Ye lust, and have not; ye kill, and desire to have, and cannot obtain" (4:2a), and he mentions *their wars:* "ye fight and war" (4:2b). A battle royal was raging both within and without.

The word for "desire" here is *zēloō*. It is a strong word. It means "to covet earnestly." The word for "war" is *polemeō*. The lusts and covetous desires of some of the professing Christians were turning the local church into a battleground. Satan's strategy is to get us fighting among ourselves instead of warring against him. Our own carnal lusts and desires are often all that is needed to stir up strife. Human passions can keep the church in turmoil.

One example of how far reckless passion can lead us to fight bitterly with our brethren comes from the story of Martin Luther. The great reformer—standing alone at Worms, defying pope and emperor alike, and refusing to retract a single word of what he had written—is a noble figure. "I cannot and I will not recant. . . . Here I stand; I cannot do otherwise. God help me, Amen."

But Luther, fighting with his brethren over the question of the sacrament, is something else. Church historian Andrew Miller tells the tale. He summarized this sad war between the saints thus:

> The position and danger of a party leader in the things of God are clearly expressed in the following opinion of Luther. "At Marburg, Luther was Pope. By general acclamation the chief of the evangelical party, he assumed the character of a despot; and to sustain that part in spiritual matters, it is necessary to create the prejudice of infallibility. If he once

yielded any point of doctrine—if he once admitted that he had fallen into error—the illusion would cease, and with it, the authority that was founded on it. It was thus at least with the multitude. He was obliged by the very position which he believed he occupied, or which he wished to occupy, to defend in the loftiest tone every tenet that he had once proclaimed to the people. . . .[10]

"Ye fight and war," James declared. Even when contending for the truth, an acrimonious spirit can assume command. Hot and carnal passions can take over. The cause of Christ can be hindered. The root of such violent squabbles is the flesh. Sometimes the flesh arrays itself in its worldly robes and plunges us into all kinds of carnal and wicked behavior. Sometimes it dons its religious robes and takes a strong stand on some doctrinal error. The flesh can exhibit itself in both the pulpit and the pew. It can pray with self-righteous eloquence. It can triumph in the deacons' meeting. It can take over the trustees' meeting. It can split churches over the color of the carpet, fine points of doctrine, or whom a church should receive into its fellowship or ordain to its ministry. The spirit of the elder brother is worse than that of the Prodigal Son.

(b) Their faulty logic (4:2c–3)

One reason for discord, divisions, and similar problems in the life of a Christian or a church often can be traced to wrong attitudes about prayer. James points to two problems—*a failure to pray personally:* "ye have not, because ye ask not" (4:2c); and *a failure to pray properly:* "Ye ask, and receive not, because ye ask amiss, that ye may consume it upon your lusts" (4:3). The word for "ask" here carries the idea of asking for something to be given in contrast to asking someone to do something.

The reason we often do not get things from God is very simple: we don't ask! The Bible contains many admonitions to pray. The Lord Jesus taught His disciples to pray. The church was born at a prayer meeting. God refuses to be left out of our affairs. So many things that we need or desire are in His hand; therefore, we must come to Him and ask. Thus, He teaches us our dependence upon Him for all things.

Prayer is a mysterious thing. It is one of the laws of the universe, as real and as functional as the laws of electricity, sound, magnetism, or light. God takes our

---

10. Andrew Miller, *Short Papers on Church History* (reprint, Fincastle, Va.: Scripture Truth Book Co., n.d.), 677–93. For more of this story, see appendix, "Luther's Rage."

prayers into consideration just as He takes the laws of chemistry, physics, or medicine into consideration. As He weighs all of the factors of matter, space, and time in the balances of His purposes, so He takes into account all of the features of our nature, persons, and personalities, along with all of the facets of our minds, hearts, and wills. Along with all of these things, He takes into consideration our prayers. The prayers of God's people are an important factor in the great equation of His involvement in the affairs of this world. We can no more define all of the implications of that—why God should be interested in and influenced by our prayers—than we can explain all the implications of nuclear science, the genetic code, or the behavior of countless galaxies in space. God assures us that our prayers count. That is what matters.

The Bible is full of illustrations of this truth. Abraham prayed for Lot the night of Sodom's overthrow (Gen. 18:17–33). Elisha prayed that the Lord would open the eyes of his companion to see what magnificent and invincible forces protected them (2 Kings 6:15–17). David—when he heard that the clever old scoundrel Ahithophel had joined Absalom's conspiracy—prayed that God would turn the counsel of Ahithophel to foolishness (2 Sam. 15:31). God answered the prayer instantly by the appearing of Hushai, a man whom God used to defeat that counsel. Hezekiah prayed when the Assyrian army surrounded Jerusalem and when a dangerous propaganda offensive was launched to subvert the loyalty of the Jewish population (2 Kings 18:17–19; 19). His prayer was answered instantly and miraculously.

Daniel prayed when he needed wisdom to tell Nebuchadnezzar the substance and significance of his dream (Dan. 2:17–23). God answered the prayer promptly. Daniel prayed when he faced the peril of the lions' den (Dan. 6:10–23). Ezra prayed for divine protection when he led a contingent of Jews back to Jerusalem. The way was dangerous, but Ezra declined politely the guard that the Persian king offered. Nor did he pray in vain (Ezra 8:21–32). Nehemiah prayed when word came to him of the desolate condition of Jerusalem (Neh. 1:1–11; 2:1–8). The Psalms are full of potent prayers. Apparently Jesus prayed through Psalm 22 while hanging on the cross. He prayed without ceasing. The early church prayed. The true church has always prayed. We should pray. James himself had a reputation for being a man of prayer.

Not only can we fail to pray *personally* but also we can fail to pray *properly:* "Ye ask, and receive not, because ye ask amiss, that ye may consume it upon your lusts" (4:3). The word for "amiss" is *kakos.* The word means "depraved," that which is bad in its very nature. Prayer is not a magic incantation guaranteed to get us whatever our hearts desire. Prayer has its rules. It must be in accordance with God's will (Matt. 26:39). It must be in faith (Matt. 21:22). It must come from a pure heart because God says that if we regard iniquity in our heart, He will not hear us (Ps. 66:18). It must be in the name of the Lord Jesus (John 14:13–14; 15:16). And it must be fervent (James 5:16).

Prayer assumes various aspects. It can be in the form of confession, supplication, intercession, petition, or adoration. James has in mind here specifically the prayer of petition—asking God for things.

Too often, we ask for the wrong things. Most of our prayers are concerned with material and physical things, with the matter of wealth or health. Often, our prayers are sheer folly in the light of God's eternal purpose. When James and John came to Jesus with their mother, she requested of Him that "these my two sons may sit, the one on thy right hand, and the other on the left, in thy kingdom." Jesus said, "Ye know not what ye ask" (Matt. 20:21–22).

Some years ago, when I was preaching in the West Indies, I heard of a man who liked to use big words, especially when he was praying. He was not an educated man and frequently used words incorrectly, not knowing their meaning. On one occasion, he had picked up an expression that had a resounding ring to it, and he was waiting for a suitable occasion to use it. Shortly afterward, he was at a prayer meeting. Request was made for a brother who was in the hospital facing a serious operation. The brother who was infatuated with big words seized his opportunity. He prayed, "Dear Lord, You know all about Brother Sam's condition. He's in the hospital, Lord. He has to have an operation, Lord. Please give him a successful postmortem! In Jesus' name, Amen."

"Ye know not what ye ask," Jesus said to His ambitious disciples. A cup had to be shared; a dread baptism had to be passed. Besides, what they requested was not His to give.

A study of Bible prayers can be most instructive, especially Paul's prison prayers. The Lord's Prayer, of course, is the model upon which all prayers should be built. Most of the petitions in Bible prayers are of a moral and spiritual nature. In answering our prayers, God reserves the right to say "No!" or "Wait!" Looking back, we can be devoutly thankful that the Lord did not answer some of our prayer requests.

In Numbers 11 is the classic example of God answering prayer to the detriment of those who prayed. The psalmist, many years later, commented on this incident: "[They] lusted exceedingly in the wilderness, and tempted God in the desert. And he gave them their request; but sent leanness into their soul" (Ps. 106:14–15).

God will not answer some prayers at all. He will not grant our request for something against which He has spoken in His Word—or, if He does, it will be in judgment. He has declared that the prayer of the wicked is an abomination (Prov. 28:9).

(c) Their fatal liaisons (4:4)

No wonder the prayers of some people rise no higher than the ceiling. James points out *the worldliness of such people:* "Ye adulterers and adulteresses, know ye not that the friendship of the world is enmity with God" (4:4a), and also *the wickedness of such people:* "whosoever therefore will be a friend of the world is the enemy of God" (4:4b).

Some believers in the Jerusalem church might well have been guilty of physical adultery. An extreme case was known, for instance, in the church at Corinth (1 Cor. 5:1–5). It called for stern discipline. Adultery is a serious offense against God. In the Old Testament, it was a capital crime (Deut. 22:24; Num. 5:11–31; John 8:1–11). Moreover, "he that despised Moses' law died without mercy under two or three witnesses" (Heb. 10:28). God is severe with cases of flagrant immorality and has a thousand ways to punish it.

I once heard Dr. Adrian Rodgers, pastor of the great Bellevue Baptist Church in Memphis, Tennessee, say, "A man committing adultery says to his children: 'Your mother is not worth much, and your father is a cheat and a liar. Honor is not as important as pleasure, and my satisfaction is more important than you.'" True words.

After David sinned with Bathsheba, he never won another victory. Other people had to do his fighting for him. He did write a half-dozen tear-drenched, penitential psalms, and he was able to save enough money to pay for the temple. But he was through as the all-victorious, God-empowered, warrior king. He resorted, instead, to counting heads. Even Joab—worldly, carnal man that he was—had more sense than that (2 Sam. 24:1–17).

Physical adultery is bad, but spiritual adultery is immeasurably worse. When we accept Christ, we are spiritually "married to another, even to him who is raised from the dead" (Rom. 7:4). Any liaison with the world constitutes spiritual adultery. James declared that the "friend of the world is the enemy of God."

We have three foes: the world, the flesh, and the Devil. Throughout the New Testament, we see that God the Father is the special enemy of the world (1 John 2:15–17), God the Son is the enemy of Satan (Matt. 4:1–11; 1 John 3:8), and God the Holy Spirit is the foe of the flesh (John 3:6; Gal. 5:16–25). By "the world," James does not mean the planet Earth in space. He means human life and society with God left out—the Devil's lair for sinners and his lure for saints. Worldliness, which includes carnality, negates prayer. The poet Margaret Mauro, having described her attraction to the world, explained in her poem "The Young Christian" why, at last, she rejects its blandishments:

> Nay world, I turn away,
> Though thou seem fair and good,
> That friendly, outstretched hand of thine
> Is stained with Jesus' blood.[11]

b. The further question (4:5)

James concludes, "Do ye think that the scripture saith in vain, The spirit that dwelleth in us lusteth to envy?" This is a rhetorical question, and it calls for a vigorous denial. No such quotation is in the Old Testament. James, therefore, must be appealing to the general tenor of Old Testament Scripture. Certainly, in the Decalogue, God proclaims Himself to be "a jealous God," One who is intolerant of rivals (Exod. 20:5). He refuses to share us with the world.

One view of this somewhat obscure verse is that the word *spirit* here refers to the human spirit. In its natural condition, it is dead toward God. Man, in his unregenerate nature, likes to indulge his selfish desires. That, in turn, causes him to envy people who possess things that he would like to have. Scripture legislates against this attitude. The tenth commandment declares, "Thou shalt not covet" (Exod. 20:17).

Another view is that the word *spirit* here really refers to the Holy Spirit. The statement, "The spirit that dwelleth in us lusteth to envy," in this case, reminds us that we have the indwelling Holy Spirit in our hearts. Paul would agree with James. He says, "The Spirit [lusteth] against the flesh" (Gal. 5:17). This concept is expanded in Romans 8:3–15. Moreover, the Holy Spirit covets our complete obedience. He wants all of our heart's desires, not just some of them.

B. Sin in the life resisted (4:6–10)
1. The call to submit (4:6–7)

James now turns our attention to *the secret of spiritual virtue:* "But he giveth more grace. Wherefore he saith, God resisteth the proud, but giveth grace unto

---

11. Margaret Mauro, "The Young Christian," *Word and Work* 13.10 (October 1920): 289.

the humble" (4:6). This statement is a quotation from Proverbs 3:34. It comes toward the end of a long monologue in which Solomon tries to warn his son and heir against the wrong choice of friends. The key is the word *grace*. That is the secret of a virtuous life. Grace, after all, is unmerited favor. It is getting something that we don't deserve. It is the driving force behind the salvation, sanctification, and security that God offers to the fallen children of Adam's ruined race. It is the key to the kingdom. It is the deathblow to our pride. It annuls all of the world's religions, which demand that we do something, earn something, or merit something. The proud man will not stoop to accept God's grace, so God resists him.

Thus, He resisted Cain, who invented the world's first false religion. Thus, He resisted Nimrod and the builders of Babel with their humanism, pride, and goals for a one-world society independent of God. Thus, He resisted Pharaoh and his disdainful word to Moses, "Who is the LORD, that I should obey his voice. . . ? I know not the LORD, neither will I let Israel go" (Exod. 5:2). Thus, He resisted the Edomites and their boast in their impregnable fortress. And thus, He resisted Naaman, Nebuchadnezzar, Haman, Herod, Balaam, and Belshazzar.

He resisted Alexander the Great, cutting off his life in its prime. He resisted Napoleon, sending snowflakes to stop his onward march against Russia. He resisted Voltaire, giving him such horrors on his deathbed as terrified his very nurse. He resisted Stalin and the Soviet Empire, tearing it to tattered shreds in a matter of months when the time came.

To accept God's grace, we must lay aside all pride and come as a repentant sinner to the foot of the cross. He "giveth grace unto the humble," adds James. God's grace does not end with our salvation; it provides us with all that we need for the journey home. God's grace set Egypt's captives free. But God not only put His people under the blood but also marched them out of the house of bondage, brought them through the water, and turned their faces toward the Promised Land. Did they need water? He brought it flowing from the riven rock. Did they need food? He sent them bread from heaven. Were they assailed by foes? He gave them victory. Did they need to know which way to go? He marched before them. Did they need protection from the smiting sun and staring moon? He spread a cloudy canopy over one and all. Did they need to cross a river? He smote it so that it parted before them. Were the walls of Jericho too great and tall and strong? He knocked them down.

It was all of grace for them. It is all of grace for us. So wrote John Newton in his hymn "Amazing Grace":

'Twas grace that taught my heart to fear,
And grace my fears relieved;
How precious did that grace appear
The hour I first believed!
Through many dangers, toils, and snares,
I have already come;
'Tis grace hath brought me safe thus far,
And grace will see me home.[12]

James mentions, further, *the secret of spiritual victory:* "Submit yourselves therefore to God. Resist the devil, and he will flee from you" (4:7). Preachers often quote the second sentence of this verse: "Resist the devil, and he will flee from you." But that is not true. Satan is not the least bit afraid of us. He is more clever than we are. He is very much stronger. He has powers above and beyond any that we possess. In terms of creation, he is far older than the human race and much higher in the order of things. He belongs with the cherubim. Before his fall, he was the highest, wisest, and most powerful of all created beings. Even in his fallen state, he is so awesome in power that not even the archangel Michael dared rail against him (Jude 9). He is the ruler of countless legions of fallen angels and demon hosts. He is the master of deception, and he knows all about us. He has had some six thousand years of practice in manipulating the human race. When he targets an individual, as he did Job, he can beggar that person, destroy his family, inflict him with incurable diseases, turn his wife and loved ones against him, and fill his life with discord and strife. Even the winds obey him.

The Devil is not afraid of *us,* nor is he going to flee from *us.* We can "resist" him as much as we like, but, when he puts forth his power, down we go.

The Holy Spirit does *not* say, "Resist the devil, and he will flee from you." That is a text taken out of context and, consequently, a pretext. What the Holy Spirit *does* say is this: "Submit yourselves unto God. Resist the devil, and he will flee from you." That changes the equation! When we submit ourselves unto God, that leaves the Devil face-to-face with *Him!* So it was when Satan tempted the incarnate Christ in the wilderness. To each temptation, the Lord responded by quoting from the written Word, the one weapon that Satan fears. Then, after the third such temptation and response, the Lord Jesus simply told Satan to go—and so he did, utterly defeated (Matt. 4:1–11).

Thus, Moses responded to the Satan-inspired rebellion of the children of Is-

---

12. From *A Collection of Sacred Ballads,* 1790.

rael in the wilderness. After the spies returned with a pessimistic majority report, the people turned on Moses. "Would God we had died in this wilderness!" they said. *It would be better,* they thought, *to elect a captain and return to Egypt rather than face the giants and walled cities of Canaan.* Moses simply fell on his face, leaving the rebels face-to-face with God (Num. 14:1–5).

It was the same when Korah, Dathan, and Abiram raised the standard of rebellion against the lordship of Moses and the priesthood of Aaron (Num. 16:1–22). Then, when judgment fell on the rebels, yet another insurrection occurred: "Ye have killed the people of the LORD," the Israelites charged. Again Moses fell on his face (Num. 16:41–45). It was the same thing all over again with the second generation. The wilderness wanderings had gone on for years. The children of Israel had now returned to Kadesh, and again the problem of water arose. The angry people accused Moses of deliberately bringing them to the site so that they would die of thirst. Once again, Moses fell on his face (Num. 20:1–6). It was the instinctive response of a man of God to provocation and problems brought about by the wiles of the Evil One. He submitted himself unto God; Satan fled from him.

2. The call to commit (4:8–10)

James is still pursuing his theme of resisting the reign of sin in one's life. The call to submit is now followed by a call to commit. We begin with *a word about coming:* "Draw nigh to God, and he will draw nigh to you" (4:8a). Between God and man is distance, distance that cannot be measured in miles. Before the Fall, no distance existed between God and man. God and Adam walked and talked together in fellowship and harmony in the cool of each day. After the Fall, however, distance existed. At the sound of God's voice, Adam and Eve fled from God, who, in infinite compassion, had come looking for them. They were lost and had to be found. That kind of distance expresses itself in rebellion, as when the Prodigal Son took his journey into the far country. That kind of distance is not measured in miles but in morals. That kind of distance expresses itself in self-righteous religion, as when the elder brother was angry and would not go in to the feast, preferring to sit outside in bitter, hypocritical scorn.

Many of our hymns address this fact of distance and the fact that God has now devised "means, that his banished be not expelled from him," as the wise woman of Tekoah reminded David (2 Sam. 14:14).

William R. Newell put it thus in his hymn "At Calvary":

> Oh, the love that drew salvation's plan!
> Oh, the grace that brought it down to man!
> Oh, the mighty gulf that God did span
> At Calvary!

Elizabeth C. Clephane borrowed a different imagery when she penned the wondrous words that caught the attention of Ira D. Sankey, D. L. Moody's song leader, and that he immortalized at one of their campaign meetings in the song "The Ninety and Nine":

> There were ninety and nine that safely lay
> In the shelter of the fold,
> But one was out on the hills away,
> Far off from the gates of gold—
> Away on the mountains wild and bare
> Away from the tender Shepherd's care.

The Good Shepherd could not be content with that. Oh, no! That lost sheep had to be sought and found. He said,

> Although the road be rough and steep,
> I go to the desert to find My sheep.

And so He did, at infinite cost. However,

> None of the ransomed ever knew
> How deep were the waters crossed;
> Nor how dark was the night that the Lord
> passed through
> Ere He found His sheep that was lost. . . .

And find it He did! The closing note of triumph, though, still conveys the thought of distance:

> But all through the mountains, thunder riven,
> And up from the rocky steep,

> There arose a glad cry to the gates of heaven,
> Rejoice! I have found My sheep.[13]

So that "great gulf fixed," such a dread reality in a lost eternity (Luke 16:26), has been bridged on this side of the grave. God has taken the initiative. He has come as far as He can. Although He stops short of violating the human will, He stands with welcoming arms outstretched and says, "Come!" He refuses to close the Book before He says it again and again—"Come! Come! Come!" (Rev. 22:17).

So, there is a word about coming. We come first as poor, lost sinners, and He puts us in His family. At times, we drift away, but He calls us back. James was, doubtless, thinking of some people who had wandered. "Draw nigh to God," he says, "and he will draw nigh to you." Straying sons are not like lost coins or lost sheep. Wayward sons have wills of their own. The father of the Prodigal Son did not run into the far country in search of his son. He watched and waited. When the prodigal came to an end of himself, arose, and came to his father, however, he had no doubt as to the reception that would be his. His father ran to meet him to welcome him home.

If we become aware that distance has grown between God and us, it is time for heart searching. Preachers like to tell an amusing story about an old couple driving along the highway. After a while, the wife spoke up. "D'yer remember back when we was courting, Henry?"

"Yep!" he said. "Sure do."

"D'yer remember how close we used to sit?"

"Sure do!"

"Well, how come we don't sit like that no more?" she asked.

Henry thought about it for a moment, then said, "I ain't moved!"

If distance has grown between God and us, we can be sure of one thing—God hasn't moved! All kinds of things contribute to distance. Failure to maintain a meaningful daily quiet time of Bible reading and prayer will do it. Entertaining known and unconfessed sin in one's life will do it. Reading certain types of books and watching tainted movies will do it. Indulging in questionable amusements will do it. Neglecting the fellowship of God's people will do it. Ignoring the prompting of a conscience quickened by the Holy Spirit will do it. Willful disobedience to God's revealed will and failure to cultivate a walk with God and a growing knowledge of Christ will do it. God's Word is clear: "Come back! Draw nigh to God, and He will draw nigh to you."

---

13. From *The Family Treasury*, 1872.

Then, James offers *a word about cleansing:* "Cleanse your hands, ye sinners; and purify your hearts, ye double minded" (4:8b). The hands and the heart go together. The hands symbolize our outward life, the life that other people see. The heart speaks of our inner life, the life that God sees. The hands speak of what we do: the heart speaks of what we are. The hands and the heart are put together because we do what we do because we are what we *are.* David's great hymn of the ascension and coronation of Christ was, perhaps, in the mind of James when he penned these words. If we wish to reign with Christ, we must be and act like Him (Ps. 24:3–4).

When we allow distance to grow between us and God, it is because we have failed to keep our heart with all diligence (Prov. 4:23). As a result, our hands get into mischief. Solomon is a glaring example of what happens when we allow distance to grow between God and us. He ended up in all kinds of sin. His book Ecclesiastes is really a wail of despair, written in his old age, over a misspent life. There came a time, with Solomon, when he no longer trusted God with all of his heart. Instead, he leaned on his own understanding. He ceased to acknowledge God in all of his ways, so God no longer directed his paths. He drifted so far from his early nearness to God that he concluded that there was no particular advantage in being either good or bad (Eccl. 7:15–16). Solomon, now an old man, with a very great distance between him and God, does not even mention *Jehovah,* the God of covenant, in the book of Ecclesiastes. He had become so backslidden that he now knew God only as Elohim, the God of creation. All the difference in the world exists between knowing God as the Creator and knowing God personally by covenant relationship. Solomon, by the time he wrote Ecclesiastes, had become completely cynical. He advised people not to be "righteous overmuch" and to "be not overmuch wicked." Pessimism ruled his aging heart. As for his hands, he had kept them busy building shrines, all over Jerusalem, to all kinds of pagan idols. Worse still, we do not find that genuine repentance and heartbroken cry for cleansing in Solomon's book that we find in David's psalms. James's appeal would fall on deaf ears with Solomon. We can perhaps detect remorse over a misspent life in Ecclesiastes, but we find no brokenhearted repentance. The best advice he can conjure for young people is to remember their Creator while they are still young.

The old-time preachers used to urge us to "keep short accounts with God." That is, the moment the Holy Spirit convicts us of something, we should confess it and seek cleansing (1 John 1:7–10). That is good advice.

Now comes *a word about crying:* "Be afflicted, and mourn, and weep: let your laughter be turned to mourning, and your joy to heaviness" (4:9). Nothing is amusing about sin. When a person, be he a sinner or a saint, comes under Holy Ghost conviction, jests die on his lips. Some people can sit through the most solemn and searching of messages and crack a joke on the way out. The Spirit of God has not touched their souls.

James piles up words. He seems to have had ascetic tendencies, but that is not what comes through here. He sees people in spiritual peril; warring and lusting and envying—and apparently carrying it all off with a jest here and a joke there. They were riding high, wide, and handsome, as we would say. He would like to pull them down off their high horse, just as Nathan pulled David down off his throne (2 Sam. 12:1–14).

The word for "be afflicted" is *talaipōreō*. Underlying the word is the root *pōros*, the word for a callous. The word conveys the thought of something miserable and painful. The word for "mourn" is *penthos*. It means to lament. The word is used to describe the distress of the world's merchants over the collapse and overthrow of Babylon and the loss of all of their investments and trade (Rev. 18:11; cf. 18:15–19). That is the kind of mourning that James had in mind.

All of this will result in weeping. The Lord Jesus wept. "He shed no tears for His own griefs," as the old hymn puts it, "but sweat drops of blood for mine." Three occasions are recorded in the Gospels when Jesus wept. He wept on His way to the tomb of Lazarus, in the company of Martha and Mary. He wept as He looked down on the city of Jerusalem and saw its doom, already written in the counsels of God. He wept in Gethsemane. Thus, He wept for an individual, a city, and all of mankind. "Man of sorrows" was His name. Sin, our sin, was a terrible reality to Him. It brought an ache to His heart and tears to His eyes. It should do the same for us. "Weep!" says James. The only reason we do not weep is that we are so insensitive to the horror of our sin, so ignorant of its consequences, and so careless about the holiness of God.

The word for "laughter" is *gelōs*. The word means "loud laughter," in contrast with unrestrained weeping. In Luke's account of the Beatitudes, the Lord says, "Blessed are ye that weep now: for ye shall laugh . . . Woe unto you that laugh now! for ye shall mourn and weep" (Luke 6:21, 25).

Solomon said, "Fools make a mock at sin" (Prov. 14:9). The great lesson of the prophet Hosea is that sin breaks not only God's law but also God's heart. James had no use for levity of that kind. He was certainly against that kind of ribald, raucous laughter that denotes a lack of conviction of sin. Very little laughter is recorded in the Bible, and such references to it as there are do not put it in a good light. Not that all humor is wrong. A man who has no sense of humor can be an absolute bore because, as Solomon said, there is "a time to laugh" (Eccl. 3:4). Just the same, one of the most terrible statements in the Bible concerns laughter—the fearful laughter of God (Ps. 2:4; Prov. 1:26).

The word for "heaviness" means "to cast down the eyes." It pictures utter dejection and sorrow. The whole picture that James painted with dark and gloomy colors is one of misery and woe. James portrays a person under deep conviction of sin. Obviously, it is not God's mind that we should remain in that condition because He says, "Weeping may endure for a night, but joy cometh in the morning" (Ps. 30:5). That was David's testimony when, the years of persecution being over and all of his enemies having been subdued, he dwelt safe and secure in his own house at last (2 Sam. 7:1–2). It was a different matter after his sin with Bathsheba. Then David learned how to weep indeed.

Finally comes *a word about contrition:* "Humble yourselves in the sight of the Lord, and he shall lift you up" (4:10). Those who have read Bunyan's *Pilgrim's Progress* will remember Evangelist. When Bunyan's Christian fled in terror from the City of Destruction, he carried a great burden on his back. The burden was the great load of his sin. He had been made conscious of it by reading the book of God. The early experiences of Christian, his false starts and mistakes, and his misery under that burden were all reflections of Bunyan's early experiences as an awakened sinner.

In due course, Bunyan's Christian met a man called Evangelist, who pointed him to Calvary. In real life, Bunyan's benefactor was Dr. John Gifford. Alexander Whyte describes him for us thus:

> John Gifford had been a John Bunyan himself, only unspeakably worse. John Gifford had at one time been a Royalist officer in the great Civil War; and like so many officers and men on that bad side, he was a man of a very bad life. In the course of the conflict he fell into the hands of his enemies, and for some transgression of the laws of war he was condemned to death. But by the devotion and the determination of his sister he managed to outwit his jailor and to escape from his prison.
>
> After some hairbreadth escapes Gifford was enabled somehow to set up as a doctor in the town of Bedford, where he continued his old life of debauchery and was notorious far and near for his hatred and ill-usage of the Puritan people. But one night after losing all his money at cards— "as God would have it," as Bunyan was wont to say—Gifford was led to open a book by the famous Puritan Robert Bolton, when something that he read in that book took such a hold of him that he lay in agony of conscience for several weeks afterward. "At last," as his old kirk-session

record still extant has it, "God did so plentifully discover to him the forgiveness of his sins for the sake of Christ that all his life after he lost not the light of God's countenance, save only about two days before he died."

No sooner did John Gifford become a changed man than, like Saul of Tarsus, he openly joined himself to those whom he had hitherto persecuted, and ultimately he became their beloved pastor. The three or four poor women whom Bunyan one day saw sitting at a door in the sun and talking about the things of God were all members of John Gifford's Free Church congregation.[14]

Mark those words: "he lay in agony of conscience for several weeks." No wonder he could minister to the guilt-ridden Bedford tinker whose conscience had been aroused by the godly conversation of those women who gathered so often to discuss the things of God among themselves. That was what James was after—conviction of sin, accompanied by the godly sorrow that leads to true repentance. That kind of sorrow brings us down, indeed, but only so that God can afterward lift us up, set our feet on the rock, and put a new song in our souls, even praise unto our God (Ps. 40:1–3).

    C. Sin in the life repudiated (4:11–12)
        1. The command (4:11)

First, *the command is expressed:* "Speak not evil one of another, brethren" (4:11a). The word that James uses means to backbite, to speak against someone, to tear someone to pieces. James is back again to sins of the tongue; to envy and spite and gossip; and to the destruction of an abler brother, a more successful preacher, and a godlier saint. The classic Old Testament example is the old prophet of Samaria. Nobody tells us about him better than Alexander Whyte.

It was an high day of idolatry at Bethel. And, all the time, Bethel, of all the cities of Israel, was one of the most ancient and the most sacred. Bethel, as its name bears, was none other but the house of God, and it was the very gate of heaven. Bethel was built on that very spot on which their father Jacob had slept and dreamed when he was on his lonely way to Padan-aram; and it is that very heaven out of which the ladder was let

14. Alexander Whyte, *Bunyan's Characters* (London: Oliphant, Anderson, and Ferrier, 1895), 81–82.

down on Jacob's pillow that is today to be darkened by the unclean incense of Jeroboam's altar-fires. It was a brave step in Jeroboam to set up his false gods at Bethel, of all places in the land. And he needed a stout heart and a profane to support him as he stood up to kindle with his own hands the heathen fires of idolatry and impurity at Bethel.

And, behold there came a man of God out of Judah by the word of the Lord unto Bethel: and Jeroboam stood by the altar to burn incense. And the man of God cried against the altar of the Lord, and said, O altar, altar! And then he foretold the fall of the altar, and with it the fall of him who stood in his royal robes that day ministering to his unclean gods at that altar. And how Jeroboam's hand was withered that moment; how it was healed immediately at the intercession of the man of God; how Jeroboam invited the prophet to come home with him to eat and to drink and to get a reward; and how the prophet answered the king that he had the command of the Lord neither to eat bread nor to drink in that polluted land, but to return home to Judah as soon as he had delivered his prophetic burden—all that is to be read in the thirteenth chapter of First Kings.

At the same time, we are not told so much as this great prophet's name. He was wholly worthy thus far to have his name held up aloft along with the names of Samuel and Elijah themselves, for he stood up alone against Jeroboam and against all Israel and nailed the curse of God to Jeroboam's altar under the king's own eyes. We would hold his name in more than royal honour if we knew it. But for some reason or other of her own the Bible holds his great name back. This great man of God comes out of a cloud, he shines for a splendid moment before all men's eyes, and then he dies under a cloud. Alas, my brother!—Come home with me and refresh thyself. But the man of God said to the king, "If thou wilt give me half thine house, I will not go in with thee, neither will I eat bread nor drink water with thee." So he went another way, and returned not by the way that he came to Bethel.

Just as the man of God is setting out to go back to Judah with a hungry belly indeed, but with a good conscience, we are taken by the hand and are led into the house of an old prophet who dwells at Bethel. Yes. There are prophets and prophets' sons all this time at Bethel. Only, they had their domiciles and their doles from Jeroboam's bounty on the strict condition that they kept at home and kept silence. Well, this old Bethelite prophet was keeping at home and was keeping silence when his sons burst in upon him with the great news of the day. Father, you should have come with us! We asked you to come. What a day it has been! And what a man of God we have seen! Till they told him all that we are told about Jeroboam, and his altar, and the man of God from Judah, and his cry that shook down the altar, and the king's withered hand, and the prayer of the man of God, and the king's hospitality, and the man of God's refusal of the king's hospitality.

"What way went he home?" demanded the old prophet of his excited sons. "Saddle me the ass," he instantly ordered. "Art thou the man of God from Judah?" he asked, as he overtook the man of God sitting under an oak. "Come home with me and eat bread." "I may not eat bread, nor drink water by the word of the Lord," said the man of God. "But I am a prophet also as thou art." But it was a lie, adds the sacred writer. So the man of God rose and went back and did eat bread and drink water. And so on; till a lion met him in the way home that night, and slew him because he had gone back. And when the old Bethelite prophet, who had deceived him, heard of it, he mourned over him, and said, "Alas, my brother!" And he said to his sons, "Bury me beside this man of God. Lay my bones beside his bones."

What is it that makes the decrepit old prophet of Bethel post at such a pace after the man of God who is on his way home to Judah? Has his conscience at last been awakened? Have the tidings of his delighted sons filled the poor old timeserver with bitter remorse for his fat table and for his dumb pulpit? Or, is it deadly envy and revenge at the man who has so stolen his sons' hearts that day till they are about to set off to Judah to go to school to this man of God? It is too late now for him to command his sons' reverence and love. And how can he ever forgive the man who has so taken from him his crown as a prophet and as a father? "Saddle me the ass," he shouted. And the decayed old creature rode down the Judean road at a pace he had not ridden since he used, as a godly youth, to be sent out on errands of life and death and mercy from Samuel's School of Mount Ephraim. If lies will do it; if flattery, flesh, and wine will do it,—that Judean prophet's pride shall be brought down today! "Saddle me the ass!" he thundered. So they saddled him the ass, and he rode after the man of God. "I am a prophet as thou art!" But he lied unto him. . . .

We are not told why this great man of God stopped short so soon on his way home from Bethel, and sat down so soon under one of the oaks of Bethel. He had done a splendid day's work. Never prophet of God did a more splendid day's work. But our hearts sink as we see him stop short, and then take his seat under that tempting tree. What was the matter? We are not told. He may have been very hungry by this time, and he may have begun to repent that he had not accepted the penitent king's hospitality. Who knows what good might have come of it had he, God's acknowledged prophet, been seen sitting in the place of honour at the royal table? Had he not been somewhat short, and sharp, and churlish after his great battle with Jeroboam's altar? . . .

Well, then, if that was the case with the man of God from Judah,— here is the forbidden fruit of Bethel back and at his open mouth this moment: "I am a prophet as thou art, and an angel spake unto me by the word of the Lord, saying: Bring him back to eat and to drink." So he went back with him to his house. . . .

It was surely a little sin, if ever there was a little sin, to sup that Sabbath night at an old prophet's table, and that, too, on the invitation of an angel. But the lion that met the disobedient prophet that night did not reason that way.

"Bury me," said the remorseful old man to his sons standing in tears round his miserable deathbed, "bury me in the same grave with the bones of the man of God out of Judah." And the old prophet's sons so buried their father. And an awful grave that was in Bethel, with an awful epitaph upon it. Now, suppose this. Suppose that you were buried on the same awful principle,— in whose grave would your bones lie waiting together with his till the last trump to stand forth before God and man together? And what would your epitaph and his be? Would it be this: "Here lie the liar and his victim"? Or would it be this: "Here lie the seducer and the seduced"? Or would it be this! "Here lie the hater and him he hated down to death"?[15]

Sins of the tongue! How terrible are sins of the tongue! Sins of the tongue can kill a person as surely as the sword. So David Livingstone discovered. His wife died a premature death, thanks to the backbiting tongues of some people in the white settlements of Africa. No wonder James waxes so eloquent when it comes to sins of the tongue!

---

15. Alexander Whyte, *Bible Characters from the Old and New Testaments,* 1 vol. (Grand Rapids: Kregel, 1990), 346–52.

b. The command explained (4:11b–c)

We note *what is involved:* "He that speaketh evil of his brother, and judgeth his brother, speaketh evil of the law, and judgeth the law" (4:11b). And we note *what is inferred:* "but if thou judge the law, thou art not a doer of the law, but a judge" (4:11c). The person who judges another brother or sister in Christ sets himself up as a substitute for the law itself. More than that, he actually becomes a critic of the law. The function of the Word of God is to monitor our lives and the lives of others. It is the work of the Spirit of God to apply the Word of God to the consciences of the people of God. That is not our work but God's work.

The entire book of Job is an exposition of this truth. Job's three friends set themselves up as authorities to lecture the long-suffering Job at considerable length and they judged him unmercifully. They accused him, in varying degrees, of having been a very great sinner indeed. He must have been wicked, they thought, to have reaped such a bumper harvest of misfortunes.

Far from convincing Job, however, they only provoked long and loud laments at the calamities that, he felt, had fallen upon him so unjustly. When they had finished slandering him, God spoke. Then, indeed, all of their merciless judging was silenced. Only God could really judge Job, and He had already declared him to be "a perfect and an upright man, one that feareth God, and escheweth [habitually avoids] evil" (Job 1:8).

When it was all over and Job stood forth, not only vindicated but also purified by the fire, God turned on Eliphaz, the first of the three "friends" who challenged and criticized Job and said, "My wrath is kindled against thee, and against thy two friends: for ye have not spoken of me the thing that is right, as my servant Job hath. Therefore take unto you now seven bullocks and seven rams, and go to my servant Job, and offer up for yourselves a burnt offering; and my servant Job shall pray for you: for him will I accept: lest I deal with you after your folly, in that ye have not spoken of me the thing which is right, like my servant Job" (Job 42:7–8).

Thus, their evil speaking against Job recoiled on their own heads. Not one of them knew why the calamities had overtaken Job. They were all presumptuous. They were all guilty of slandering Job and arguing out of sheer ignorance. They had become a law unto themselves and were in dire peril of perishing according to God's law, a law about which they were abysmally ignorant.

2. The comment (4:12)

"There is one lawgiver, who is able to save and to destroy: who art thou that judgest another?" God alone is omniscient. Only He knows all of the facts, and only He can lay down the law. He alone has absolute power of life and death. How foolish we are to imagine that we can act as someone else's judge. Even in secular society, under common law, we are called upon to give people the benefit of the doubt and to adjudge the accused to be innocent of all charges until such time as he is proven guilty. Why cannot we be equally charitable toward our brothers and sisters in Christ?

PART 7

The Christian and His Boasting
James 4:13–5:6

A. Boasting about our plans (4:13–17)
   1. The proposal (4:13)

"Go to now," says James, (or, as we would put it today, "Come now") "ye that say, Today or tomorrow we will go into such a city, and continue there a year, and buy and sell, and get gain." We have numerous proverbs that warn against such overconfidence. One says, "Man proposes, but God disposes." Another warns, "There's many a slip twixt cup and lip." We say, "Don't count your chickens before they are hatched."

Here, James visualizes people making plans, plans for today and tomorrow, plans for now and for a year from now, plans to travel and plans for trade. And, as far as we can tell, they are legitimate plans, the kind of plans that we make all of the time, the kind of plans that any businessman has to make if he is to prosper. So, what is James's problem? Doubtless, when he was in business as the village carpenter, he had been obliged frequently to make similar plans. The problem that James underlines is simple, common, and serious—these plans are made without any reference to God.

The Lord Jesus provides us with the classic illustration. He told once of "a certain rich man" whose bumper harvest prompted him to do some thinking and to devise some plans. It would be a good idea, he decided, not to dump his grain on the market right now because that would only depress prices still further—the law of supply and demand worked in his day as much as it does in ours. What he would do, the rich man decided, was hold his grain in store until leaner times came. When grain was in short supply, prices would rise, and he could really cash in. That was only common sense. He was a rich man, and he could affort to wait. But where was he to store the grain in the meantime? His current facilities were inadequate. The solution was simple: invest in bigger and better barns!

So far, apart from a certain selfishness and callousness about it all and a total disregard for the plight of the poor, it was a valid business proposal. The Lord, however, read this man's heart. He saw a thoroughgoing materialist and opportunist, a man who had not a single ounce of spirituality about him. He heard him as he talked to himself: "Soul, thou hast much goods laid up for many years; take thine ease, eat, drink, and be merry."

Jesus called this man a fool, "a senseless one," because he left God out of his plans. He made three common mistakes. First, *he mistook his bankbook for his Bible.* He judged his success in life by what he read in his bankbook rather than by what he read in God's Word—if he ever read his Bible at all. Many passages of Scripture are addressed to rich people.

Moses, for example, wrote, "Beware that thou forget not the LORD thy God, in not keeping his commandments, and his judgments, and his statutes, which I command thee this day: Lest when thou hast eaten and art full, and hast built goodly houses and dwelt therein; and when thy herds and thy flocks multiply, and thy silver and thy gold is multiplied, and all that thou hast is multiplied; then thine heart be lifted up, and thou forget the LORD thy God, which brought thee forth out of the land of Egypt, from the house of bondage . . . and thou say in thine heart, My power and the might of mine hand hath gotten me this wealth. But thou shalt remember the LORD thy God: for it is he that giveth thee power to get wealth. . . . And it shall be, if thou do at all forget the Lord thy God. . . . I testify against you this day that ye shall surely perish" (Deut. 8:11–14, 17–19).

No doubt this "certain rich man," of whom Jesus spoke, attributed his bumper harvest to his own acumen as a farmer, as proof of his skill in managing his estates. It never occurred to him to give the glory to God. He was rich, Jesus said, but he was "not rich toward God" (Luke 12:21). He had no thought for God.

Neither did he have a thought for the poor. Yet, Moses had written about this subject too: "If there be among you a poor man of one of thy brethren within any of thy gates in thy land which the LORD thy God giveth thee, thou shalt not harden thine heart, nor shut thine hand from thy poor brother: but thou shalt open thine hand wide unto him. . . . Thou shalt surely give him, and thine heart shall not be grieved when thou givest unto him. . . . For the poor shall never cease out of the land" (Deut. 15:7–8, 10–11). So far as we can see, this "certain rich man" left the poor out of his calculations as readily as he left out God.

Next, *he mistook his body for his soul.* Listen to him as he talks to his soul. He talks to his soul as though he were talking to his body. "Soul," he said, "thou hast much goods! Soul, eat! drink!" A soul has no use for barns and bumper crops. It has no use for beef steak and beer. The rich fool failed to discern between his physical, material part and his soul. He seems to have had very confused ideas about his soul and its needs, and he knew nothing about his spirit at all.

Finally, *he mistook time for eternity.* "Thou hast many years," he said. Evidently, he was still a young man. He thought that he had a long time to live, and he had plans to spend those years in pleasure and selfish indulgence. As a matter of fact, however, he was going to be dead before the morning. No wonder Jesus called him a fool (Luke 12:16–21).

James addresses people with similar ideas. They had elaborate plans for the future, but they left God out of those plans.

2.   The problem (4:14)

James points to two factors in this equation. First is the factor of *our hidden future*. "Whereas ye know not what shall be on the morrow" (4:14a). God has drawn a veil between today and tomorrow.

A traveling preacher used to come our way once in a while when I was a boy. My parents were hospitable people, and traveling preachers from all around knew that they were good for a meal at our place, even in the war years when everything was heavily rationed. This particular preacher told us of an encounter he had recently had with an old gypsy woman.

"Cross my palm with silver," she said to him, "and I'll read your fortune for you, mister."

"Do you mean to say," replied the preacher, "that if I give you some money you'll tell me what is going to happen to me in the future?" She assured him that she would.

"Well," he said, "let's get specific. If I give you some money, can you tell me what I'll be doing this time tomorrow?" She assured him she could.

"Ah!" he said, "but you see, my friend, I don't believe you can tell me what I'll be doing tomorrow. But I'll cross your palm with silver twice if you'll just tell me what I was doing yesterday!" The deal was off!

We can plan for the future. We ought to take thought for the future. The Bible reminds us that even the little ant does that. But we cannot know the future. Only God knows that. Even our weather forecasters, with all the latest gadgets of science and technology, cannot predict tomorrow's sky accurately.

Yet, we have a great yearning to know the future. Nowadays, astrologers, spiritists, soothsayers, and so-called psychics have again become popular. People long for a guide to take them past the forbidden frontier and on into the hidden mysteries of the morrow. Some of them, like Jeanne Dixon, who supposedly forecasted the death of President Kennedy, achieve a measure of dubious fame. Their track record, however, is very poor. Jeanne Dixon, for instance, also predicted that Jacqueline Kennedy would not remarry and that Walter Reuther, the prominent labor leader, would run for the presidency of the United States. She was wrong on all counts. Hitler, Himmler, and the other leaders of the Nazi movement were all members of a satanic occult-oriented lodge. Hitler kept a court astrologer and consulted him regularly. Nancy Reagan, wife of President Ronald Reagan, achieved a few moments of notoriety when it was learned that she consulted psychics.

It is all a sad spectacle because only God can prophesy. As the old hymn put it:

> God holds the key to all unknown,
> And I am glad.
> If other hands should hold that key,
> Or if He trusted it to me,
> I might be sad.[1]

One of the things that sets the Bible apart from all other books is its ability to predict the future accurately. It contains hundreds of prophecies. It foretold accurately the birth of the Lord Jesus in Bethlehem, described His career, and gave many details regarding His death, burial, and resurrection. It foretold His death by crucifixion, that He would be betrayed by a friend, that He would be offered vinegar to drink, that people would gamble for His clothes, and that He would be in the tomb for a total of three days and three nights.

Many other prophecies focus on His return. This subject is mentioned 1,845 times in the Old Testament and is referred to in 318 verses of the New Testament. It is found in twenty-seven of the thirty-nine books of the Old Testament and in seventeen of the twenty-seven books of the New Testament. We can rest assured that all of these Scriptures will be fulfilled as accurately as were the prophecies connected with His first coming. Signs of their impending fulfillment are all about us.[2]

Often, foolish people, misunderstanding the prophetic Scriptures, make lamentable mistakes. Some years ago, a considerable amount of commotion was stirred up in the United States by a certain Edgar C. Wisenant who wrote a little book titled *Eighty-Eight Reasons Why the Lord Will Come in Eighty-Eight*. Although the book was based on a number of false premises, the author accumulated an astonishing assortment of facts and misinformation and set a date for the Rapture.[3] His preferred

---

1. J. Parker, "God Holds the Key," in *Sacred Songs and Solos,* ed. Ira D. Sankey.

2. See John Phillips, *Exploring the Future* (reprint, Grand Rapids: Kregel, 2001).

3. For instance, Wisenant said that when the Bible says that we cannot know the date of the Rapture, it really means that you can know. He mistakenly assigned the Old Testament Feast of Trumpets to the church when it belongs to Israel. Moreover, he invented an entity that he called "Gentile Israel" (a contradiction in terms) and said that he could find two hundred references to the United States in the Old Testament. In fact, we would be hard pressed to find one.

date was Monday, September 12, 1988, the Jewish New Year, but he hedged a little by also proposing the day before and the day after as possibilities.

Like all other people who set dates for the Rapture, the man was wrong. Not that he admitted that he was wrong in principle, in setting a date for the Rapture, because when the blessed event failed to materialize, he promptly did some fresh calculations and set a new date-September 1, 1989.

Wisenant was very bold in giving his readers all kinds of details. In his original book, he stated that the Antichrist would sign a treaty with Israel on September 21, 1988. The 144,000 witnesses would be sealed on September 26. World War III would break out on October 4 and would last for three and a half weeks. The two witnesses would be killed on March 9, 1992. The Battle of Armageddon would be fought on October 4, 1995, and the Millennium would begin on December 23, 1995.

Bold predictions! And all wrong!

One of my preacher friends decided to put Mr. Wisenant to the test. When the original book came out, he received a copy of it, read it, and then called the man on the phone.

> "Are you Edgar C. Wisenant?" he asked.
>
> "Yes, sir!"
>
> "The former NASA space engineer?"
>
> "Yes, sir!"
>
> "Are you the man who wrote the book *Eighty-Eight Reasons Why the Lord Will Come in Eighty-Eight?*"
>
> "Yes, sir, I am."
>
> "Tell me, Mr. Wisenant, are you sure the Lord is coming this September? September 11, 12, or 13?"
>
> "Yes, sir!"
>
> "You're quite sure?"
>
> "Yes, I am."
>
> "Very well, then, Mr. Wisenant, I'd like to buy your house and your car. I'll give you $5,000 for your house and $1,000 for your car. I will have the legal documents made out and pay you the cash right now. I'll take possession on September 14."

I asked my friend what happened. "He refused to sell," he said.

So, James is quite right. We cannot tell the future, "not even tomorrow." But God can. Therefore, we ought to take God into our reckoning when making any plans. In practical terms, that means that we ought to be taking God into consideration moment by moment because we do not even know what is going to happen the next moment, let alone the next year. We cannot afford to live one moment without God.

The second factor in James's equation is that of our *human frailty:* "For what is your life? It is even a vapour, that appeareth for a little time, and then vanisheth away" (4:14b). What is our life, after all? It is like steam rising from boiling water. It dances in the sunlight for a moment and then vanishes into thin air.

This illustration sets before us a graphic picture of a *transient life.* As the old hymn says,

> Life at best is very brief,
> Like the falling of a leaf,
> Like the binding of a sheaf.[4]

We are here today and gone tomorrow and, for most, soon forgotten. Nobody knew this fact better than Moses when he wrote the ninetieth psalm. God had just passed the sentence of death upon the children of Israel in the wilderness. They had come to Kadesh-barnea and were poised for the conquest of Canaan. Then, when the spies came back with news of the giants, the people crowned all of their other complaints with the lament, "Would God that we had died in this wilderness!" (Num. 14:2).

God said, "Prayer answered! So you shall!"

Moses recorded God's verdict: "Because all those men which have seen my glory, and my miracles, which I did in Egypt and in the wilderness, and have tempted me now these ten times, and have not hearkened to my voice; surely they shall not see the land which I sware unto their fathers, neither shall any of them that provoked me see it: . . . Your carcases shall fall in this wilderness; and all that were numbered of you, according to your whole number, from twenty years old and upward, which have murmured against me . . ." (Num. 14:22–23, 29).

When Moses wrote Psalm 90, he had that generation—his generation—in mind. Everyone in that generation, aged twenty and older, was now condemned to forty years of wilderness wanderings until the last of them (including Moses himself) died in the desert on the wrong side of the Jordan. So he wrote in his psalm, "Thou carriest them away as with a flood; they are as a sleep; in the morning they

---

4. Anonymous, "Life at Best is Very Brief," 19th century.

are like grass which groweth up. In the morning it flourisheth, and groweth up; in the evening it is cut down, and withereth. . . . For all our days are passed away in thy wrath: we spend our years as a tale that is told. The days of our years are threescore years and ten; and if by reason of strength they be fourscore years, yet is their strength labour and sorrow; for it is soon cut off, and we fly away. . . . So teach us to number our days, that we may apply our hearts unto wisdom" (Ps. 90:5–6, 9–10, 12).

The "threescore years and ten" (seventy years) referred to the length of life in the wilderness. Those who were twenty when the sentence was passed would be sixty when the forty-year wanderings were over. The "four score years" perhaps referred to Moses himself, who was about eighty years old at the time the sentence was passed, and to those people who were forty at the time the sentence was passed.

So, Psalm 90 illustrates James's point for us. The psalm was a dirge, occupied with the sorrows of the vast multitude (associated with the 603,550 "men of war" who had recently been numbered for impending battle in Canaan) in the wilderness. They had been numbered "from twenty years old and upward" (Num. 1:19–46) and were now being sentenced to death. If a man was twenty when he was numbered as an enlisted warrior, he would die at, or before, the age of sixty. If he was numbered at thirty, he would die at, or before, seventy. If he was forty when he was numbered, he would die at or before he was eighty. The average age would be thirty. So the shadow of death overhung the camp as surely as the Shechinah cloud.

That same shadow hangs over us as well. We must always consider the uncertainty of life. We are reminded of the sinner's dream, in which he saw himself clinging to a rope suspended over a river. He had ventured out on the rope to escape from a tiger. Looking down, however, he could see a crocodile lurking in the river below. And there, gnawing at the rope, was a rat. The tiger was his past, which pursued him. The rope was his present situation, representing a temporary reprieve. The crocodile stood for his future. And the rat was time, gnawing at his life.

We all arrive on earth with a figurative hourglass suspended over us. We cannot see it, but God can. The sand runs down, day and night, relentlessly, continually, as our moments speed by. We do not know how much sand is still left in our glass. All we know is that it is less now than it was an hour ago. Ours is a transient life. It is a vapor in the air.

When Solomon wrote the book of Ecclesiastes, he was haunted by a ghost, the ghost of death. He keeps on mentioning it because if there was one thing he did *not* want to do, it was die. He tells us of "the fly in the ointment," and, of course, it was a *dead* fly because that *is* the fly in the ointment—death! No matter how fragrant life was for that pampered and perfumed king, nothing was more certain than the fact that one day he was going to die, and no ointment or embalmment would prevent the stench and corruption of death from doing its work.

The vapor, however, has another message. It reminds us not only of a transient life but also *a transformed life.* "What is your life?" James insists. "It is even a vapour." And what is vapor? Nowadays we call it steam. In chemical composition, it is H_2O—water. However, it is water the nature and behavior of which has been changed. Water *obeys* the downward pull of this world; steam, or vapor, *overcomes* the downward pull. Water always seeks the lowest level; steam, or vapor, soars to its highest level. Water gravitates toward the sea; vapor rises to the sky. Water has its place on earth; it belongs eventually in the sea. Vapor has its seat in the heavenlies; it belongs ultimately with the clouds.

What is it that seats vapor in the heavenlies? The sun! It draws the water to itself and seats it on high. Not all water responds to the drawing power of the sun, but that which does dwells above. So it is with us. Some respond to the Lord Jesus, "the Sun of righteousness" (Mal. 4:2). Those who do are seated with Him "in heavenly places" (Eph. 2:4–6).

Vapor has one other lesson for us. It speaks to us of *a triumphant life.* The idea for the steam engine was born when a thoughtful scientist observed an iron pot, which was sitting on the fire, full of water. As the water temperature began to increase, the heavy lid of the pot began to rise. The scientist observed that this action allowed the steam to escape. Millions of other people had observed this penomenon, but this scientist carried the observation further. He concluded that as weak, unsubstantial, and vaporous as steam was, it must possess considerable power to lift that heavy iron lid. It then occurred to him that if that steam, or vapor, could be contained and channeled properly, it could be put to work. In time, it was used to push pistons, which, in turn, were harnessed to wheels. All kinds of steam devices were invented. Some were set to work to pull trains along tracks. Others were made to drive the engines of the Industrial Revolution. Feats long impossible to men became everyday events. Factories sprang up all over the world. Men had learned how to put vapor to work. It simply needed to be channeled.

James never dreamed of that possibility! But it is so! And it has a lesson for us. Our lives can be dissipated, wasted, allowed to drift like vapor in the air until we vanish away. Or we can be changed and channeled and accomplish great things for God. So much, then, for our frailty.

3. The proposition (4:15)

"For that ye ought to say, If the Lord will, we shall live, and do this, or that."
James brings us back to his original thought. We should not announce boastfully
our plans for the future. We should acknowledge reverently that we are completely dependent on the will of God for the accomplishment of anything. The
Lord can bless our plans, or He can blight them. What matters is that, even in
forming our plans, we should seek the Lord's will humbly and involve Him in even
the mundane, ordinary affairs of life. Failure to do that makes us presumptuous.
Involving God, right from the start, in the decision-making process, is the way of
wisdom.

The book of Joshua supplies us with several instances of the folly of making
decisions without God. After the spectacular fall of Jericho, a formidable fortress,
Joshua became complacent. The next city scheduled for conquest was Ai. Following
the pattern that had proved so helpful at Jericho, Joshua sent some spies ahead to
evaluate what the army would be facing. "Let not all the people go up; but let
about two or three thousand men go up and smite Ai; and make not all the
people to labour thither; for they are but few" (Josh. 7:3). That was the assessment
of the situation as voiced by worldly wisdom.

The result of depending on human opinion was disastrous. The Israelites suffered
a humiliating defeat. They had not consulted God. Moreover, sin was in the camp.
One might protest that Joshua had no way of knowing that an obscure soldier
named Achan had imperiled the whole enterprise by stealing from Jericho plunder
that had been dedicated publicly to God. That argument might be so, but God
knew it. Joshua's mistake was in making plans for the conquest of Ai based on
human reasoning and without ascertaining God's will. When later, he did find
out how God wanted to move against Ai (Josh. 8:1–29), he discovered that God's
will was quite different from the worldly reasoning of Joshua's spies. Indeed, the
spies, themselves, had been sent on their expedition without seeking God's will.

The next mistake was even more disastrous because it involved an action quite
contrary to the revealed will of God in His Word. God had commanded, through
Moses, that Israel was to make no treaty with the nations entrenched in the
Promised Land (Exod. 23:32; Deut. 7:1–5; Judg. 2:1–3).

While Joshua was pondering his next move, the Gibeonites came. Their strategy
was simple. They knew that the Israelites had been commanded to destroy all of the
inhabitants of the land of Canaan (Josh. 9:24), so they sent a delegation to Joshua,
suing for peace and pretending to have come from a distant land (Josh. 9:8–11).

As proof of their claim, the Gibeonite embassy produced dry and moldy bread, which, they claimed, had come hot and fresh from the oven on the day of their departure. They pointed to their worn-out clothes and shoes, which, they declared, had been new when they left home. All the while, they were near neighbors—the next nation, in fact, slated for destruction. Gibeon was only half a dozen miles or so from Ai.

Once again, Joshua acted without seeking God's will. We read that he "took of their victuals, and asked not counsel at the mouth of the LORD. And Joshua made peace with them, and made a league with them, to let them live: and the princes of the congregation sware unto them" (Josh. 9:14–15). Three days later, they discovered their mistake. And a costly one it turned out to be. God made Joshua honor his ill-advised commitment with the Gibeonites. What the people of Gibeah were like we learn from the book of Judges (chaps. 19–20). They were as bad as the men of Sodom, and they were a thorn in Israel's side for centuries.

The Lord Jesus is the supreme example of One who never acted without ensuring that He had the mind of God and that He was moving along the line of His will. Luke's gospel is particularly helpful in pointing out this fact. Luke tells us, for instance, that the Lord was praying at the time of His baptism (Luke 3:21) when the Holy Spirit came down and anointed Him for His ministry.

He retired into the wilderness to pray at a time when He was riding the crest of popularity and fame. He returned to face a delegation of Pharisees and doctors of the law that had assembled from every town in Galilee and Judea and even from Jerusalem (Luke 5:16).

He sought the silences and solitude of the mountain to pray when He had provoked the fury of the Pharisees by healing a handicapped man in the synagogue on the Sabbath. He returned to appoint the twelve apostles who were to carry on His work after He was gone (Luke 6:12).

He withdrew from the thousands of people whom He had just fed with a few loaves and a couple of fishes to pray. Immediately, He challenged the disciples to declare who He really was and received Peter's noble answer, "The Christ of God" (Luke 9:20).

Eight days later, we see Him praying once more, this time amid the snows of Hermon. At once, He was transfigured before them and then began to make His disciples aware of the fact that He was now on His way to death on a cross (Luke 9:28).

He was praying again when His disciples, so impressed by His prayer, asked Him to teach them to pray. He gave them "the Lord's prayer," as we call it, and went on to teach as no man before or since has ever taught.

Next, Luke shows us the Lord praying in Gethsemane (Luke 22:41) and giving voice to the very words that James employs: "Father, if thou be *willing*, remove this cup from me: nevertheless not my will, but thine, be done" (Luke 22:42).

Then, too, we see the Lord praying on the very cross itself. Surely, if the Lord found it necessary thus to seek God's will at every step of His earthly journey, how much more do we need to seek His will daily and hourly!

4. The prohibition (4:16)

"But now ye rejoice in your boastings: all such rejoicing is evil." James had in mind people who were taking pride in their ability to plan their own future. Instead of seeking God's will, they were boasting in their own cleverness. James prohibits such pride. He is on solid ground here. Solomon had said, "Boast not thyself of tomorrow; for thou knowest not what a day may bring forth" (Prov. 27:1).

Perhaps James had his friend Peter in mind. Simon Peter had made up his mind. He would never, ever deny the Lord. Not that he believed all of this talk about crucifixion. That simply had to be incredible. He knew Jesus to be the Christ, the Son of the living God. He had not only stated that to be so but also had been congratulated on his perception. That Jesus should be about to die was unlikely enough—given the fact that all power was His to command. Why, here was One who could walk upon the heaving waves and still the howling winds! Here was One who could feed people by the thousands with a little lad's lunch! Here was One who could heal the leper and the lame, One who could actually raise the dead! Who in all of this world could put such a One to death? Still less, the death of a cross! Why, that would mean that He would die accursed. Incredible! Impossible! Inconceivable!

Still, there was no denying that the situation was threatening. But circumstances had been threatening before. Jesus had weathered all such storms with astonishing ease. Angels marched all about Him. All power was His. In any case, he, Peter, would never deny Him. He had made up his mind about that. He even boasted about it. Not today, or tomorrow, or ever! James and John might deny Him. Thomas and Matthew might deny Him. But he, Peter, would never deny Him. The idea was preposterous. He said so.

Jesus warned him. "Peter, before the cock crows twice tomorrow, you will deny me three times."

"Not me, Lord," Peter declared. He took pride in his ability to handle the future. The Sanhedrin and the synagogue had turned hostile. Caiaphas and his crowd were hatching plots against Christ. Peter and the others knew that (John 11:7–16).

But, so what? To be on the safe side and to ensure that he had the wherewithal to strike a blow or two himself, if it came to a showdown, Peter slipped away to the market and purchased a sword. With the sword strapped to his thigh under his robe, Peter, with Christ, could take on the Romans themselves.

Peter's pride in himself, and his planning for the future with such absolute self-confidence, was entirely misplaced. All such boasting is. Before the dawn broke the next morning, Peter had bungled his attempted defense of Jesus, had taken to his heels, had fraternized with the world, and had three times denied that he had ever known Christ—once with oaths and curses. So much for a cocksure attitude toward one's own plans, preparations, and prognostications!

5. The principle (4:17)

"Therefore to him that knoweth to do good, and doeth it not, to him it is sin." Much of God's will is revealed in the Scripture. We are held responsible to know what God says about all of the great issues of life. We are held accountable to bring our wills under the supreme authority of God's will. God holds us just as accountable for what we do *not* do as for what we *do*. Indeed, at the great coming judgment of the nations in the Valley of Jehoshaphat, at the return of Christ, that will be the whole criteria for those who are condemned (Matt. 25:41–46).

Years ago, when my children were still young, our daily family devotions brought us one evening to this verse: "To him that knoweth to do good, and doeth it not, to him it is sin." I explained that it was just as bad *not* to do a good deed as it was actually to *do* a bad one. I posed an example.

"Suppose that you came in from school one day and saw your mother lying on the couch, exhausted and unwell. Then you went into the kitchen and saw that the sink was full of dirty dishes. What would you do?"

My young son responded at once. He said, "I'd give her some Geratol (a much advertised patent medicine) for iron-tired blood!" We laughed! But that was not the answer I had expected, and it wasn't what James had in mind.

The classic New Testament illustration is found in the Lord's parable of the Good Samaritan. The unfortunate traveler on the downward Jericho road had fallen among thieves. He had been beaten, robbed, and left by the roadside half dead.

Along came a priest—Jericho was a bedroom community for many of the priests. This man was on his way home from Jerusalem, where he had been attending to his religious duties. He had been handling holy things, officiating at the altar, advising people regarding their sacrifices, helping them with their offerings. He might even, perhaps, have had his turn ministering in the sanctuary itself. His mind had been occupied with his religious duties. If ever a man knew to do good, surely this was the man. He could not help but see the wounded man. What did he do? Nothing! He "passed by on the other side." He wrapped his robes about him and scuttled past on the opposite side of the road. This man was a hypocrite. James has the word for him: "Pure religion and undefiled before God and the Father is this, to visit the fatherless and widows [and beaten-up travelers!] in their affliction" (James 1:27).

Then along came a Levite. In New Testament times, the Levites were the experts in the law. If ever a man knew to do good, it was him. He spent his whole life studying the Scriptures, especially the Mosaic Law. He knew, for instance, the law that stated,

> Thou shalt not see thy brother's ox or his sheep go astray, and hide thyself from them: thou shalt in any case bring them again unto thy brother. And if thy brother be not nigh unto thee, or if thou know him not, then thou shalt bring it unto thine own house, and it shall be with thee until thy brother seek after it, and thou shalt restore it to him again. In like manner shalt thou do with his ass; and so shalt thou do with his raiment; and with all lost thing of thy brother's, which he hath lost, and thou hast found, shalt thou do likewise: thou mayest not hide thyself. Thou shalt not see thy brother's ass or his ox fall down by the way, and hide thyself from them: thou shalt surely help him to lift them up again. (Deut. 22:1–4)

In fact, the Mosaic Law went even beyond the preceding statement. The Hebrew was to do as much for an enemy: "If thou meet thine enemy's ox or his ass going astray, thou shalt surely bring it back to him again. If thou see the ass of him that hateth thee lying under his burden, and wouldest forbear to help him, thou shalt surely help with him" (Exod. 23:4–5).

The Levite knew all about these commandments of the law. Now, here at hand, was an opportunity for him to put to work what he knew. The fallen man was of far greater worth than an ox or a sheep. The law commanded him to do a good work. What did he do? He crossed over the road, took a good look at the poor man, crossed back over the street, and "passed by on the other side." This man's religion was as vain, empty, and futile as that of the priest. It took a journeying Samaritan, a man whom both the priest and the Levite would have despised, to show true religion and true good works by helping the man in his need (Luke 10:1–37). James would have approved of the Lord's parting shot: "Go," He said to the lawyer who had been heckling Him, "and do likwise."

    B.   Boasting about our prosperity (5:1–6)
        1. The rich men's woes described (5:1–4)
           a. The prophetic declaration (5:1)

James is still pursuing the subject of boasting. A person might not be so much inclined to boast about his plans, perhaps, as he is to boast about his prosperity. Rich people often like to display their wealth. Let them beware, James warns. Rich people are a ready target for the thief, the envious, and the oppressed. Indeed, James now becomes somewhat of a prophet: "Go to now, ye rich men, weep and howl for your miseries that shall come upon you."

It was the abject poverty, misery, and despair of England's working class that kindled the fires of fury that burned in the souls of Friedrich Engels and Karl Marx and led them to write the *Communist Manifesto* and caused them to call upon the workers of the world to unite. The rich were getting richer, and the poor were getting poorer. The Industrial Revolution was creating a new class of people, the *nouveau riche,* the great tycoons of business and commerce.

About the same time that the steam engine changed the world, a new economic invention came along too—the joint-stock company. Suddenly, family businesses discovered that they could acquire vast amounts of capital by issuing stocks and shares. Enormous business enterprises could be launched with an independent life of their own. Impersonal investors put money into impersonal companies run by boards of trustees responsible to only the stockholders, who had only one concern—profits! These new, giant business enterprises had an independent life of their own. They were legal entities in themselves, but they were business institutions that had no soul, no conscience, and no obligation to be fair to their workers. They existed only to produce goods as quickly, as efficiently, and as cheaply as possible and at as great a profit as possible.

Books have been written on the plight of the new poor. They were serfs forced to work for their new masters on starvation wages for endless hours and without regard to their health, safety, or well-being and without regard to their age or sex. They slaved at monotonous and dangerous tasks. They were exposed to toxic substances and placed in peril of their lives amid thundering, throbbing belts, wheels, and rollers driven at full speed from early morning until late at night. They dug for coal in dark, satanic mines, where no regard was paid to their safety. They worked harder than the brute beasts that were harnessed alongside them, were treated with less consideration, and were paid starvation wages. If they failed to produce their quota or if they were injured or became sick, they were sacked and thrown out to starve. They were drafted by this great industrial Moloch at a tender age, and they grew old and died before their time.

They lived in squalor in frightful hovels with not enough to eat and no time for proper rest. Open sewers, where rats and disease found a congenial breeding ground, ran down the middle of their narrow, cobbled streets. They were crowded into dismal dens, where they sought to drown their sorrows in debauchery and drink.

Such were the scenes that inspired Charles Dickens to write his famous novels and Marx to issue his call for a radical, violent, godless change.

The ideas of Marx and Vladimir Lenin took root. The oppressed workers of the world, bullied and defrauded by a system that favored the rich and crushed the poor, took heed and found hope. Communism gave them a weapon with which to avenge themselves upon the rich. Communism and socialism were twins, born of despair, that grew rapidly and changed the face of the world.

What the world saw in the next seventy-five years was a dress rehearsal for end-times events, a foreshadowing of that coming catastrophic collapse of the world economic system foretold in Revelation 18. Babylon, the Antichrist's coming economic capital, is to be overthrown violently, bringing about the final ruin of the unscrupulous and oppressive business tycoons of the world.[5] James saw a similar, if not the same, collapse of the world's economic system in the end times.

With astonishing speed, the ideas of Marx, honed and sharpened by the genius of Lenin, took over Russia. The Bolshevik Revolution sliced away all opposition. The Czar and his family were murdered. The workers triumphed. The state seized all land, all property, and all businesses. The state collectivized the farms and factories. The "workers' paradise" was born. "From each according to his ability; to each according to his need" was the promising slogan.

In the West, change was less violent but equally successful. Trade unionism gave birth to socialism. Socialism became a political power. It arranged for a gradual, "legal" massive transfer of wealth from the rich to the poor. Its theories took firm root in the universities, where much sympathy was generated for Marxist ideas and passed on to successive waves of students from home and abroad.

The world's infatuation with communism spread. The Soviet Union was born. By means of force, aggression, adroit planning, and clever propaganda, communism spread from country to country. It seemed to be invincible. At one period, right after the Second World War, the communists were actually conquering territory

---

5. See John Phillips, *Exploring Revelation* (reprint, Grand Rapids: Kregel, 2001).

at the rate of forty-four square miles an hour. The communists took over China, and more millions of people were added to the fold of communism. Then, as suddenly as it had arisen, the Soviet Union collapsed. The poor of the world discovered that the system did not work. It simply bankrupted countries that embraced it and gave rise to a new breed of tyrants, the elite party members who ran things. Nevertheless, despite the impressive demonstration of the bankruptcy of communism, it still flourishes. Some people in Russia and some of the former satellites of the former Soviet Union would like to give communism another chance. In China, communism is still in vogue. In Western universities, a die-hard elite still promote communism. The poor are still poor. The rich are still rich. The world awaits a new messiah, a new siren call. It now awaits the Antichrist.

James's warning still stands. He advises the rich men to weep and howl. The word for "howl" is *ololuzō.* It is described as an "onomatopoeic" word—a word that expresses its significance in its sound. It was a word commonly used for crying aloud to the gods. The word for "miseries" is *talaipōria.* It conveys the idea of distress. The word suggests hardship, suffering, and wretchedness.

b. The prophetic details (5:2–4)
(1) The depreciated value of their wealth (5:2)

James now expands on his prophetic utterance. He says, "Your riches are corrupted, and your garments are motheathen," a graphic description of lost wealth. The word for "riches" here is *ploutos,* the word for wealth. It carries the idea of abundance. The Lord used the word in His parable of the sower to describe the seed that fell among thorns. One of the things that chokes out the seed is "the deceitfulness of riches *(ploutos),*" He said (Matt. 13:22). Paul told Timothy to warn the believers at Ephesus against "uncertain riches" (1 Tim. 6:17). The word is used in describing the coming fall of Babylon: "For in one hour so great riches *[ploutos]* is come to nought" (Rev. 18:17).

The picture that James paints, then, is of rich men suddenly stripped of their wealth. The word for "motheaten" points us to a garment full of holes. A man once arrayed in rich apparel but now reduced to covering himself with moth-eaten garments is a picture of destitution indeed. Such a person has certainly come down in the world. Because riches can vanish so easily, the Lord Jesus, in the Sermon on the Mount, warns, "Lay not up for yourselves treasures upon earth, where moth and rust doth corrupt, and where thieves break through and steal: But lay up for yourselves treasures in heaven, where neither moth nor rust doth corrupt, and where thieves do not break through nor steal" (Matt. 6:19–20).

(2) The damning voice of their wealth (5:3a)

"Your gold and silver is cankered; and the rust of them shall be a witness against you, and shall eat your flesh as it were fire." Money that is kept in circulation does not usually tarnish. Rather, it shows evidence of wear and tear. The picture we can paint from all of this is that of rich people being forced to disgorge their buried treasure. All about them are the world's poor. They have ignored terrible cases of need. They have salted their wealth away in vaults and treasure chambers. Now, forced to reveal where their hoarded wealth is concealed, it is dug up; and the evidence is all too clear. The buried treasure has tarnished. On the day of reckoning, that very tarnish will witness against the misers. They will dread the sight of it. It will be too hot for them to hold. They will recoil from it because its very presence witnesses against them.

"Your gold is cankered," James declares. The word that he uses means "rusted." Of course, gold does not tarnish, although silver tarnishes quickly enough. The word that James uses for "rust" is *ios.* It can also mean "poison." James piles up the words to make his case against the rich who get richer and richer, hoarding their wealth, while the poor get poorer and poorer. He anticipates the day when the rich will find their treasures a terrible liability rather than an asset.

In a different context, we have the case of Judas. He sold the Son of God to Caiaphas for thirty pieces of silver. But he soon found that the money that he received was accursed. It seemed to burn and scorch his fingers even as it seared his soul. It was the price of innocent, precious blood. He never spent a single shekel of it. Before long, he was back in the temple. He flung those accursed coins onto the marble mosaic of the temple floor. Those coins rolled and rattled here, there, and everywhere, and the greedy priests chased after them. They counted them. They were all there. While Judas went out to hang himself, the priests debated what to do with this unexpected windfall. It would not be appropriate, they decided, to put the tainted coins in the temple treasury; so they used the money instead to buy a worked-out potter's field to use as a cemetery for strangers.

James realized that hoarded wealth is much the same. It recoils upon the heads of those who own it. If not now, then later, when the day of reckoning comes.

(3) The detailed vision of their wealth (5:3b–4)
(a) As to the day of reckoning (5:3b)

"Ye have heaped treasure together for the last days." Paul foretold these days more specifically in his final epistle (2 Tim. 3:1–9). He describes them not only as "the last days" but also as "perilous times." It is worth noting that both James, the first New Testament writer, and Paul, in his last New Testament epistle, point to the catastrophic age yet to come.

The concept of "the last days" reaches back to the first book of the Bible. When Jacob was about to die, he summoned his boys around his bed and told them that he intended to tell them "that which shall befall you in the last days" (Gen. 49:1). He then proceeded to foretell the future of the Jewish people from that day to this and on into ages yet unborn.[6] Jacob's amazing reference to the last days is the first of fourteen such references in the Old Testament (Gen. 49:1; Num. 24:14; Deut. 2:28; 4:30; 10:14; 31:29; Isa. 2:2; Jer. 23:20; 30:24; 48:47; 49:39; Ezek. 38:16; Hos. 3:5; Mic. 4:1). These accumulated prophecies embrace both comings of Christ.

Doubtless, James was familiar with this extensive body of truth. A well-developed end-times eschatology was to be found in the Old Testament. The apocalyptic writings of Daniel and Zechariah throw considerable light on the character of the end times. It would be interesting to know if James ever discussed the subject with Jesus during the Nazareth years. The Lord Jesus had a complete grasp of these things; and it came out, from time to time, in His parables and preaching (Matt. 24–25).

James was fascinated by just one feature of the end times, and he stands almost alone in pointing it out—labor-management relations. He saw the accumulation of vast fortunes on the one hand, some of them based on callous exploitation of workers. We have seen, in our own times, the emergence of giant multinational corporations competing fiercely for the world's business. James saw, also, an unconscionable exploitation of the workforce. Gone are the days when big companies looked after their workers in reward for loyal, lifelong service. Today, giant corporations dread a hostile takeover more than they fear their competition. Mergers of giant corporations tend to throw thousands of people, labor and management alike, out of work with total disregard for years of faithful service. Unscrupulous manipulators buy well-established companies that have provided work and security to their workers and staff. They plunder these companies of their assets, force them into bankruptcy, and then make off with millions of dollars. Automation and the relocation of factories to countries that allow the ruthless exploitation of labor aggravate matters. As for the plight of workers in some of the Third World countries, they need a modern Dickens to describe them. Anyone who has been to places such as Rio de Janeiro, Calcutta, or Cairo and seen the plight of the poor will understand James's wrath.

---

6. See Phillips, *Exploring the Future.*

James was a poor man. His father had been a poor man. He had experienced the scorn and anger of the rich. His sympathies were all on the side of the poor.

"Ye have heaped treasure together for the last days," was James's word. The word for "treasure" means "to store up." The idea is that the treasure is piled up in a place of safe keeping. These miserly rich do not spend this wealth. They have far more money than they could ever spend, so they pile it up.

I was reading recently of some of the oil-rich sheiks of Arabia who have more money than they know what to do with. Their extravagance has never been surpassed in history. One petty princeling of a royal house built a multimillion-dollar palace. When it was finished, he didn't like it, so he bulldozed it to the ground and built another one. Another young princeling wastes his money on cars. He will buy a new Rolls Royce. Because it comes with a tankful of gas, he drives it until the tank is empty. Then he throws it away and buys a new one—with a tankful of gas. This kind of prodigality goes on in a part of the world where poverty abounds. Such senseless abuse of wealth is by no means restricted to oil barons. Some of the drug czars are equally prodigal.

James sees this kind of thing becoming increasingly prevalent as the end times draw near. Once the last days dawn, of course, events will take over with a vengeance as the pace of things is suddenly greatly accelerated. The opulent rich will not have time to spend their accumulated billions, even if they want to. Not enough time will be left. The final judgments will come in like a flood. The rich will be swept away by war, persecution, disease, or natural disaster. Their piled-up treasure will be left behind to witness against them at the Great White Throne.

(b) As to the details of reckoning (5:4)

James gets down to specifics. First, *their fraud is described:* "Behold, the hire of the labourers who have reaped down your fields, which is of you kept back by fraud, crieth . . ." (5:4a). The word *hire* is *misthos*. It refers to the wages of the day laborers who toiled so hard to bring in the rich man's harvest. The powerful landowner, however, withholds their wages. "Kept back by fraud!" is James's pointed way of putting it. The word that he uses means "to deprive" or "defraud."

James, of course, was aware of the requirement of the law on the prompt payment of the laborer: "Thou shalt not oppress an hired servant that is poor and needy, whether he be of thy brethren, or of thy strangers that are in thy land within thy gates: At his day thou shalt give him his hire, neither shall the sun go down upon it; for he is poor, and setteth his heart upon it; lest he cry against thee unto the LORD, and it be sin unto thee" (Deut. 24:14–15).

The honorable landowner settled with his hired hands at the end of each day (Matt. 20:1–16). Doubtless, James knew of instances where workers went unpaid. Some people seem to get a perverse satisfaction, a sense of power, from making people wait for the settlement of their accounts. God calls that kind of thing sin. It is bad enough when a small-time, hard-pressed businessman holds out on the payroll. It is unconscionable when a rich man delays paying those who have done work for him.

James reminds us that *their fraud is discerned:* "and the cries of them which have reaped are entered into the ears of the Lord of sabaoth" (5:4b). The Lord of Sabaoth! The Lord of hosts! This is the only place where this Old Testament title of Jehovah is actually used in the New Testament—although it is quoted from Isaiah 1:9 by Paul in describing God's past dealings with the Hebrew people in Romans 9:29. The title is first used in connection with Elkanah and Hannah, the parents of Samuel. We are told that they made an annual pilgrimage "to worship and to sacrifice unto the LORD of hosts in Shiloh" (1 Sam. 1:1–3). This is the first of 281 occurrences of this particular Jehovah title. It speaks of God as the Lord of all of the hosts of heaven and earth.

James, with the fervor of an Old Testament prophet, reminds the unscrupulous rich people of this world that their wicked oppression of the poor does not go unnoticed.

One of the dramatic occasions when this title was used was in connection with the killing of Goliath. The Philistine and Israelite armies were drawn up in battle array on either side of the Valley of Elah. The Philistine champion swaggered out each day to challenge the Hebrews to find a man to come and fight him in a duel. David, a mere youth, a shepherd boy, volunteered to go, something that no one else in Israel, from the king on down, dared to do. The scene was dramatic indeed. There was the giant! There was young David! There were the hosts! It seemed like a hopeless situation. All of the power seemed to be on the side of the monstrous man who stood forth arrayed in solid steel and wielding a vast spear and a mighty sword. He looked with the utmost contempt at David, who stood there alone with just a staff and a sling in his hands.

"Am I a dog?" the Philistine roared, "that thou comest to me with staves?" He cursed him in the name of his gods. He sneered, "Come to me, and I will give thy flesh unto the fowls of the air, and to the beasts of the field" (1 Sam. 17:43–44).

David was unperturbed. "Thou comest to me," he said, "with a sword, and with a spear, and with a shield: but I come to thee in the name of *the Lord of hosts*" (1 Sam. 17:45, emphasis added). It seemed that all of the might and power were on the side of the mighty Goliath and the sophisticated Philistines. Not so! David had "the Lord of hosts" at his side. Goliath never had a chance!

It often seems that the powerful rich have the upper hand. Not so! The poor have the Lord of hosts, unseen, but at their side. Napoleon once remarked cynically, "God is on the side of the big battalions." Well, so He is. But the "big battalions" are not those that are visible to the eyes of men—a lesson that Elisha had to teach to his young colleague (2 Kings 6:14–17).

2. The rich men's wickedness disclosed (5:5–6)

James continues his theme by underlining three specific areas of abuse common to unscrupulous plutocrats. He speaks of *their pleasure:* "Ye have lived in pleasure on the earth, and been wanton" (5:5a). The expression "lived in pleasure" comes from a word that means to live a voluptuous life or to give oneself up to pleasure. The Lord Jesus told of one such man. He was very rich. He was clothed in purple and fine linen like a royal prince. He fared sumptuously every day. He lived in gorgeous splendor. At the gate of his palatial mansion lay a beggar named Lazarus. His disease-ridden, emaciated body spoke eloquently of his need. All he hoped for was for a crumb or two to fall his way when the rich man's servants were taking out the garbage. He hoped in vain. The scavenger dogs of the city were kinder to him than the rich man. Both men died. The rich man had a funeral, doubtless commensurate with his opulent lifestyle. The body of the beggar was dumped in a pauper's grave. So ends the story.

No indeed! So *begins* the story. The Lord lifted the veil that hides from our eyes what goes on in the spirit world. The Lord of hosts had been watching this stark but all-too-common tragedy on earth. The roles were reversed in eternity. Now the rich man becomes the beggar, and he begs in vain. Now poor Lazarus lies at rest, luxuriating in well-being and peace. What the oppressive rich people forget, in their dizzy round of pleasure and as they indulge their every whim at the expense of those whom they have swindled, is that a day of reckoning is to come.

James speaks also of *their plunder:* "Ye have nourished your hearts, as in a day of slaughter" (5:5b). One view of this verse is that the rich men—indulging themselves, careless of all consequences, and spending on their lavish lifestyle wealth plundered from the poor—are like cattle in the field adjacent to the slaughterhouse, feeding on the grass, feeling quite secure, and oblivious to the doom that awaits them on the morrow.

Another view pictures quite a different scene, one that draws its strength from the expression "the day of slaughter." These men are like the ghouls who descend on a battlefield at the end of a day of slaughter. They go here and there, looting the bodies, picking out what they want from the corpses of the dead. They are no better than vultures.

James speaks, too, of *their power.* They seem to live charmed lives. Their abuses seem to go *unprevented:* "Ye have condemned and killed the just" (5:6a); and their abuses seem to go *unpunished:* "and he doth not resist you" (5:6b). They have condemned and ruined and even killed innocent people, who have been power-less to defend themselves. When people are determined to become rich and abandon all scruples, there are no crimes that they will not commit. "The love of money," Paul wrote, "is the root of all evil" (1 Tim. 6:10).

The seeming prosperity of the wicked has puzzled many a thoughtful person. David wrote about it (Ps. 37), and so did Asaph (Ps. 73). David, who had known many years of persectuion, calmly compared and contrasted the two lifestyles: that of the poor, suffering saint of God, and that of the wicked who do not get the best of it after all, even down here. Asaph was more impassioned. He seemed to think that the wicked *do* prosper. Many of them even die in bed, free from pain and the pangs of remorse. Indeed, contemplation of these things almost made him give up his faith. What saved him was his going into the sanctuary. Then he understood their end, that is, their final end in the hereafter.

James wrestled with things more along the line of Asaph than along the line of David. And he comes to much the same conclusion: "Be patient!" That is to be his closing word on this issue.

PART 8

The Christian and His Burdens

James 5:7–20

A. The burden of poverty (5:7–11)
1. A call for simple patience (5:7–8)
a. The prospect (5:7)

James produces two reasons for patience. The first is a *biblical reason:* "Be patient therefore, brethren, unto the coming of the Lord" (5:7a). James wrote in the early days of the church; some scholars think that he wrote before the Jerusalem conference. If that was so, it was only a little more than a dozen years since the Lord had returned to heaven. Hope of His sure and soon return still burned brightly in many hearts. Little did those early believers know that the Lord's return was to be delayed for some two millennia and that the church would be called upon to develop an agelong patience. The fact that many centuries would intervene between the promise and the advent really was immaterial. Each generation has hoped that His coming would be in its lifetime. Anticipation of His soon return burns as brightly as ever today. The date of the Rapture is the best kept secret in the universe. "Perhaps today" has been the motto of all those who love His appearing, in all of the ages of the church's sojourn on earth.

It was no idle thing, then, for James to point the suffering saints to the Lord's return as a reason for patience. His second coming will be a time when all wrongs will be redressed. James would have us put our case into the capable hands of the Lord Jesus.

The return of the Lord is to be in two stages. First is what we call the *Rapture* (1 Thess. 4:13–5:11). At that time, the church will be caught away to be with Christ, and Christians will appear at the judgment seat of Christ (1 Cor. 3:12–15; 2 Cor. 5:10; Rom. 14:10). There, unconfessed and unrequited wrongs between believers will be settled. Then is the actual *return,* the second advent of the Lord to establish His millennial kingdom (Matt. 24:1–31). This long-anticipated and frequently heralded event will be preceded by the judgment of the surviving nations in the Valley of Jehoshaphat (Joel 3:9–21; Matt. 25:31–46). That great assize will settle accounts among the survivors of the end-times judgments. All remaining wrongs will be dealt with at the Great White Throne in preparation for the establishment of the eternal kingdom (Rev. 20:11–15).

The Bible nowhere promises that wrongs and injustices will be settled on earth in our own particular lifetime, but it does promise that they will be redressed justly and adequately. James, like other prophets, sees the second coming of Christ as the time when all accounts will be settled. He urges us to be patient and leave things in the capable hands of Christ.

He has a second reason for advising patience, *a biological reason:* "Behold, the husbandman waiteth for the precious fruit of the earth, and hath long patience for it, until he receive the early and latter rain" (5:7b). The one thing a farmer can not do is hurry the seasons. His one necessary virtue is patience. In the very nature of things, he can do nothing but sow his seed and then wait. Above all, he cannot command the rain, as James points out. Dr. George Adam Smith describes the weather of the Holy Land thus:

> The ruling feature of the Syrian climate is the division of the year into a rainy and a dry season. Towards the end of October heavy rains begin to fall for a day or several days at a time. These are what the English Bible calls the early or former rain, literally the Pourer. It opens the agricultural year; the soil hard and cracked by the long summer is loosened, and the farmer begins ploughing. Till the end of November the rainfall is not large, but increases from December to February, abates in March, and is practically over by the middle of April. The latter rains of Scripture are the heavy showers of March and April. Coming before the harvest and the summer drought, they are of more importance to the country than the rains of the winter, and that is why these are passed over in Scripture, and emphasis is laid on the early and the latter rains. This has given most people the idea of only two intervals of rain in the Syrian year, at the vernal and the autumnal equinox; but all winter is the rainy season, as we are told in the Song of Songs:

> > Lo, the winter is past,
> > The rain is over and gone.

During most winters both hail and snow fall on the hills. Hail is common and often mingled with rain and thunderstorms, which happen at intervals through the winter, and are frequent in spring. The Old Testament mentions hail and thunder together. On the Central Range snow is known to reach nearly two feet and lie for five days or more, and pools at Jerusalem are sometimes covered with ice. But this is rare: on the Central Range the ground seldom freezes, and the snow disappears in a day. On the plateaus east of Jordan, snow lies for days every winter, and on Hermon, fields of it last through the summer. None has been seen in the tropical Ghor. This explains the feat of Benaiah, who went down and slew a lion in the midst of a cistern in the day of the snow. The beast had strayed up from Jordan and been caught in a snowstorm. Where else could lions and snow come together?

In May showers are rare, and from then till October not only is there no rain, but a cloud seldom passes over the sky, and a thunderstorm is a miracle. Morning mists are not uncommon-in midsummer, 1891, we twice woke into one as chill and dense as a Scotch "haar"-but are soon dispersed. In Bible lands vapour is the symbol of what is frail and fleeting, as it cannot be to us northerners, to whose coasts the mists cling with a pertinacity suggestive of opposite ideas. On the other hand, the dews of Syrian nights are excessive; on many mornings it looks as if there had been heavy rain, and this and mist are the sole slackening of the drought from May till October. Through summer prairie and forest fires are not uncommon. The grass and thistle of the desert will blaze for miles, driving scorpions and vipers from their holes, as the Baptist describes in one of his vivid figures; sometimes, as the prophets tell us, the air is filled with the smoke of a whole wood.[1]

James, of course, was familiar with the weather patterns of his native land. Like the Palestinian farmer of old, we can no more control the weather than we can the seasons. All we can do is wait. In due time, the appointed weather comes along, and the seeds germinate, grow, flower, and produce the harvest. Everything proceeds at a slow pace; and, ultimately, all is in the hands of God. James sees in all of this a pointed illustration of the need for patience. God refuses to be hurried; He sees all but bides His time.

We get impatient when injustice seems to triumph. In the days of Israel's bondage in Egypt, God waited for centuries. The explanation He confided in Abraham was that "the iniquity of the Amorites is not yet full" (Gen. 15:16)—a similar explanation is given to us by Peter (2 Peter 3:3–10). God had not forgotten either His promise or His people down there in Egyptian bondage. When He called Moses to emancipate the Israelites from their bondage in Egypt, He said, "I have surely seen the affliction of my people which are in Egypt, and have heard their cry by reason of their taskmasters; for I know their sorrows" (Exod. 3:7).

---

1. George Adam Smith, *The Historical Geography of the Holy Land* (New York: Harper and Row, 1966), 62–64.

God was just as concerned for "the Amorite," however, as He was for the Israelite. He was as patient with the Egyptian as He was with Moses. God's timetable is not the same as ours. Moreover, He takes into full consideration all of the factors of any given equation before He acts. We must learn to wait.

b. The promise (5:8)

God says, *"Be still":* "Be ye also patient" (5:8a), and He says, *"Be strong":* "stablish your hearts: for the coming of the Lord draweth nigh" (5:8b). The rich man might have the power that comes from the ability to buy whatever he wants, including henchmen and crooked lawyers and judges. But the believer has character. He has the inner strength that comes from knowing God.

Simon Legree, the wicked landowner in Harriet Beecher Stowe's novel *Uncle Tom's Cabin,* had power. Poor, bullied, and beaten, Uncle Tom had strength. In the end, character won out over cruelty. When Simon Legree threatened to roast Tom over a slow fire, the powerless slave replied that although his master could do many cruel things and could even kill his body, all eternity would come after that. Uncle Tom had learned to be still and to be strong.

The prophet Isaiah lived in dark and dangerous days. The ominous Assyrian Empire was on the rampage again—and not a country in the Middle East failed to tremble when the Assyrian army was on the march. In due time, the Assyrians overran the Promised Land. They destroyed the northern kingdom of Israel and deported its people. The Babylonians invaded the little land of Judah and captured most of its cities. They surrounded Jerusalem itself, and there seemed to be no hope.

Isaiah the prophet had warned and warned, but he had preached—for the most part—to deaf ears. Hezekiah the king, however, was willing to listen. He instituted many reforms, but they were legislated by the throne and did not represent a grassroots revival. So the prophet's messages assumed an apocalyptic tone. Current events were merged and mingled with end-times events. The Assyrians merged with the Antichrist and current disasters mingled with future disasters in the terrible "day of the Lord." Probably not even Isaiah himself could have unraveled the one from the other. He saw war and famine, death and disaster, and oppression and panic. But there was still God! Isaiah had a word for the king and everyone else who would listen: "Thou wilt keep him in perfect peace, whose mind is stayed on thee," he said, adding, "because he trusteth in thee" (Isa. 26:3). James agreed with that assurance.

2. A call for sufficient patience (5:9)

James interjects two warnings. He tells his oppressed readers to *beware of complaining:* "Grudge not one against another" (5:9a). The word for "grudge" refers to an inward and unexpressed feeling of sorrow. It is used of the Lord Jesus on the occasion when He healed a man who had a speech impediment. The man seems to have become deaf and, as a result, had developed a speech problem. The Lord dealt with him in a somewhat unusual way in the process of which He looked up to heaven and "sighed." This is one of two miracles that only Mark recorded (7:31–37; 8:22–26). They are both unusual because, in each case, the Lord healed by a process. When Mark says, "he sighed," the word that he uses can be translated "groaned." It suggests how deeply Jesus felt for the ills of men.

The apostle Paul uses the same word and its cognates in describing the three-fold groaning of the creation, the Christian and the Comforter. "The whole creation *groaneth,*" he says (Rom. 8:22, emphasis added). We ourselves "*groan* within ouselves," he adds (8:23, emphasis added). "Likewise," he declares, "the Spirit itself maketh intercession for us with *groanings* which cannot be uttered" (8:26, emphasis added).

Some of this groaning is natural, understandable, and perfectly legitimate. The sufferings that some people are called upon to undergo generate these inward groans. God Himself groans with us. But James uses the word somewhat differently. He uses the word in the sense of murmuring or holding a grudge. We never see the Lord doing that. We are to beware of complaining.

We are to *beware of condemnation:* "Lest ye be condemned: behold, the judge standeth before the door" (5:9b–c). James implies that possibly the one who is doing the murmuring is the one at fault. Our reactions to wrongs can be as bad as the wrongs inflicted on us. In any case, the judge Himself is at the door. That should put a swift stop to our murmurings.

3. A call for sublime patience (5:10–11)
a. The prophets (5:10)

James is by no means finished with his exhortation. He has in mind sublime, even supernatural, patience, and he has two examples. First, "Take, my brethren, the prophets, who have spoken in the name of the Lord, for an example of suffering affliction, and of patience." Hardly any of the prophets were welcomed by their contemporaries. The two who did have instant and spectacular results were Jonah and Nahum, both of whom prophesied regarding Ninevah. In the one case, instantaneous repentance resulted; in the other case, instantaneous and spectacular ruin occurred.

For the most part, the prophets were highly unpopular preachers to the consciences of their countrymen. Hosea was a man of sorrows and acquainted with grief. Amos was doubtless popular enough in Israel—as long as he denounced the surrounding nations—but the high priest of the calf cult threatened him at once when he denounced Israel. Micah was the first prophet to threaten Jerusalem with destruction. He must have been about as popular as a skunk at a Sunday school picnic! Habakkuk was called upon to utter woe after woe against his countrymen. Haggai saw success, but his contemporary and colleague Zechariah was murdered. Isaiah, after a distinguished career, was sawn in half in a hollow tree by Manasseh. And as for Jeremiah, he wept his way through life. John the Baptist was murdered, and so was Jesus.

A prophet arose in Israel only in a time of crisis or apostasy. Prophets were not commissioned to "make friends and influence people." Nor were they promised "success." They were not attracted to the pulpit by glamorous, four-color brochures. They were not called to build crystal cathedrals and promote "possibility" thinking. The basic requirements of a prophet were conviction and courage, along with patience. Often, the things that the prophets revealed belonged in the future. Sometimes the prophetic focus was on events far removed by time to dim and distant ages. More often than not, the things that the prophets foretold had both a near and a far fulfillment. The local, impending fulfillment, in that case, was a mere dress rehearsal, so to speak, for the far-off, full, and final fulfillment. The prophets soon learned that God's calendar was very much bigger than theirs. Patience was the essence of their call.

b. The patriarch (5:11)

James again presents two facts. First, he draws our attention to *a point to ponder:* "Behold, we count them happy which endure" (5:11a). That is, those who hold on to the end are usually those whom we count as blessed. Those who cave in when the going gets tough do not usually win our applause. The classic Old Testament example of one who failed to remain constant is Michal.

Michal was King Saul's younger daughter. She fell in love with David right after David's monumental triumph over Goliath (1 Sam. 18:20, 28), and she married him. David's popularity and the way he reigned in the affections of Michal, her brother Jonathan, and all Israel quickly alarmed Saul, Michal's father. He became jealous of David, came to hate him, and spent years persecuting him.

Nor did it take long for his murderous envy to bear fruit. He hurled a javelin at David but missed. David escaped and made his way home. Michal assisted him to make his getaway and, consequently, was hauled before her furious father. Instead of standing up for David, she made the false excuse that David had threatened to kill her if she did not assist him and cover his tracks.

Meanwhile, David became not only a fugitive but also an outlaw chief with an ever growing band of refugees about him. He transformed this ragtag-and-bobtail band into a group of mighty men. Saul chased David from one end of the country to the other but could never succeed in capturing him. Time and again, God delivered Saul into David's hand, and David loyally, magnanimously, and royally let him go.

Michal did not share in David's rejection. She stayed in Jerusalem, and King Saul married her off to a man named Phalti, a native of Gallim, a small town just north of Jerusalem. Michal seems to have acquiesced passively in this bigamous arrangement. It was a gross denial of David and a mean-spirited betrayal of him. Indeed, Michal never did seem able to stand up under the threat of persecution. Although she was David's wife, the Holy Spirit usually calls her "Michal, Saul's daughter."

After the death of Saul and the surrender of the ten tribes to David, Michal's adulterous relationship with Phalti was terminated. David took her back as the beloved wife of his youth, but she remained "Saul's daughter" after all because when David brought the ark of the covenant back to Jerusalem, amid the rejoicing of the nation, Michal simply sneered. When David arrived home, she made some cutting remarks to him that showed, once again, what a shallow, worldly, and carnal person she was.

So Michal stands forth as the classic example of a person too devoid of courage and conviction to be true to her vows and loyal to her Lord. She could not endure. We do not count her as blessed.

Abigail is a marked contrast. She comes into the story at about the time Michal betrayed David and took up with Phalti. Abigail was the wife of Nabal, a born fool if ever there was one, a man who lived up to his name, which means "fool." Nabal, a wealthy farmer, pigheadedly refused to pay even nominal tribute to David, even though David and his freebooting irregulars had often protected both Nabal's flocks and his shepherds. This fool of a man abused David's messengers with harsh words and sent them packing back to David. The man was a boor, a drunkard, and "a son of Belial."

Yet, Abigail remained loyal with patient endurance to this her graceless husband. She did more. She came to David to try to disarm his vengeance. No less than fourteen times, in an eloquent appeal, she called David her "lord." And three times David called her "blessed" or "happy." She had learned how to endure hardship and to develop character along with conviction and courage. Her example is a point to ponder. James would have approved of Abigail.

James, however, has a different illustration. He sets before us *a person to ponder:* "Ye have heard," he says, "of the patience of Job, and have seen the end of the Lord; that the Lord is very pitiful [not just pitiful], and of tender mercy" (5:11b–c). James uses a couple of superlatives here. The word for "very pitiful" is *polusplanchnos.* It means to be full of pity. It is made up of *polus* ("much") and *splanchnon* ("heart"). It has been rendered "full of understanding" pity. The psalmist David put it thus: "Like as a father pitieth his children, so the LORD pitieth them that fear him. For he knoweth our frame; he remembereth that we are dust" (Ps. 103:13–14). It means to be compassionate. David said, "The mercy of the LORD is from everlasting to everlasting . . ." (Ps. 103:17). Indeed, he expresses the Lord's mercy not only in terms of time, as in this verse, but also in terms of space. He gives the vertical dimension: "as the heaven is high above the earth, so great is his mercy toward them that fear him." Then he gives the horizontal dimension: "As far as the east is from the west, so far hath he removed our transgressions from us" (Ps. 103:11–12). Both dimensions are infinite.[2]

James carries all of this over to the story of Job. Job was a remarkable person, a man greatly beloved in heaven and pronounced "perfect" by God. He was compassed with blessings. He was rich and increased with goods and had need of nothing. Moreover, he had a large and loving family, enjoyed good health, and was a man highly regarded by his peers. When Satan, in the course of his endless walking about, presented himself before God, God confronted him with the case of Job. He was both a good man and a godly man. Job himself tells us that he never looked with lust, that he was a friend of the fatherless and widows, and that no stranger ever escaped his boundless hospitality. He was devout and godly, a man who prayed and fasted systematically for the welfare of his children.

Then came the upheaval. His whole world caved in. In one disasterous day, all of his wealth was swept away. Worse still, all of his children were killed in a tornado. Then his health broke down, and he was smitten with a painful, disfiguring, and incurable disease. As though that were not enough, his wife turned against him and advised him to curse God and commit suicide.

The remarkable thing about Job was his patience in all of this. The word that James used to describe Job's patience refers to the patience that grows only under

---

2. See John Phillips, *Exploring Psalms* (reprint, Grand Rapids: Kregel, 2002).

trial. It means patient endurance. It conveys the idea of holding out or of bearing up under a trial. It is used of "the patience of Christ," or "the patient waiting for Christ," as the King James text puts it (2 Thess. 3:5). The idea here is that the Lord is seated on His Father's throne in glory, waiting patiently for the day when His enemies will be made His footstool. Just so, we should wait patiently for Him, being as patient in our sufferings as He was in His.

Thus, Job bore up under the hammer blows that were rained upon him. After the loss of his fortune and his family, "Job arose, and rent his mantle, and shaved his head, and fell down upon the ground, and worshipped, and said, Naked came I out of my mother's womb, and naked shall I return thither: the Lord gave, and the Lord hath taken away; blessed be the name of the Lord." To which the Holy Spirit adds, "In all this Job sinned not, nor charged God foolishly" (Job 1:20–22).

When Job was inflicted with his mysterious disease and his wife turned on him, he simply responded, "Thou speakest as one of the foolish women speaketh. What? shall we receive good at the hand of God, and shall we not receive evil?" The Hebrew word for *evil* speaks of the "breaking up of all that is good or desirable." Again, the Holy Spirit comments, "In all this did not Job sin with his lips" (Job 2:10).

Such was the patience of Job. It was sorely tested under the false accusations and wordy arguments of his friends. Even so, his forbearance was remarkable. When he was vindicated in the end, he harbored no malice but prayed for the well-being of his critics.

The whole point of all of this was that neither Job nor anyone else around him had the slightest idea why all of these calamities had overtaken him, a person renowned as a man of great integrity and piety. We know why these things happened. We know about Satan's slanders. We know that God permitted Satan to strike Job—although with certain limitations. We know all about the titanic struggle in the unseen world. But Job knew none of this. He was completely in the dark. Yet, as blow after blow fell upon him, he bore up bravely and with sublime patience.

James, under the inspiration of the Holy Spirit, reveals something about this whole business that is not mentioned in the Job narrative: he tells us of the Lord's pity and tender mercy. The context leads naturally to the conclusion that James still has Job in mind. It was not as though the Lord sat on His throne high and lifted up, distant and remote, watching the entire spectacle of Job's struggle and distress, with impassive indifference. On the contrary, He knew all about Job's bewilderment, bankruptcy, and brokenness. His heart went out to Job, even though He allowed Satan to have his way and allowed Job's friends to antagonize him. He was right there, suffering with Job, listening to his every word, in rhythm with the beating of his heart, treasuring up his tears, and planning his bright reward. So He is with us in our trials.

James draws our attention, too, to "the end of the Lord," and that is one of the most wonderful things about the book of Job. The story had a good ending. Job had dark days when he not only did not know why these disasters had overtaken him, but also he did not know if they were ever going to end at all. But they did. Job came through the ordeal a humbler, happier, and holier man. Moreover, God gave him double what he had before! The end of the story was very good indeed—and God had that end in mind from the very beginning. And so He does for us. Our story, too, is to have a good ending in a land of fadeless day; there awaits us "joy unspeakable and full of glory" and the Lord's resounding, "Well done!"

B. The burden of proof (5:12)

James continues. He's back to the tongue again. Under trial, we are apt to say far too much. Job almost did so when defending himself against the false accusations of his friends. James tell us *what to avoid:* "But above all things, my brethren, swear not, neither by heaven, neither by the earth, neither by any other oath" (5:12a); and he tells us *what to avow:* "but let your yea be yea; and your nay, nay; lest ye fall into condemnation" (5:12b–c). This is an echo from the Sermon on the Mount (Matt. 5:33–37). We have all met people who think that they have to swear some kind of an oath every time they make an affirmation. A little of that kind of thing goes a long way. We doubt the honesty and integrity of the person who has to swear to the truth of his every remark. Constant appeals to this, that, or the other as confirmation of one's words cheapens the whole point of such affirmation. Appealing to God or to Christ soon degenerates into taking the Lord's name in vain.

The believer is to be so much a man of his word that no oaths are necessary. There was a time in English history when honor was prized as the highest virtue. A man who broke his word was the lowest form of cad. A common saying in lands where the flag of the empire was displayed was, "It is the word of an Englishman."

We find an echo of that attitude in the words that David Livingstone so often wrote into his diary. At every great crisis, he retreated back upon his favorite text: "lo, I am with you alway, even unto the end of the world" (Matt. 28:20). He said, "It is the word of a gentleman of the strictest and most sacred honor—and that's an end of it!" And so it was. A Christian's word should be his bond. When he gives his word, that should be enough. People ought to know that he will fulfill his promise, no matter how inconvenient it might become, for the simple reason that, having given his word, it would never occur to him to go back on it.

   C. The burden for prayer (5:13–18)
     1. The hypotheses (5:13–14a)

James turns now to the availability of prayer, the great resource of all of those who are undergoing trial and the ready source of solace and strength for God's people in all ages and under all conditions.

He begins with a threefold word. He points us to *the man who is overwhelmed:* "Is any among you afflicted? let him pray" (5:13a). He is to speak—to God. The word here for "afflicted" means "suffering hardship." It refers to those who are in trouble. As long as we are in this world, we are in enemy territory, as Job discovered. However, we are not left to our own resources, left to grope along as best we can. We have a grand highway blazed for us straight into the throne room of the universe (Heb. 10:19–22). As Paul puts it, "If God be for us, who can be against us?" (Rom. 8:31).

Our anchor is cast "inside the veil." It is both sure and steadfast (Heb. 6:19). In her song "We Have an Anchor," hymn writer Priscilla J. Owens asks the following question:

> Will your anchor hold in the storms of life,
> When the clouds unfold their wings of strife?
> When the strong tides lift and the cables strain,
> Will your anchor drift or firm remain?

Then comes the answer:

> It is safely moored, 'twill the storm withstand,
> For 'tis well secured by the Savior's hand;
> And the cables passed from His hand to mine
> Can defy that blast thro' strength divine.

And following each verse comes the chorus:

> We have an anchor that keeps the soul,
> Steadfast and sure while the billows roll,

> Fastened to the Rock which cannot move,
> Grounded firm and deep in the Savior's love.[3]

James moves on. He considers now *the man who is overjoyed:* "Is any merry? let him sing psalms" (5:13b). The word for "merry" has to do with strong feelings of well-being. It means to be cheerful. The only other time the word occurs in the New Testament was under very adverse circumstances indeed: Paul was a prisoner on his way to trial before Nero at Rome.

At Myra, a seaport on the coast of Asia Minor and one of the chief ports for the grain fleet that sailed between Egypt and Rome, Paul embarked with his guard and numerous other passengers. It proved to be rough sailing once they put out to sea. After a difficult passage, they came to Fair Havens, a small bay on the island of Crete. It was an incommodious anchorage. The captain advised making a dash for a better harbor farther along the coast. But Paul, a seasoned traveler, advised staying where they were. The dangerous winter months were at hand. The centurian had the deciding vote. He opted for the captain and a bold attempt to reach the better port of Phoenix. Soon after this decision was reached, a favorable wind sprung up and, in spite of Paul's warnings, they set sail.

Suddenly, however, the wind changed, and the nightmare voyage began. The sailors recognized in the wind their old enemy, Euroclydon, a hurricane not at all uncommon in those waters. The ship was now caught in the gale. They were driven past the small island of Clauda. The brief respite it gave allowed them to haul the ship's dinghy on board and to tighten up the ship. The next day, with the gale still howling around the ship, the sailors began to jettison the cargo and some of the spare gear. Then followed eleven days and nights of terror. The ship was leaking. The sailors had no idea where they were. It was almost impossible to prepare food. Everyone was terrified. And fear of shipwreck loomed large.

That's when Paul spoke up. His words struck an incongruous note, but what words they were: *"Be of good cheer!"* he said. He said it twice (Acts 27:22, 25). Nor was it a shallow, baseless optimism. The angel of God had visited him and assured him of several things. Come what may, he must stand before Nero—so he could not be drowned. Moreover, God promised him that everyone on board would be saved. They were to be shipwrecked, but that was no cause for alarm! James would have called for a song! Paul advised everyone to get something to eat!

James moves on yet again—to *the man who is overcome:* "Is any sick among you? let him call for the elders of the church" (5:14a). The word for "sick" means

---

3. Priscilla J. Owen, "We Have an Anchor," 1882.

to be weak, feeble, or diseased. Christians are not exempt from the sicknesses that assail the human race. In the ordinary course of events, when a person is sick he goes to the doctor. In the early days of the church, the gift of healing was still extant, so it was not unreasonable to send for the elders. However, as James develops this theme, there seems to be more to it than that.

2. The healing (5:14b–16)
    a. The prayer (5:14b)

"And let them pray over him." James was a great believer in the power of prayer. He had a reputation as a prayer warrior. To this day, the church believes in the efficacy of prayer. And, judging by the high proportion of prayer requests at local church prayer meetings for the healing of sick people, we still believe that God is able to heal.

That is not by any means the same as saying that we believe in healers. The gifts of healing, miracles, and tongues, like the gifts of apostles and prophets, were temporary and suited to an age of transition. The "sign" gifts were for Israel; when the nation of Israel, at home and abroad, rejected the Spirit of God, as the Jews in the Promised Land had rejected the Son of God, the sign gifts were withdrawn (1 Cor. 1:22; Eph. 2:20).

The "healers" who perform on television and at giant rallies nowadays frequently resort to all kinds of tricks. They specialize, too, in psychosomatic healings and frequently leave a trail of disappointment and disillusionment behind them. Often, their failures are blamed on the sufferer, who is accused of lack of faith. Modern "healers" could earn some much-needed credibility for themselves if they would take a tour through the local hospitals, emptying the wards by the exercize of their "gift."

In spite of all this lamentable hoopla, God does heal. He sometimes even heals at healing meetings in spite of the so-called healers. But when God heals, it is in answer to the earnest prayers of His people, and it is in accordance with His will. He does not guarantee to heal everybody. Much illness is salutary. Some of it is disciplinary. The gift of healing died out of the church by the end of the apostolic age. Paul himself needed the constant ministration of Luke, "the beloved physician." He left Trophimus at Miletum sick (2 Tim. 4:20), and he advised Timothy to take a little wine for his stomach's sake and for his frequent infirmities (1 Tim. 5:23).

Even in the early days of the church, when the sign gifts were fully operational, James advised the sick to summon the elders—not the healers. It is possible that, among the elders in the early church, some people had the gift of healing. James, however, emphasizes neither the doctor nor the healer but rather the *elder* for a reason.

b. The procedure (5:14c–d)

James now describes an almost Old Testament-like procedure, one that was followed in the Jerusalem church when a sick person summoned the elders to his bedside. He mentions the *sanctifying oil:* "and let them pray over him, anointing him with oil" (5:14c), and he mentions *the sovereign name:* "in the name of the Lord" (5:14d).

Throughout history, oil has been used for its medicinal properties. When I was a boy, a popular remedy for earache was olive oil. If we had a bad cough, mother used camphorated oil. Constipation called for cod liver oil.

The use of oil recommended by James was possibly symbolic—an appeal to the Spirit of God—just as calling on the name of the Lord was an appeal to the Son of God. If we take the use of oil literally, then it is possible that here we have a combination of medicine and miracle. In any case, this procedure was recommended in a day when the church was young. Moreover, it was recommended to churches that were largely Jewish in composition. It is extremely unlikely that it was ever intended to be a blanket formula for universal healing.

When our second daughter was born, she had a severe cross to one eye. It was very pronounced, and, naturally, we were very concerned. At the time, we were living in a remote town, and no professional advice was available. We had started a small church and particularly appreciated the teaching and insight of a resident missionary who was also gifted in the Word and was a successful soul winner.

One day he approached us. "Have you considered James 5:14–16?" he asked. He explained to us his interpretation of this passage. We should call a meeting of the elders of the church. We should anoint the child with oil. We should claim the promise and pray that the child's eye might be healed.

We accepted his counsel and one evening gathered the elders in the little one's bedroom. Our friend poured some oil on the child's head. We all placed our hands upon her, and each prayed that the Lord would work a miracle and heal the child's eye. Nothing happened. The next morning, we rushed into the bedroom to see. The little one's eye was unchanged. A day passed, a week, a month. It was very evident that the Lord was not going to perform a miracle.

But two things did happen. First, we heard of an ophthamologist in Vancouver, some five hundred miles away, who specialized in children's eye problems. We took her to him. He examined her and said, "This is a very common eye problem and nowadays a simple one to remedy. Bring the child back when she is two years old, and we'll take the eye out, tighten the muscle, put the eye back, and she'll be fine." So that is what we did, and that is what he did—and that is what the Lord did.

The second thing that happened to me on that occasion was that I realized
that I could not depend upon a secondhand theology. I needed to do my own
hermeneutics and exegesis. It became obvious to me that the passage in James did
not say what my teacher-evangelist friend said it said; otherwise, the Lord would
have performed the requested miracle. Evidently, this much-abused passage is
not a blanket prescription for healing.

I learned, also, that the kind of teaching to which I had listened raised false
hopes that, as often as not, ended in disappointment. Also, it led to self-incrimi-
nation. Maybe I was at fault for not having enough faith. But then, what about
the faith of the other elders, and what about the faith of my missionary friend? It
was years before I saw through the fallacy of that line of thinking—that the fault
was mine for not having enough faith. It is a favorite cop-out of healers when
their gimmicks fail to produce lasting results. Moreover, it is cruel to add to the
sufferings of the sick the burdening thought that "You are not healed because
you don't have enough faith." A friend of mine was driven to distraction when
his much-loved wife was dying of cancer and some "charismatics" told him that
it was his fault; if he had enough faith, she could be healed. The obvious fallacy
in that line of "exegesis" is that it persuades people to put their faith in their
faith—a self-defeating process. The false theology behind that is the idea that the
more faith we have, the more results we get—a barefaced contradiction of the
teaching of the Lord Himself (Luke 17:5–6).

> c. The promise (5:15)
> > (1) What is asserted (5:15a–b)

So we come back to the passage. We cannot dismiss it as belonging solely to
the apostolic age of miracle. That there is a definite promise here is self-evident.
If James is not giving us a blank check for healing, for us to fill out when and
where we please, what is he offering?

We note two things in his assertion. We note first *the authority of the prayer
involved:* "And the prayer of faith shall save the sick" (5:15a). We emphasize the
word *shall.* We cannot hedge here. The assertion is positive and categorical and
leaves no room for doubt or debate. The prayer of faith is a force to be reckoned
with in the universe. Millions of people in all ages have proved it so. We would be
cold-blooded atheists to deny it.

We note also *the authority of the person invoked:* "and the Lord shall raise him
up" (5:15b). Again we underline the word *shall.* This assertion is equally as positive
and categorical as the first one. The appeal is to the Lord, the Creator and Sustainer

of the universe, the One who, throughout His earthly ministry, healed people by the thousands, cast out countless evil spirits, cleansed all kinds of lepers, and even raised the dead. The appeal is not to a cult leader, a phony healer, or a dead saint. The appeal is to the Lord, who has absolute authority in heaven and earth and who says so (Matt. 28:17).

So, what is asserted is positive and undeniable. So why doesn't this formula of calling for the elders and anointing with oil work every time? Because we take the words out of context—and a text without a context is a pretext. Note the following.

(2) What is assumed (5:15c)

"And if he have committed sins, they shall be forgiven him." That is the key to the whole problem. That is why the sick person (not his friends or relatives) calls for the elders rather than for the doctors.

Here is the crux of the whole matter. The person involved who, when sick, calls for the elders of the local church, is a person who is guilty of some sin. We can carry that a step further; he is under the discipline of the elders of the church, and his illness is a direct result of that discipline (1 Cor. 11:28–31; 5:1–13).

The word *if* in the New Testament always should be examined in the light of its context. Four conditional structures are in the Greek New Testament. The first-class *if* means "because." It assumes the certainty, not the contingency. The second-class *if* means "if it were so," but it isn't. It assumes the contrary to be the fact. The third-class *if* (used here) means "more than likely." The assumption is that it is most likely that the person has sinned. The fourth-class *if* means "more remote or less likely." Perhaps the reason why the third-class *if* is used here is because God, in grace, does sometimes heal those who appeal to this passage even though they incorrectly apply the passage.

The word for "sick" here is *kamnō*. The word used in verse 14 is *astheneō*. The word *astheneō* is the usual word for an illness, for sick people in general (Matt. 10:8), and for people suffering from a disease. It speaks of weariness, often an accompaniment of sickness. It is used of the great multitude of "impotent" (*astheneō*) folk who congregated at the pool of Bethesda (John 5:3).

The word *kamnō* means "to be weary" and is so used in Hebrews 12:3. It is translated "fainted" in Revelation 2:3. W. E. Vine sees a significance in the choice of this word here in James 5:15 rather than the repetition of the word just used in verse 14. He says that the deliberate use of this word "is suggestive of the common accompaniment of sickness, weariness of mind (which is the meaning of this verb), which not infrequently hinders physical recovery; hence this special cause is here intimated in the general idea of 'sickness.'"[4] It would seem, then, that the person whom James has specifically in view here is not only sick but also has something weighing on his mind. This thought is strengthened by James's concluding remarks (5:19–20).

So, then, the person whom James has been describing is worn out by a sickness brought upon him as a result of church discipline because of some excommunicating sin. He calls for the elders. He confesses his sin. He is forgiven. The elders anoint him with oil and pray for him. He gets better. It works every time. One reason we do not see this kind of healing is because most of our modern churches do not have spiritual elders. In any case, they are so often so anemic that they do not carry out church discipline.

d. The postscript (5:16)

James concludes this subject by making a general statement. There is a *requirement:* "Confess your faults one to another" (5:16a). There is a *response:* "and pray for one another, that ye may be healed" (5:16b). And there is a *reason:* "The effectual fervent prayer of a righteous man availeth much" (5:16c).

The word for "faults" here has to do with a falling aside when one should have stood upright. It indicates a falling away from truth, a moral fall, a fault or trespass. It means a false step. This kind of behavior needs to be confessed, hopefully before it gets to the point where disciplinary action has to be applied. A person attending a church where an atmosphere of holiness and spirituality exists will not be able to stand any cover-up of a secret sinful condition. The early Jerusalem church was like that. When Peter disciplined Ananias and Sapphira, "great fear came upon all the church." Many people exercised self-discipline because they were afraid to join such a church (Acts 5:1–13).

The word for "healed" here is *iaomai*, used both of physical and spiritual healing. Here in James 5:16 it is probably used in both ways. This use strengthens the thought that the circumstances in view here are those that Paul had to correct at Corinth (1 Cor. 11:30). The offenders had brought chastisement on themselves.

James calls for "effectual fervent" prayer. Behind this expression is the idea of energy *(energeomai),* the mighty energy of the Holy Spirit of God. Great is the power and strength of a godly person's supplication. It avails much in its outworking. It releases tremendous power.

---

4. W. E. Vine, *Vine's Expository Dictionary of New Testament Words,* 1 vol. (London: Oliphants, 1952).

Charles G. Finney, the revivalist, was such a man of extraordinary prayer and power. Many stories are related about the effect that just his presence had on people. He frequently preached extemporaneously and with a rare anointing of the Holy Spirit.

On one occasion, he was preaching in the vicinity of Utica, New York. He tells us what happened.

A circumstance occurred in this neighborhood, which I must not fail to notice. There was a cotton manufactory on the Oriskany creek, a little above Whitesboro, a place now called New York Mills. It was owned by an unconverted man, but a gentleman of high standing and good morals. My brother-in-law was at that time superintendent of the factory. I was invited to go and preach at that place, and went up one evening, and preached in the village school-house, which was large, and was crowded with hearers. The word, I could see, took powerful effect among the people, especially among the young people who were at work in the factory.

The next morning, after breakfast, I went into the factory, to look through it. As I went through, I observed there was a good deal of agitation among those who were busy at their looms, and their mules, and other implements of work. On passing through one of the apartments, where a great number of young women were attending to their weaving, I observed a couple of them eyeing me, and speaking very earnestly to each other; and I could see that they were a good deal agitated, although they both laughed. I went slowly toward them. They saw me coming, and were evidently much excited. One of them was trying to mend a broken thread, and I observed that her hands trembled so that she could not mend it. I approached slowly, looking on each side at the machinery, as I passed; but observed that this girl grew more and more agitated, and could not proceed with her work. When I came within eight or ten feet of her, I looked solemnly at her. She observed it, and was quite overcome, and sunk down, and burst into tears. The impression caught almost like powder, and in a few moments nearly all in the room were in tears. This feeling spread through the factory. The owner of the establishment, was present, and seeing the state of things, he said to the superintendent, "Stop the mill, and let the people attend to religion; for it is more important that our souls should be saved than that this factory run." The gate was immediately shut down, and the factory stopped;

but where should we assemble? The superintendent suggested that the mule room was large; and, the mules being run up, we could assemble there. We did so, and a more powerful meeting I scarcely ever attended. It went on with great power. The building was large, and had many people in it, from the garret to the cellar. The revival went through the mill with astonishing power, and in the course of a few days nearly all in the mill were hopefully converted.[5]

The early church, over which James presided in Jerusalem was a church like that. Revivals broke out constantly. People were saved by the thousands. The church lived in an atmosphere of power. Prayer was as natural as breathing. It was "effectual" and "fervent," energized by the Spirit of God. Things happened. Even the unconverted stood in awe. The early chapters of the book of Acts are unique in all of history. Periodic outpourings of the Spirit of God have occurred from time to time, but what happened in the years right after Pentecost is unique.

3. The hero (5:17–18)
   a. Elijah and his passions (5:17a)

The introduction of Elijah here is not so abrupt as it might seem. The age in which he appeared was one of overwhelming apostasy. Israel was sick unto death. The miracle-working Elijah was the great physician, sent by God to deal with the cancer of corruption that Ahab and Jezebel introduced into the northern kingdom. Elijah was an extraordinary person, a Melchizedek among the prophets, introduced full grown "without beginning" (as it were) "and without ending of days." He was a man of might and miracle who went from one triumph to another and who ended his days on earth by being caught up living into heaven with an angel escort and a chariot of fire.

Yet, he was "a man subject to like passions as we are." Several words are used for man in the New Testament. James uses the word *anthrōpos,* which emphasizes the fact that he was just an ordinary human being. He was made from the same kind of clay as we are. He was a man of like feelings too. James uses the word *homoiopathēs,* which means to be subject to like feelings or affections. He was just like us. Paul and Barnabas used the word when, at Lystra, the mob wanted to worship them as incarnate gods because Paul had healed a lifelong cripple. They

---

5. Charles Finney, *Memoirs* (New York: Fleming, 1903), 183–84.

hailed Barnabas as Jupiter (Zeus, the father of the gods) and Paul as Mercury (Hermes, the messenger of the gods). Paul and Barnabas were horrified. They rent their clothes. They ran in among the people, saying, "We also are men of like passions *(homoiopathēs)* with you" (Acts 14:11–15).

Elijah had his ups and downs. Sometimes he lived spiritually on the mountaintop, sometimes in the valley. Some days, he lived in victory; other days were filled with doubt, depression, and defeat. He had his moods and temperamental highs and lows.

b. Elijah and his prayers (5:17b–18)

James focuses on Elijah's two outstanding prayers, prayers in which he was able to command the very clouds of heaven: "and he prayed earnestly that it might not rain: and it rained not on the earth by the space of three years and six months. And he prayed again, and the heaven gave rain, and the earth brought forth her fruit."

These were not the only recorded prayers of Elijah. He prayed two remarkable prayers, for instance, in connection with the death and resurrection of the widow's son. But James is particularly interested in the two prayers that brought judgment and then relief to an apostate land.

James says that Elijah "prayed earnestly." The word used is *proseuchē*. The literal rendering of the phrase would be "he prayed in his prayer." The expression denotes earnest, fervent prayer. Alexander Whyte says that Elijah put his passions into his prayers.

The two prayers are joined in the Old Testament story by the twin phrases "Go hide thyself" and "Go show thyself" (1 Kings 17:3; 18:1).

The prayer that God would withhold the rain was in accordance with the Mosaic Law and the Palestinian covenant (Deut. 28:23–24). Drought was one of the punishments for apostasy. Similarly, a repentant people could expect God to be bountiful with the annual rainfall (Deut. 28:1–12). Elijah then had a solid basis in Scripture for his soaring faith.

Suddenly, he appeared in the presence of weak King Ahab and Ahab's wicked wife, Queen Jezebel, an unscrupulous princess from the neighboring city of Sidon. This utterly pagan princess imported into Israel the foul worship of the Phoenicians, along with some 850 false prophets to staff the cult.

"As the Lord God of Israel liveth, before whom I stand," he declared, "there shall not be dew nor rain these years, but according to my word" (1 Kings 17:1).

Then he turned on his heels, marched out of the presence of the dumbfounded king, and vanished.

Famine and drought gripped the land. It continued for three and a half years, just like the coming Great Tribulation. Except those days had been shortened, no flesh would have been saved in Israel. Elijah remained hidden while Ahab and his aides scoured the country looking for him and while Jezebel breathed out threatenings and slaughter. Men tightened their belts and perished with hunger. Elijah's prayer brought judgment on the land.

"Go show thyself!" When the time was ripe, Elijah returned from his seclusion. He accosted Ahab and arranged for a test of strength on Mount Carmel. Elijah, having exposed the utter futility of the cult and its priests, prayed again—and down came the rain.

James was impressed with that display. He had come to know Jesus as the Lord God of Israel, the living God. "A greater than Elijah is here," he infers. Elijah was James's hero; Jesus had become his God.

D. The burden for people (5:19–20)

He closes his epistle on a threefold note. He is burdened for people. He presents before us, first, *the careless backslider:* "Brethren, if any of you do err from the truth . . ." (5:19a). Evidently, James knew some backsliders. At any rate, he knew how easy it was for a person to drift from the truth. The twin perils of prosperity on the one hand and persecution on the other make backsliding a real possibility. It takes commitment to keep moving ahead for God. The Bible is full of illustrations of backsliders, from Lot in the Old Testament to Demas in the New Testament. Also, countless errors are in circulation, so it is easy to "err from the truth." Backsliding is usually a gradual process. It is critical that we be like Enoch, who "walked with God" (Gen. 5:22, 24). A few days neglecting our daily quiet time with God, and the subtle drift begins, although it often takes time before the fatal flaw begins to show.

A famous violinist was asked how long he practiced every day. He replied that he spent ten to twelve hours a day with his instrument. "What would happen if you slacked off?" he was asked.

"After one day," he said, "I would know it. After two days, the conductor would know it. After three days, the orchestra would know it. After that, everybody would know it."

That is how backsliding works too. Only the backslider, if he is careful, can deceive people for much longer than that. However, he does not deceive himself or the Lord.

James mentions next *the concerned believer:* "If . . . one convert him . . ." (5:19b). Usually, someone has to go after the backslider. The lost sheep of Matthew 18:12 is not the lost sinner but the careless backslider. The chapter is a prophetic cameo of the local church. It depicts the threefold function of the local church-the reception of the believer, the restoration of the backslider—and the reconciliation of the brethren. The wandering sheep needs someone with a shepherd's heart to track it down and bring it back.

Finally, James leaves us with *the consequent benediction:* "Let him know, that he which converteth the sinner from the error of his way shall save a soul from death, and shall hide a multitude of sins" (5:20). It is far better to cover someone's sins than to gossip about them. Blessed is the man or woman who has a heart for the wayward. Great is their reward in heaven.

After I had been in the Lord's work full time for some fifteen years, I ran into a difficulty. At the time, I was directing the global outreach of a Christian organization. A decided difference arose as to how things should be done, especially as to how it should be financed. The divergent viewpoints became more and more irreconcilable, so I tendered my resignation.

By that time, I had become disillusioned with full-time Christian work and went back to secular employment. I was working for a friend of mine who owned a very large business. He treated me well, paid me well, and liked me well. But I was thoroughly miserable! On weekends, I preached in several churches in the area. I was not doing anything wrong, but neither was I doing what was right.

After about a year, a brother in Christ, an elder of one of the local churches where I preached periodically, took me out for lunch. After we had ordered our meal, he looked me in the eye and said, "John, you are wasting your time. With your gift, you belong in full-time Christian work. We need you. The church needs you. What sense is there in your sitting at the phone all day ordering spare parts for trucks? Anyone can do that. But not everyone can preach like you do. . . ." A few weeks later, I was back in full-time Christian service.

Roy Waters was that elder's name. Great will be his reward in heaven. Since then, I have preached throughout the length and breadth of Canada, the United States, and overseas. The Lord has opened doors to some of the biggest churches in the country. By His grace, too, numerous commentaries have been written. All because a brother, with a shepherd's heart, went out of his way to track me down! Had it not been for him, I likely would still be wasting my time buying spare parts for trucks or—as seems very likely because the company has since gone out of business—I would be out of a job altogether and looking for work.

So, James ends on a practical note. He shows us his pastor's heart. After all, that was what moved him to write this letter in the first place—a burden for "the twelve tribes which are scattered abroad" (James 1:1), those other sheep who were not directly of his fold (John 10:16). In this sense, he was just like Jesus after all.

Luther's Rage

The doctrine of the real presence of Christ in the Eucharist had been established in the Romish Church since the fourth Lateran Council in the year 1215. For three hundred years the mass and transubstantiation had been the principal bulwarks of Rome, and her greatest blasphemy. The idea of the corporeal presence of Christ in the holy supper threw a halo of sacred importance around it, excited the imagination of the people, and fixed it deeply in their affections. It was the origin of many ceremonies and superstitions, of great wealth and dominion to the priesthood; and the most stupendous miracles were said to be wrought by the consecrated bread, both among the living and the dead. It thus became the cornerstone of the papal edifice.

Luther, as a priest and a monk, firmly believed in this mystery of iniquity and never was, throughout his whole career, delivered from its delusion. . . . Transubstantiation, or the actual conversion of the bread and wine into the real body and blood of Christ, by priestly consecration, was then, as it still is, the recognized doctrine of the Church of Rome. . . .

As a reformer, Luther gave up the term transubstantiation and adopted, if possible, the still more inexplicable term of consubstantiation. He renounced the papal idea that the bread and wine after consecration remained no longer, but were changed into the material body and blood of Christ. His strange notion was that the bread and the wine remained just what they were before—real bread and real wine—but that there was also together with the bread and wine, the material substance of Christ's human body. No invention of man, we may freely affirm, ever equalled this Popish doctrine in absurdity, inconsistency, and irreconcilable contradictions. "The hands of the priests," said the Pontiff Urban, in a great Roman Council, "are raised to an eminence granted to none of the angels, of creating God, the Creator of all things, and of offering Him up for the salvation of the whole world. This prerogative, as it elevates the Pope above angels, renders Pontifical submission to kings an execration." To all this the sacred synod, with the utmost unanimity, responded, Amen. Surely this is the last test of human credulity, and the consummation of human blasphemy.

Ulric Zwingle, the great Swiss Reformer, and compeer of Luther, differed entirely from both the teaching of Rome and the Saxon Reformers as to the real presence of Christ in the Holy Supper. The Swiss had long held opinions contrary alike to the Roman and the Saxon. At an early period of Zwingle's Christian course his attention had been attracted by the simplicity of Scripture on the subject of the Lord's Supper.

The words of our blessed Lord: "This is My body," "This is My blood," Zwingle maintained to be figurative in their character, and to imply nothing more than that the sacramental bread and wine were simply symbols or emblems of Christ's body; and that the ordinance or institution is commemorative of His death for us. This do in remembrance of Me. For as often as ye eat this bread and drink this cup, ye do show forth the Lord's death till He come (1 Cor. 11:22–28).

For several years Zwingle had privately entertained these views of the Lord's Supper, but knowing the hold that the old church doctrine had on the minds of the ignorant and superstitious people, he did not openly avow them. But believing that the time would soon come for the public promulgation of the truth, and forseeing the opposition he would have to encounter, he diligently, though in a private way, sought to spread the truth and strengthen his position. . . . But while Zwingle was thus quietly waiting for the right moment to speak aloud, another, with more zeal than wisdom, imprudently wrote a pamphlet against Luther's doctrine of the Lord's Supper, and raised the storm of controversy, which raged with great violence for four years.

Andrew Bodenstein, better known as Dr. Carlstadt, once a professor at Wittemberg, commenced the attack. . . . He would have all the images destroyed, and all the rites of Popery abolished at once. We have met with him before. He was one of the earliest and warmest friends of Luther, but he had rejected Luther's notion of the real presence in the Eucharist, and that was the unpardonable sin in the eyes of the Reformer. . . .

In refutation of Dr. Carlstadt, Luther wrote a pamphlet against these prophets in 1525, in which he says: "Dr. Carlstadt has fallen away from us, and become our bitterest foe. Although I deeply regret this scandal, I still rejoice that Satan has shown the cloven foot, and will be put to shame by these His heavenly prophets, who have long been peeping and muttering in concealment, but never would come fairly out until I enticed them with a guilder: that, by the grace of God, has been too well laid for me to rue it. . . ."

Zwingle was now persuaded that the time for silence was past. Although he sympathised with Carlstadt's views of the Eucharist, he greatly objected to his offensive style and levity.

He published in the year 1525, an important treatise "concerning true and false religion." His own view of the Eucharist are fully and clearly stated in this book, besides his utter condemnation of the seditious spirit of the Anabaptists, and the errors of the Papists on the subject in dispute. An opponent soon appeared in a pamphlet, "against the new error of the Sacramentaries." To this Zwingle replied in the same year, 1525; and took occasion to remind his opponents, the Lutherans, that they should be less personal in their abuse, and more rational and Scriptural in their arguments. There was a mildness and respect in the writings of the Swiss, to which the Saxons were utter strangers; even Melanchthon, at times, became the reflection of his violent master. . . .

Thus, the controversy went on. Luther was deeply grieved and astonished to find so many learned and pious men holding the same views as Zwingle; and many of whom he had entertained the highest opinion now expressed themselves favourable to the new views. This was gall and wormwood to the spirit of Luther, and filled him with inexpressible grief and anger. In his letters and writings at this time he expressed himself in the most unmeasured and unguarded terms. He calls them "his Absaloms, sacrament-conjurors, in comparison with whose madness the Papists are mild opponents—the Satanic instruments of my temptation." Luther's followers took up the tone of their master, and he transferred to this controversy all the vehemence and obstinacy of his own nature. From about the close of the year 1524 till the year 1529, Luther had written so violently against the Swiss, and so little against the Papists, that it was sarcastically said by Erasmus "the Lutherans are eagerly returning to the bosom of the church. . . ."

The Landgrave evidently grieved over this division more than the theologians of Wittemberg, and now determined without further delay to bring about a conference, and if possible, a reconciliation between the leaders of the different parties. On the great fundamental truths of revelation, the German and the Swiss reformers were agreed. Only on one point did they differ—the manner in which Christ is present in the bread and wine of the holy Eucharist. It appears that Philip thought the whole question little more than a dispute about words, as he says: "The Lutherans will hear no mention of alliance with the Zwinglians; well then, let us put an end to the contradictions that separate them from Luther." Accordingly, he summoned the principal divines of Saxony, Switzerland, and Strasburg, to meet together at Marburg in the autumn of 1529.

Zwingle accepted the invitation with all gladness, and made ready to appear at the time appointed. But Luther-generally so bold and dauntless, as we have repeatedly seen-expressed the greatest unwillingness to meet Zwingle. . . . The Landgrave's repeated entreaties, however, at length prevailed. . . .

The general conference was held in an inner apartment of the castle, in the presence of the Landgrave and his principal ministers, political and religious, the deputies of Saxony, Zurich, Strasburg, and Basle, and of a few learned foreigners. A table was placed for the four theologians—Luther, Zwingle, Melanchthon, and Ecolampadius. As they approached, Luther, taking a piece of chalk, steadily wrote on the velvet cover of the table in large letters, *"Hoc est corpus meum"*— "This is My body." He wished to have these words continually before him, that his confidence might not fail, and that his adversaries might be confounded. "Yes," said he, "these are the words of Christ, and from this rock no adversary shall dislodge me. . . ."

He continued: "I protest that I differ from my adversaries with regard to the doctrine of the Lord's Supper, and that I shall always differ from them. Christ said, "This is My body.' Let them show me that a body is not a body. I reject reason, common sense, carnal arguments, and mathematical proofs. God is above mathematics. We have the Word of God; we must adore and perform it." Such was the commencement of this celebrated debate. The impetuous head-strong Saxon had written his text on the velvet, and was now pointing to it, and saying, No consideration shall ever induce me to depart from the literal meaning of these words, and I shall not listen either to sense or reason, with the words of God before me. And all this was done and said, be it observed, before the deliberations were so much as opened, or a single argument had been advanced. This declaration, coupled with the notorious obstinacy of its author, was enough to crush every hope of a satisfactory termination to the conference. . . .

When the conference was ended, nothing had been done toward unanimity. Philip and other mediators endeavoured at least to establish an understanding of mutual toleration and unity. The theologians, one after another, were invited into his private chamber; there he pressed, entreated, warned, exhorted, and conjured with them. "Think," said he, "of the salvation of the Christian republic, and remove all discord from its bosom. . . ."

The Swiss doctors entered most heartily into the wishes of the Landgrave. "Let us," said Zwingle, "confess our union in all things in which we are agreed, and as for the rest, let us forbear and remember that we are brethren. Respecting the necessity of faith in the Lord Jesus, as to the grand doctrine of salvation there is no point of discord."

"Yes, yes!" cried the Landgrave, "you agree! Give then a testimony of your unity, and recognise one another as brothers." "There is no one upon earth," said Zwingle, "with whom I more desire to be united than with you," approaching the Wittemberg doctors. Ecolampadius, Bucer, and Hedio said the same.

This most Christian movement seemed for the moment to produce the desired effect. Many hearts were touched even among the Saxons. "Acknowledge them! acknowledge them!" continued the Landgrave, "acknowledge them as brothers!" Even Luther's obduracy seemed to be giving way. The keen eye of Zwingle seeing what he hoped was a measure of relenting, he burst into tears—tears of joy— approaches Luther, holds out his hand, and begged him only to pronounce the word "brother. . . ." Luther coldly rejected the hand thus offered, with this cutting reply, "You have a different spirit from ours," which was equal to saying: "We are of the Spirit of God, you are of the Spirit of Satan." "These words," says D'Aubigne, "communicated to the Swiss, as it were, an electrical shock. Their hearts sank each time Luther repeated them, and he did it frequently." "Luther's refusing to shake hands with Zwingle," says Principal Cunningham, "which led that truly noble and brave man to burst into tears, was one of the most deplorable and humilating, but at the same time solemn and instructive exhibitions of the deceitfulness of sin and the human heart the world has ever witnessed. . . ."

The Swiss had exhausted their soliciations. "We are conscious," said they, "of having acted as in the presence of God." They were on the point of leaving. They had manifested a truly Catholic Christian spirit: and the feeling of the conference was in their favour and also of their doctrine. Luther perceiving this, and especially the indignation of the Landgrave, appeared to soften down considerably. He advanced toward the Swiss and said: "We acknowledge you as friends, we do not consider you as brothers and members of Christ's church; but we do not exclude you from that universal charity which we owe even to our enemies."

Although this concession was only a fresh insult, the Swiss resolved to accept what was offered them without disputation. The Swiss and the Saxons now shook hands, and some friendly words passed between them. . . .

A "Formula of Concord" was immediately drawn up by Luther. It consisted of fourteen articles; rather general in their character—such as the Trinity, Incarnation, Resurrection, Ascension, Original Sin, Justification by Faith, the Authority of the Scriptures, the Rejection of Tradition, and lastly, the Lord's Supper, which was spoken of as a spiritual feeding on the very body and very blood of the Lord Jesus Christ. To the thirteen articles as they were read, one by one, the Swiss gave their hearty amen. And although the terms in which the fourteenth was expressed appeared to them objectionable, yet being somewhat obscure and capable of different interpretations, they agreed to sign the articles without causing further discussion. This important document received the signatures of both parties on 4th October, 1529. A desire was expressed to cherish toward one another the spirit of Christian charity, and to avoid all bitterness in maintaining what each deemed to be the truth of God.[1]

1. Andrew Miller, *Short Papers on Church History* (reprint, Fincastle, Va.: Scripture Truth Book Co., n.d.), 677–93.

Explore the
BIBLE
in greater depth with the
John Phillips
Commentary Series!